Barker Review of Land Use Planning

Final Report - Recommendations

Kate Barker

December 2006

£25.00

This document can be found on the Barker Review website at:

www.barkerreviewofplanning.org.uk

HM Treasury contacts

For general enquiries about HM Treasury and its work, contact:

Correspondence and Enquiry Unit
HM Treasury
1 Horse Guards Road
London
SW1A 2HQ

Tel: 020 7270 4558
Fax: 020 7270 4861
E-mail: public.enquiries@hm-treasury.gov.uk

ISBN-10: 0-11-840485-7
ISBN-13: 978-0-11-840485-3

Printed by The Stationery Office   12/06   349591

Printed on at least 75% recycled paper.
When you have finished with it please recycle it again.

PU062

Contents

Foreword

Dear Chancellor and Secretary of State,

The Interim Report to this Review set out the importance of the planning system as a vital support to productivity and economic growth. The recommendations in this Final Report, which build on the recent planning reforms, aim to create planning policy and processes in England that give appropriate weight to economic benefits, are more responsive to changing circumstances (including environmental pressures), and deliver decisions in a more transparent and timely manner. I believe these objectives can be achieved in ways that will also enhance the ability of local and central government, businesses, community groups and other stakeholders to work together in delivering thriving communities, tackling regeneration and protecting the natural environment.

Planning policies and decisions require the consideration and weighing of a range of factors: local, regional and national interests, environmental issues and economic growth. In part, planning policy is a set of regulations aimed at correcting market failure – in which context climate change is becoming increasingly important. But planning should also play a central role in delivering the vision that regional and local government has for its area, and it should enable development to fulfil that vision. This also implies that the planning system needs to be accessible to the community, and that community engagement should take place at the right time, when development plan documents are being drawn up and before major new development takes place.

The Interim Report set out a number of major challenges for planning policy and processes in England: the rapid pace of structural economic change driven by the pace of globalisation; projections for increased population growth; and the need to consider the mitigation of, and adaptation to, climate change and the development of biodiversity policy. The remit for the Review focused on how the planning framework in England could better deliver economic growth and prosperity alongside other sustainable development goals. In the Interim Report a wide range of evidence was set out which suggested that, while there had been recent improvements to the planning framework, some aspects of planning policy and planning processes still tended to have a negative impact on the five drivers of productivity, contributing to the UK's productivity gap with our major competitors. At the same time, there is particular concern that necessary infrastructure, including that which is environmentally desirable, is not being delivered quickly enough.

As discussed in the Interim Report, there are no silver bullets to resolve the weaknesses that that report identified. Rather, a wide-ranging package of reform is needed, addressing three key issues:

Flexibility and responsiveness

The Interim Report discussed the inevitable tensions between rapidly changing economic (and to some extent environmental) circumstances, and the development of plans with a 15-20 year time horizon. The recommendations aim to ensure that regional and local plan documents are as timely as possible, and that they take full account of the requirements of economic growth alongside social and environmental needs. The key proposals under this heading include:

- the updating of planning policy with regard to economic development: clarifying the need to take full account of economic benefits from development applications;

- modifications to ensure that the new development plan documents can be delivered more quickly, generating efficiency savings for local authorities;

- a policy framework which encourages, within the context of the plan-led system, a more positive attitude to development; and

- setting out the case for local planning authorities to have better financial incentives and flexibility to promote economic development more effectively – detailed proposals in this area are under consideration by the Lyons Inquiry into Local Government.

Efficiency of process

The reforms proposed here aim to achieve an improved framework for the delivery of major infrastructure projects, a simpler national policy framework and decision-making processes focused on outcomes. Specific recommendations cover:

- a substantial reform of the planning process for major infrastructure projects, the key elements of which are ministerial engagement and public consultation at the start of the process, resulting in a clearer national policy framework, and final decisions being taken by a new independent Planning Commission (these proposals have been developed in collaboration with the Eddington Transport Study);

- streamlining of policies and processes, including a simplification of national policy; further rationalisation of consent regimes; a reduction in the emphasis on targets for decision-making, and a greater use of Planning Delivery Agreements so that local planning authorities can focus on outcomes;

- enhancing skills and resources, including raising the status of the Chief Planner, training for Committee Members, and an expanded role for the central support function ATLAS to remove bottlenecks in the processing of major applications; and

- improving the efficiency of the planning application procedure, including more partnership working with the private sector, a reduction in the information requirements for applications, fewer central government call-ins and a new Planning Mediation Service.

More efficient use of land

No-one needs reminding that England is a small and relatively densely-populated country. Over the coming decades, decisions about where development should take place are likely to become more difficult. Central projections suggest that population growth will be a little faster in the future, with the population rising to 55 million by 2026. The Stern Review on the economics of climate change made clear the challenges and uncertainties around both mitigation and adaptation – ranging from flooding, to changes in agriculture, to the need to accommodate shifting biodiversity requirements. Against this background, there are three main proposals:

- the Government should consider fiscal changes to encourage business property to be kept in use, and to incentivise the use of vacant previously developed land;

- planning authorities and regional planning bodies should continue to review green belt boundaries to ensure that they remain appropriate given sustainable development needs, including regeneration; and

- steps should be taken where possible to improve the quality of green belt land, and to ensure that valued green space in urban areas is protected and enhanced.

As I have commented before, it is inevitable that some individuals and groups will be adversely affected by particular planning decisions, and in that sense planning will always be controversial. But I hope that this package of measures will offer a real chance for planning to reach its full potential by shifting the focus of activity towards the strategic level by reducing administrative burdens and complexity. Economic, social and environmental goals will be attained more readily by a planning system that is focused more on outcomes, and less on processes.

This Review has benefited greatly from many thoughtful responses to both the initial Call for Evidence and to the Interim Report. I am also very grateful to those who contributed to the consultation we conducted in the form of workshops and study visits and to those who were prepared to comment on the thinking as it emerged, enabling us to draw on a wealth of experience. Members of the Panel of Experts and of the Academic Panel have been both very generous with their time and frank with their contributions although, as with the Interim Report, this does not imply they necessarily agree with the conclusions of the Review.

Finally, I owe a big debt of gratitude to every member of the team that has worked with me over the past year: in particular Hugh Harris and Alison Moore, who have led the work in a very skilful manner. The remainder of the team – Rachel Blake, Siobhan McAndrew, James Meadway, Anne Perryman-McDonald, Natalie Turner and John Watson (thanks are due to the City of London for seconding John to us) – have also shown impressive commitment and much good humour.

Executive Summary

Terms of reference

1.   The Chancellor and the Deputy Prime Minister commissioned this review of the planning system in England in December 2005, with the following terms of reference:

To consider how, in the context of globalisation, and building on the reforms already put in place in England, planning policy and procedures can better deliver economic growth and prosperity alongside other sustainable development goals. In particular to assess:

- *ways of further improving the efficiency and speed of the system;*

- *ways of increasing the flexibility, transparency and predictability that enterprise requires;*

- *the relationship between planning and productivity, and how the outcomes of the planning system can better deliver its sustainable economic objectives; and*

- *the relationship between economic and other sustainable development goals in the delivery of sustainable communities.*

Introduction

Interim Report findings

2.   The planning system has a profound impact on our quality of life. Its outcomes influence the quality of our urban environment, the price and size of our homes, the employment opportunities available to us, the price of goods in the shops and the amount of open space we have in our towns and countryside. The Interim Report focused in particular on understanding how the planning system impacts on economic growth and employment, through analysis of its impact on the key drivers of productivity: enterprise, competition, innovation, investment and skills. It also discussed the wider context of the long-term challenges faced by the planning system. Key findings included:

- planning is a valued and necessary activity. While the nature and extent of the relationship between planning and productivity can be debated, business is clear about the need for a high-quality planning system – 79 per cent believe that planning is important to supporting their competitiveness;

- plans and planning decisions can deliver positive economic outcomes through providing greater certainty for investors about the likely shape of future development; helping deliver public goods; supporting regeneration; and countering market power where the landowner is in a monopoly position, for example via the use of compulsory purchase orders. Planning also delivers important social and environmental objectives;

- the context for the planning system is becoming even more challenging. This includes rapid and significant changes in technology, production and trading patterns due to globalisation. Planning plays a role in the mitigation of and adaptation to climate change, the biggest issue faced across all policy areas. The English population is growing more rapidly, projected to reach 55 million by 2026. Increased prosperity also has implications: the better off people become, the more they seek to buy larger homes, to travel, and to have more opportunities for recreation. Policy seeks to create desirable communities that are cohesive and sustainable;

- recent reforms have started to deliver the response needed to support economic growth and productivity. The £600 million Planning Delivery Grant (PDG) has helped local planning authorities speed up decision-making against a background of rising caseloads. The Planning and Compulsory Purchase Act 2004 introduced a number of reforms to the plan-making system aimed at increasing its transparency and flexibility. Changes to planning policy for housing are underway, tackling the housing supply shortfall;

- despite this progress further action needs to be taken to deliver an *efficient* planning system, by reducing delays, addressing unnecessary complexity and increasing certainty. Unnecessary delays have a number of hidden economic costs in addition to direct financial costs, including reducing competition within markets by delaying or deterring new entrants. Major infrastructure projects in particular are often subject to substantial delays, with harmful spillover effects for the rest of the economy. The complexity of the planning system also reduces certainty, for example if there are delays to delivering local development documents caused by over-engineered processes; and

- progress is needed in terms of delivering an *effective* planning framework. In economic terms, 69 per cent of firms are dissatisfied with progress made by local planning authorities in improving their planning system, while planning is regularly one of the top six concerns for inward investors to the UK. Among the structural issues underlying these concerns is the absence of a clear financial incentive for local authorities to promote growth. This is particularly important since the costs of development are often local, visible and short-term, while the benefits may be diffuse (as when jobs are provided for a wide area), invisible (as when a new store offers lower prices) and long-term. The failure of planning to respond sufficiently to market and price signals, including the impact on land prices of restricted supply, needs to be addressed, particularly in the context of the likely contribution of land supply constraint to high occupation costs. It is also critical to the success and credibility of the planning system that there is effective and timely engagement with communities, and that policies and processes deliver the right level of protection and enhancement to the natural environment.

Context of reform 3. The Interim Report[1] of this Review was clear that, in considering options for reform, a number of factors needed to be taken into account. These included the importance of public participation and democratic accountability within the system; the principle that economic objectives should not be pursued above other sustainable development goals; and an appreciation that there have been a number of changes made to the planning system in recent years; and that constant change bears its own costs. It also recognised that reform options needed to consider the emerging findings from related reviews such as the Energy Review, the Eddington Transport Study and the Lyons Inquiry into Local Government.

Policy objectives 4. This Final Report sets out recommendations to ensure that the planning system better supports economic growth, while maintaining or enhancing delivery of wider objectives, including ensuring community involvement, supporting local democracy and protecting and enhancing the environment. The key themes are: enhancing the responsiveness of the system to economic factors; improving the efficiency of the system to reduce the costs associated with delivering desired outcomes; and ensuring that there is an appropriate use of land. These are considered under seven specific headings:

---

[1] The executive summary of the Interim Report is at Annex D.

1. ensuring that the planning system is more responsive to the market while delivering sustainable development;

2. managing growing demand for development land, both by ensuring more efficient use of urban land and ensuring that the environment is protected and enhanced within the context of more land being required;

3. enabling the effective delivery of necessary infrastructure while protecting the need for democratic accountability;

4. streamlining the planning system to increase certainty, reduce complexity and cut costs for the private and public sectors while ensuring that systems support effective community involvement;

5. enhancing the speed and quality of local authority decision-making, so that firms and other applicants are provided with the level of service they have a right to expect;

6. improving the appeals system, to reduce substantially the lengthy delays currently experienced, while providing Planning Inspectors with the resources to make high-quality decisions; and

7. improving wider incentives to support this more responsive system, in particular the fiscal incentives facing local authorities.

Supporting environmental goals 5. The key recommendations of the review are listed below (page 10). While the focus of the review has been on economic issues, the recommendations have also sought to advance environmental goals. The recent Stern Review made a clear case for early action to reduce the future economic costs of climate change, and for further steps to be taken to ensure adaptation.[2] The Government is already taking steps in this area: the Secretary of State for Communities and Local Government will be announcing measures to tackle climate change through planning, building regulations and the Code for Sustainable Homes. A number of recommendations in this Review are made in this context. In particular, considerations about emissions may need to be given greater weight in decisions about where to accommodate the development needs of expected population growth. The long-term flooding risks will also need to be given careful consideration. Fiscal changes are proposed which would encourage the development of vacant previously developed land and the early reuse of vacant buildings. This Review also suggests extending permitted development rights to microgeneration in commercial settings, in parallel to the extension for households, and supports the approach that for new development the outcomes – in terms of lower carbon emissions – should be specified, rather than the means used to achieve them, in order to enable developers to choose the most cost-efficient approach in different settings. The proposals for major infrastructure should also improve the delivery of renewable energy sources, including wind farms.

---

[2] Nicholas Stern, *Stern Review on the Economics of Climate Change* (2006).

Key Recommendations

- Streamlining policy and processes through reducing policy guidance, unifying consent regimes and reforming plan-making at the local level so that future development plan documents can be delivered in 18-24 months rather than three or more years;

- Updating national policy on planning for economic development (PPS4), to ensure that the benefits of development are fully taken into account in plan-making and decision-taking, with a more explicit role for market and price signals;

- Introducing a new system for dealing with major infrastructure projects, based around national Statements of Strategic Objectives and an independent Planning Commission to determine applications;

- Promoting a positive planning culture within the plan-led system so that when the plan is indeterminate, applications should be approved unless there is good reason to believe that the environmental, social and economic costs will exceed the respective benefits;

- In the context of the Lyons Inquiry into Local Government to consider enhancing fiscal incentives to ensure an efficient use of urban land, in particular reforming business rate relief for empty property, exploring the options for a charge on vacant and derelict previously developed land, and, separately consulting on reforms to Land Remediation Relief;

- Ensuring that new development beyond towns and cities occurs in the most sustainable way, by encouraging planning bodies to review their green belt boundaries and take a more positive approach to applications that will enhance the quality of their green belts;

- A more risk-based and proportionate approach to regulation, with a reduction in form-filling, including the introduction of new proportionality thresholds, to reduce the transaction costs for business and to increase the speed of decision-making;

- Removing the need for minor commercial developments that have little wider impact to require planning permission (including commercial microgeneration);

- Supporting the 'town-centre first' policy, but removing the requirement to demonstrate the need for development;

- In the context of the findings of the Lyons Inquiry into Local Government, to consider how fiscal incentives can be better aligned so that local authorities are in a position to share the benefits of local economic growth;

- Ensuring that Secretary of State decisions focus on important, strategic issues, with a reduction by around 50 per cent in the volume of Secretary of State call-ins;

- Ensuring sufficient resources for planning, linked to improved performance, including consulting on raising the £50,000 fee cap and allowing firms to pay for additional resources;

- Enhancing efficiencies in processing applications via greater use of partnership working with the private sector, joint-working with other local authorities to achieve efficiencies of scale and scope, and an expanded role of the central support function ATLAS;

- Speeding up the appeals system, through the introduction of a Planning Mediation Service, better resourcing, and allowing Inspectors to determine the appeal route. From 2008-09 appeals should be completed in 6 months; and

- Improving skills, including through raising the status of the Chief Planner, training for members and officers, and wider use of business process reviews.

1. Increasing responsiveness

6.   Firms of all sizes, from SMEs to FTSE-100 companies, and all types of development – retail, commercial, residential, industrial and warehousing – need development plans and planning decisions that are sufficiently responsive to the pressures discussed above so that they can expand their businesses and serve the needs of their customers. The OECD has suggested that ensuring planning takes better account of economic considerations is one of the key microeconomic challenges facing the UK.[3]

Reforming national policy

7.   In the light of the above, a number of reforms to national planning policy are proposed:

- updating national policy on economic development to stress the positive role that planning can play to promote sustainable economic growth and to ensure that all direct and indirect benefits of development are fully factored into plan-making and decision-taking. This new Planning Policy Statement on Economic Development should stress the importance of taking account of market signals. It should also seek to adopt a positive approach to changes of use where there is no likelihood of demonstrable harm. Plans should, of course, continue to make clear where it is inappropriate for development, or certain types of development, to occur, in order to protect the environment and deliver social goals;

- other future national policy statements should be flexible, strategic, based on a robust evidence-base and avoid unnecessary costs and burdens on businesses. In particular the Government should ensure that planning is used as a tool for achieving wider policy goals only when it is an efficient and effective means of delivery; and

- ensuring that planning is based on the consideration of spillover effects, rather than trying to predict market demand. Planners should not be attempting to determine if there is sufficient 'need' for a given application – rather the applicant, who is bearing the risk, should be responsible for assessing that likely demand is sufficient to make the development viable. This has implications for the 'town-centre first' policy. Protecting the vitality and viability of town centres is, rightly, an important policy priority. There are a number of means whereby this goal is promoted, including the sequential test and the impact tests of Planning Policy Statement 6. These should be retained. But the requirement for applicants to demonstrate need should be removed, and can be done without harm to the overall policy. In addition, where there are concerns about potential consumer detriment caused by restricted competition in local retail markets, should the Competition Commission conclude that there is evidence of anti-competitive conduct, the Government will also need to consider whether the planning system should play a role in encouraging new entrants to a market when a new site becomes available.

A framework for positive planning

8.   There is also the need to reform the wider planning framework. The plan-led system brings with it many benefits. It provides business with a greater degree of certainty about likely development than would otherwise be the case and enables communities to engage in developing a vision of the future of their area. It also supports the coordination of investment and the realisation of positive spillovers. To maximise these benefits, it is important that development plan documents are up-to-date and provide clear policy, and that applications in accordance with the plan are approved unless other material considerations indicate otherwise. A number of recommendations in this Report are aimed at delivering this. But there will always be circumstances when the development plan does not provide a clear guide. In these circumstances

---

[3] OECD, *Economic Policy Reforms: Going for Growth* (2005), p. 116.

firms require greater certainty about how their applications will be assessed. This should be provided by establishing that where development plan provisions are indeterminate or where they are not up to date, the application should be approved unless there is a good reason to believe that the likely environmental, social and economic costs of the development will outweigh the respective benefits.

Supporting economic outcomes through plan- making 9.   Statutory development plans, prepared by regional planning bodies and local authorities, should ensure that their policies support economic growth together with environmental and social objectives. Where possible, these should be based on outcomes rather than processes. There are some concerns that issues relating to economic development do not receive proportionate consideration at either regional or local level. But the importance of other economic issues, such as the need for a range of high-quality sites for small businesses to grow, should not be neglected. A marked reduction in the extent to which sites are designated for single or restricted use classes could improve efficient site provision. At a regional level, better integration of the Regional Economic Strategies and Regional Spatial Strategies is needed. Given the time frames for plans to be developed, it is also important to ensure that decisions on major applications should not be delayed pending completion of site allocation and area action plans, particularly where master plans have already been drawn up and have had robust community engagement.

Levels of decision- making 10.   In terms of the planning application process, a strategic issue to be considered is the spatial level at which decisions are taken. For many large developments, the spillover effects are often felt well beyond the boundary of the determining local authority, as when, for example, travel-to-work areas suggest much of the employment gain will be felt elsewhere. And it is notable that while there are three layers of policy in planning – national, regional and local – there are only two layers of decisions for planning applications, with the exception of London, where there are welcome proposals for the Mayor to have jurisdiction over certain strategic applications. In this context local authorities should be encouraged to work together in determining planning applications of strategic importance.

2. Managing growing demand for development land

11.   Successful containment policies pursued over the post-war period have curtailed the spread of major towns and cities in England. Despite widespread perceptions to the contrary (a survey carried out for the review suggests 54 per cent of people think that around half or more of England is developed), available estimates suggest that less than 13.5 per cent of the country is developed. The success of green belts and other policies has been notable, and has produced a number of important benefits, including maintaining valued open space for recreation and preserving the intrinsic character of the English countryside.

12.   There will, however, be a number of pressures on land supply in coming decades. This is a result of a growing population and changing household structures caused in part by growth in single occupier households (average household size has fallen from 2.9 people in 1971 to 2.4 in 2004). Over the 2003-26 period, the central expectation is for 209,000 extra new households to form each year. Rising incomes also increase pressures on land, with more demand for larger homes and for related services such as schools, universities and hospitals, in addition to increased retail space. Growth in demand for office space in many areas will also be high – in London, for example, it is estimated that an additional 6.6–8.9 million square metres of additional office space will be needed by 2026, in addition to the 2005 stock of 28.5 million square metres.

More efficient use of urban land 13.   This raises the question of how this increased demand for space can be best accommodated. In the short term, a significant proportion can and should take place within existing urban envelopes. Much previously developed land can be made available for redevelopment, although some sites may be too complex to develop, have 're-greened', or are located where people do not wish to live or companies to locate. The Government should make better use of fiscal interventions to encourage an efficient use of urban land. In particular, it should reform business rate relief for empty property and consider introducing a charge on vacant and derelict previously developed land. It should also consult on reforms to Land Remediation Relief to help developers bring forward hard-to-remediate sites.

Ensuring sustainability of additional land supply
14.   Densification can also make the best use of available land, but there are limits to how far this can go. Although in some urban areas it is possible to build at very high densities, this may be less acceptable elsewhere. The savings of land which come from building at 50, rather than 40 dwellings per hectare are smaller than those from building at 30 rather than 20 per hectare. Densification also comes at a cost, given the clear preference in England for living in houses rather than flats. And the amount of suitable previously developed land is limited – at a density of 30 per hectare and based on current permissions already granted it is estimated that fewer than 1 million dwellings could be accommodated on the presently identified stock of vacant previously developed land.

15.   If more land is likely to be required for development, the question arises of where it would be most environmentally sustainable to develop. Certain areas are in need of particular protection. This includes those currently protected by a number of important land use designations, including Areas of Outstanding Natural Beauty (15.6 per cent of total land in England), National Parks (7.6 per cent) and Sites of Special Scientific Interest (8.2 per cent). A survey conducted for this Review confirms that these are areas that people would most like to see free of development (see Chart 1 below). Further, the recent Stern Review drew attention to the issues around developing in areas that may be at longer-term risk from flooding.[1]

Use of land near towns and cities
16.   Conversely, the land that can be developed with the least likely environmental or wider social impact is low-value agricultural land with little landscape quality and limited public access. This will also often be near towns and cities. In part this is because urban fringe land is often run-down due to its location. But it is also because encouraging development away from major towns and cities has the effect of increasing average commuting distances, thereby increasing carbon emissions, as currently occurs when commuters 'jump' the green belt. Much of this land currently falls within green belt classification. Green belt is an important planning policy tool. In many areas it is vital to support regeneration or to preserve the character of historic towns. However, the green belt now covers almost 13 per cent of England, and in light of the discussion above, regional and local planning bodies should review their green belt boundaries to ensure they remain relevant and appropriate, and so ensure that planned development takes place in the most sustainable location.

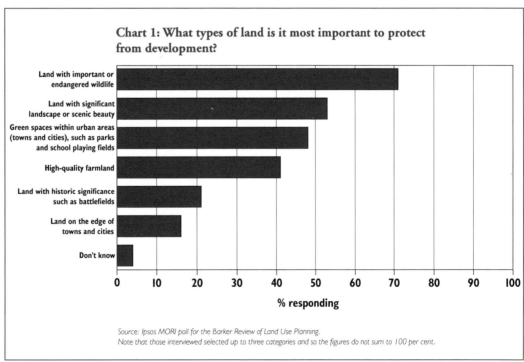

Chart 1: What types of land is it most important to protect from development?

Source: Ipsos MORI poll for the Barker Review of Land Use Planning.
Note that those interviewed selected up to three categories and so the figures do not sum to 100 per cent.

---

[1] N. Stern, *Stern Review on the Economics of Climate Change* (2006).

Enhancing the quality of green belt land

17.   Enhancing the quality of green belt land could enable the land protected within them to deliver valued environmental and social objectives. Contrary to widespread belief, the green belt is not an environmental designation but has a range of planning purposes (set out in Chapter 2). Green belt land is of varying quality, and some is previously developed land. Local planning authorities should therefore adopt a more positive approach to applications that included measures to enhance the surrounding area, for example through the creation of open access woodland. This would enable green belts to perform some of the roles for which they were originally intended, such as providing public space for recreation. The Government should also review the merits of other models of green space provision (drawing on the views of the full range of stakeholders), such as the green wedge/corridor models adopted in other countries.

3. Delivering major infrastructure

18.   Major infrastructure projects (MIPs) were identified in the Interim Report as being subject to particular delay – creating considerable uncertainty for affected local communities and for business decisions, and delaying the benefits expected to flow from these projects. These are often much needed projects – energy infrastructure, including renewable energy sources, is required to promote energy security and ensure adequate supply to meet growing demand, while transport infrastructure helps promote labour and product market flexibility. All firms therefore benefit from effective infrastructure delivery, either directly or indirectly. However, these planning cases are also often complex, and schemes that come forward can be controversial within the local community. Sufficient time must be taken to assess fully the potential impacts and the views and interests of local communities. But the very lengthy delays at present, and the high costs associated with them, indicate that major reform should be urgently considered. The proposals below were developed in conjunction with the Eddington Transport Study.

Clearer policy direction

19.   The main priority here is for a clearer policy framework within which planning applications and consents for major infrastructure can come forward. The Government should draw up Statements of Strategic Objectives for major infrastructure, including transport, energy, strategic waste and water projects. These Statements where possible should integrate environmental, economic and social interests so that policy advances sustainable development. They would need to be drawn up following full public consultation with all interested parties, including affected local communities where the Statements have a spatial element. Importantly, these Statements would have to be reviewed regularly to ensure they remained up to date. Regional planning bodies would then factor the policies contained within the Statements into Regional Spatial Strategies. A clear Statement of Strategic Objectives, with spatial specificity where possible, would have a number of advantages:

- it would increase certainty and reduce the time spent in inquiry on debating whether or not there is a national need for a project;

- in some cases, it would also reduce the costs associated with discussing whether there is a need for the development in a broad spatial area; and

- it would support a more integrated framework for infrastructure provision, with new Government policy being formulated in the context of clear policy statements in other sectors.

New Planning Commission

20.   Alongside clearer national policy, an independent Planning Commission – which would consist of a panel of experts drawn from a range of professional fields – should be established and charged with assessing applications against this strategic framework alongside other considerations such as local and environmental impact. By setting out a clear framework upfront for decision-making through Statements of Strategic Objectives, democratic accountability is established from

the outset. The time taken to reach decisions could then be reduced to some extent by cutting out the Ministerial decision-making phase, in addition to stricter timetabling of decisions, ending joint and linked decisions, changes to the inquiry process, and bringing together into a single process the range of consents often required. The Planning Commission would operate within a legal framework established by Parliament to ensure appropriate accountability. Given the requirement for proper public consultation over the Statements it will be some time before this new system can be fully operational. As an interim measure, timetabling should also be introduced for Ministerial decision-making, through rolling-out the approach of the Department of Communities and Local Government (this has halved the average time taken for Secretary of State decisions under Town and Country Planning legislation, with 80 per cent of cases determined within 16 weeks).

21.   Decision-making should be made at the most appropriate spatial level. An independent Planning Commission could decide projects of national importance once Ministers have set a strategic framework. Decisions that have only a local impact should be decided at the local level by the local planning authority. This Review does not recommend that there should be a change to Ministerial decision-making under the Town and Country Planning legislation. In the future, it may be appropriate for the Government to look again at the need for Ministerial involvement in decision-making on planning applications made under the Town and Country Planning legislation. However, there is a case for keeping the Ministerial role in decisions made by local planning authorities to a minimum. Further progress should be made to reduce the volume of cases called-in and appeals recovered by the Secretary of State for Communities and Local Government. The Government should review the directions that lead to call-in, withdrawing those that are not needed and providing a higher threshold before Government Offices need to be informed. The aim should be to reduce significantly the number of applications numbers referred by local authorities and then the number of those called-in by the Secretary of State.

4. Streamlining the planning system

22.   This Review makes a number of recommendations for the streamlining of the planning system in order to remove unnecessary levels of complexity. Complexity is inevitable in a system that governs the use of land in a small, densely populated island, but it should not add unnecessarily to uncertainty, delay and resource pressures. Improvement is needed in all main areas of planning: policy, plan-making and managing development:

- the planning framework: where secondary legislation is particularly complex, with over 200 statutory instruments. Consolidating the General Development Procedure Order should be the priority here. However, it is more important to deliver on the Green Paper reforms to streamline national planning policy – the genuine national spillover issues, while important, are relatively few in number and could be articulated briefly. The Government should commit to a substantial streamlining of national policy, including considering the potential to expand PPS1 in place of updating some of the current range of PPGs, and it should commit to publishing any necessary guidance either alongside or within four months of publishing new policy;

- plan-making: a priority is to streamline the new plan-making processes. The objective should be to secure a process whereby plan documents can be delivered in less than two years. Specific recommendations include ensuring current sustainability appraisal requirements are proportionate, and, in the next phase of development plan documents, removal of the formal requirement for an issues and options phase of development plan documents. With regard to the latter, local authorities would still have to demonstrate in their preferred options phase the original options they considered and the reasons for their preferred options, but without a formal six-month process that often adds little value but can add significantly to resource pressures. There are also concerns about the danger of consultation fatigue, which runs the risk of limiting effective public participation in planning. Local authorities should continue to endeavour to reduce the length and complexity of their plans, not least to facilitate effective community involvement; and

- the **planning application process**: the clear priority is to reduce the amount of information required to support applications. Local planning authorities should operate on a more risk-based and proportionate system, to cut applicant costs and free up planning departments resources. This should be achieved by introducing proportionality thresholds, establishing strict criteria which would have to be met before new burdens were imposed and working to raise the threshold and limit the information associated with Environmental Statements (which can cost upwards of £100,000 to prepare). Other aspects of the application system could also be made less onerous. In particular, the Government should set out how it proposes to conduct the next stage towards the unification of consent regimes, following the proposed merger of listed building and scheduled monument consents.

5. Improving performance at local authority level

23.   Alongside the more wide-ranging reforms, concerns about the efficiency of the processes around planning decisions and outcomes need to be addressed. In a number of respects, performance has improved, particularly among best-practice authorities, but there is a set of useful reforms that take this further:

- **extended permitted development rights and side-agreement system**: planning resources should be able to focus more on the larger scale applications, rather than the small-scale permissions which have little impact on the wider public interest. To achieve this, the principle of the Householder Development Consent Review (that permitted developments rights for householders should be extended based on an 'impact' principle) should be rolled-out to minor applications. This should include extending permitted development in microgeneration of power to commercial settings, supporting the planning system's role in combating climate change. If extending those rights resulted in only a 10 per cent reduction in minor cases, this would imply 12,000 fewer applications per year. In addition, a system based on the New Zealand model of side-agreements should be introduced, where if potential applicants can come to an agreement with all affected third-parties there should be no requirement for full planning permission. This is most likely to be applicable only for minor developments, both commercial and household;

- **efficiency**: process reforms are needed to ensure more efficient use of limited resources and improve the quality of outcomes. These should include an increased use of pre-application discussions, which aid the quality and efficiency of the planning process. Planning authorities should be able to charge for these as necessary. Planning Delivery Agreements should also be rolled-out so that major applications with an Agreement in place are released from the current 13-week target; revising current thresholds for 'majors' would help here. Local authority members should seek to delegate more planning decisions to their officers – 90 per cent of cases are currently delegated, but only 3 per cent of cases are for major developments. This suggests that in some cases members determine cases where it is less important to deploy their democratic mandate – which is used to best effect in setting out the vision for the area through the local development plan. A review of the statutory consultee arrangements with the aim of encouraging earlier and better engagement of consultees is needed. In this context, some of the recent concerns raised to the Transport Select Committee regarding delays caused by the Highways Agency require resolution. Focus is also needed on speeding up the final stages of the process, for getting to the point where the development can start. The costs, complexity and timescales of legal proceedings remain a cause of concern here, as are delays caused by difficulties discharging conditions (some of which may be dependent on third-party actions). As part of the overall framework, the Government also needs to ensure robust management of poor planning authority performance. This should include requiring tendering of services as a last resort. There is also a role for applicants – the efficient delivery of planning services can be hampered by the submission of incomplete or inadequate applications;

- resources: local planning authorities and other bodies involved in planning, such as the Environment Agency, Highways Agency and Natural England, need to resource their planning function appropriately. The Government should therefore review current arrangements, in particular regarding the £50,000 cap on fees for planning applications and the potential (if propriety can be assured) for applicants to pay for additional consultants to help process their application. Any new arrangement must be careful to avoid anti-competitive bias, where larger incumbent firms could gain an advantage over SMEs or new entrants. The role of ATLAS should be expanded to remove bottlenecks in the delivery of commercial development as well as housing, and to extend its current range beyond its focus on southern regions. Public-sector funding for planning must also be maintained. In particular, there continues to be a role for some form of Planning Delivery Grant to resource the system effectively so that the quality of the planning system is maintained and enhanced; and

- skills and culture: further progress is needed in supporting the skills-base of planners on top of current initiatives, such as the Academy for Sustainable Communities and the funding of over 400 post-graduate bursaries. Decentralising planning in both policy and process would help to empower local planners, which could aid recruitment and retention of high-quality staff. However, this could only be achieved in the medium-term and alongside further local government reform. For more immediate impact there should be increased use of joint-working with private-sector providers, greater use of shared services with other authorities, and the use of accredited consultants to undertake technical assessments. In addition, the status and professionalism of Chief Planners should be raised to put a confident and properly resourced planning department at the heart of each local authority with the right links to key related functions. There should be continued funding for the Planning Advisory Service to promote continuous improvement, training for members and officers and wider use of business process reviews, so that planning technicians can be used for simpler tasks, freeing up professional planners for strategic issues.

Better design 24. These improvements in quality of service should not, however, mean less focus on wider quality outcomes. Good building design and urban open space are paramount for quality of life, efficient use of space and productivity of working buildings. The planning system has a role in securing high-quality design. While recent prestige projects are highly acclaimed, too many new housing and smaller-scale commercial developments are perceived to be of low quality. Design coding, design review panels, design champions and pre-application discussions are tools which the planning system should use to deliver a high-quality built environment.

6. Improving the appeals system

25.   Over 20,000 applicants each year enter into the appeals system, a little over 4 per cent of total applications. There is much about the current appeals system that is good; surveys consistently show that the majority of appellants are satisfied with the way their appeal is handled. However, there are real problems concerning the speed of decision-making. In 2001-02, for example, only 6.1 per cent of appeals determined by hearings took over 24 weeks. By 2005-06 this had grown to 49.3 per cent. There is a risk that this situation will worsen, as a growing proportion of Planning Inspectorate resource is taken up testing new local development documents for soundness. For many firms, timely decision-making is crucial, and the current length of time taken to process their appeals is unacceptable.

26.   To speed up decision-making, stricter targets are needed. In principle there is no reason why appeals should take any longer than the 8 and 13-week time limits imposed on local authorities and from 2008-09 it should be possible for all to be processed in six months. The following reforms are needed to help achieve this:

- **tackling demand:** a Planning Mediation Service should be introduced, to address the 64 per cent rise in appeals from 1997-98 to 2004-05. Mediation has the benefits of being quick, cheap, flexible, voluntary, non-confrontational and – importantly – offering a win–win solution rather than the win–lose of imposed decisions. A recent pilot study found that 65 per cent of pilot projects were successful in delivering an outcome and that only a minority of cases went on to appeal. The Government should also reduce the non-appeal demands made on the Planning Inspectorate;

- **improving efficiency:** in addition to setting out further proposals to improve productivity levels, the Planning Inspectorate should be able to determine the most appropriate appeal route so that resources can be channelled where they are most effective (the 16,500 written representations in 2005-06 took on average one day of Inspector resource to process while 995 inquiries took 8,300 days of resource). The mechanism for doing so should be based on clear criteria, and holding oral hearings on just part of a case should be made possible. There should also be a reduction in case-creep at appeal, through placing limits on the issues and material to be considered to those that were originally put before the local authority, although the Inspector would retain the power to ask for additional information; and

- **ensuring adequate resourcing:** consideration should be given to providing an additional £2 million of public funding to the Planning Inspectorate for appeals to increase Inspector resources. Cost-recovery for foregone expenses on withdrawn appeals should be introduced. Existing powers to award costs for unreasonable behaviour leading to unnecessary expense should be extended.

7. Improving incentives

27.   One of the principles advanced in this review is that decision-making should be made at the appropriate level. This is most often local, by representatives of the communities most affected. However, for this approach to deliver the right development outcomes, it is vital that the incentives facing decision-makers are aligned with the benefits of development. Support for development can be weakened in instances where the costs of development are local, short-term and highly visible, while the benefits may be regional, long-term and less apparent – such as promoting wider employment and competition in product and labour markets. This is exacerbated by the present system of local government finance, which does not offer balanced incentives to planning authorities. As a recent report from the Lyons Inquiry into Local Government noted:

'The current system offers relatively little in the way of direct financial benefits for authorities to enhance local well-being and prosperity... we should consider reforms to the funding system which would enable local authorities to share in the benefits of economic growth.'

Enhancing current mechanisms

28.   There are current policies that can help address this issue. To counteract the increase in infrastructure costs associated with new development, section 106 payments are increasingly being used. They have raised over £1.15 billion in revenue in 2003-04, though the use of planning obligations is proposed to be scaled back alongside introduction of the proposed Planning-gain Supplement (PGS). PGS would be hypothecated to support local and regional infrastructure provision, enabling the local community to share better the value uplift accruing to land going through the planning process. Finally, the new Local Authority Business Growth Initiative (LABGI) scheme, intended to offer local authorities incentives to expand their business property tax base, also has the potential to make an impact in this area. LABGI is expected to provide £1 billion of additional funds to local authorities in the three years to 2007-08.

Potential wider reforms

29.   The interim report of the Lyons Inquiry into Local Government, published in December 2005, identified a range of options for further improving local authority incentives, enabling them to capture and retain some of the value created locally from business growth. These include:

- retained and variable business rates;

- reform of the revenue support grant; and

- local service charges and new local taxes.

30.   A further option is to enable the leveraging of future revenues, by encouraging the use of councils' new prudential borrowing powers. This could further support growth by allowing a loan to be written against the value of future tax revenues and so creating immediate access to significant funds of money. A system of this kind (called Tax Increment Financing, or TIF) operates in the United States and is a popular means of funding urban regeneration. In the context of the final findings of the Lyons Inquiry, the Government should therefore consider further fiscal options for how authorities can share in the benefits of local economic growth.

31.   There are also further options for incentivising communities. In particular, developers could use community good-will payments – on a strictly voluntary basis – to pay households a fixed sum to help gain their acceptance for a project they would otherwise object to. These projects would still, of course, require planning permission. The case for operating a land bid scheme, where the local authority offers farmers and landowners the option of selling their land on a closed-bid basis to the authority who could then buy some of it, rezone it for development, and then sell, could also be explored.

Conclusion

32.   The English planning system performs a vital role in contributing to the quality of the lives of people and the communities in which they live. The Government has brought about a number of changes in recent years, with the aim of helping ensure that the benefits of effective planning are delivered in a timely and efficient manner. The proposals outlined above aim to build on these reforms, with the particular objective of ensuring that the planning system is better able to support economic growth and prosperity alongside delivering wider sustainable development goals in the context of climate change. They will help ensure that critical infrastructure is delivered in a timely manner, that small and medium-sized enterprises can access high-quality premises at affordable prices, that competition is promoted so that prices are driven down and quality improved, that high-tech clusters can expand and prosper, that businesses do not suffer unnecessary costs and delays in processing planning applications, and that inward investment is encouraged to

support higher living standards and better job opportunities for people in all regions. At the same time they will ensure that wider environmental and social goals – including democratic accountability and community involvement – are protected or enhanced.

33.   Although some recommendations require legislative change, a number could be implemented over the course of the next 18 months, so that the benefits they will bring are felt at the earliest opportunity. To ensure that the necessary progress is made, the Government should publish a report by the end of 2009 setting out the action that has been taken against proposed recommendations, drawing on the views of key stakeholders and users of the planning system, including business applicants.

1

A more responsive planning system

INTRODUCTION

1.1   This chapter focuses on how the planning system, in a period of rapid economic change, could be more capable of producing outcomes that support economic growth and prosperity (in the form of employment opportunities, greater consumer choice and lower prices) as part of delivering its broader sustainable development goals. The recommendations are fundamentally about ensuring plans and planning decisions respond positively to changing circumstances.

1.2   The context of these recommendations is the evidence presented in the Interim Report, which suggested that while effective planning can help support economic growth, it also has the potential to impact negatively on all five drivers of productivity. The OECD has argued that giving greater weight to economic considerations within the planning system is one of the main structural reforms needed in the UK to help promote productivity growth,[1] while according to United Kingdom Trade and Investment planning issues consistently rank as one of the top six concerns of companies looking to invest in the UK.[2] The British Chambers of Commerce (BCC) has noted the danger of the UK losing out to our competitors as a result of a planning system that 'often seems set against development which would promote economic growth'.[3] As the CBI has argued, 'we need the system to be part of the solution, helping to promote enterprise and growth, rather than part of the problem'.[4]

1.3   The Government has begun to address some of these issues as part of its drive to secure a culture change within the planning profession. Planners and related professionals are increasingly being encouraged to take a positive approach to delivering change that will be of net benefit to society. And it should be recognised that the planning system does enable substantial levels of investment in fixed capital. Over 300,000 business applications are processed each year, of which around 75 per cent are approved, while £12 billion of new orders were received by contractors in 2004, many of which will have required planning permission.[5] But further reforms are needed. The Interim Report identified a number of structural features of the planning system that mean the economic benefits of a planning application may not receive their due weight in decision-making, as when there are strong local interests against development.[6] And in the context of the important role the planning system plays in supporting productivity it is right to examine how better it can promote sustainable economic development. The recommendations set out in this chapter should embed culture change more firmly within the planning system so that it can be part of the response to the challenges of globalisation and structural economic change, for the benefit of all. It focuses on:

- delivering a more supportive framework for the planning system;

- ensuring national policy helps deliver sustainable economic growth;

---

[1] OECD, *Economic Policy Reforms: Going For Growth*, p. 116, 2005.
[2] UK Trade and Investment, *Response to the Barker Review of Land Use Planning Call for Evidence*, 2006.
[3] British Chamber of Commerce, *Response to the Barker Review of Land Use Planning Call for Evidence*, 2006.
[4] CBI, *Response to the Barker Review of Land Use Planning Call for Evidence*, 2006.
[5] K Barker, *Barker Review of Land Use Planning Interim Report*, 2006, p. 83-84.
[6] For a fuller discussion of these structural issues see *Barker Review of Land Use Planning Interim Report*, 2006, p. 92-94.

- improving the economic content of development plan documents at local and regional level; and

- ensuring decisions on strategic development are made at the right level.

A MORE SUPPORTIVE PLANNING FRAMEWORK

1.4   The statutory framework in place since 1991, endorsed in the Planning and Compulsory Purchase Act 2004 (PCPA 2004), is often known as the 'plan-led' system. Until 1991, the planning system operated with a presumption in favour of development, which only a strong public interest test could override. The planning guidance at the time stated that:

> '*applications for development should be allowed,* **having regard to** *the development plan and all material considerations, unless the proposed development would cause demonstrable harm to interests of acknowledged importance.*'[7] (emphasis added)

1.5   This framework was superseded by Section 54A of the Town and Country Planning Act 1990 (TCPA 1990), which removed the presumption and strengthened the status of the development plan in decision-making so that the provisions of the plan became the primary point of reference. It stated that:

> '*determination shall be made* **in accordance with** *the plan unless material considerations indicate otherwise.*'[8] (emphasis added)

The value of the plan-led system   1.6   While it might be thought that a system based on a presumption in favour of development would support economic growth better than one based on plans, this plan-led approach is to be supported as it provides an effective balance between certainty and flexibility. There were concerns under the previous system that a lack of certainty over the framework within which decisions were made fostered an attitude of 'planning by appeal'. Under the current system, developers should know that if they put forward proposals in accordance with the development plan they are more likely to succeed than if they bring forward proposals not in accordance with the plan. This provides greater certainty of outcomes, a key requirement for investors. But unlike planning systems in most other European countries, there is still sufficient flexibility to take other factors into account since the development plan itself is not legally binding. This helps make the system more responsive to changing circumstances than would otherwise be the case – a factor of growing importance in a period of rapid economic change. In addition to this critical point, the plan-led system has further benefits:

- it supports effective place-shaping and enables a community to articulate its vision for the area by contributing to the preparation of local and regional development documents. This community engagement also helps facilitate consensus around the nature of future development in an area;[9]

- it ensures that development is brought forward in a co-ordinated manner. It provides for infrastructure to be planned in a way that facilitates development and for planned infrastructure to be used optimally; and

- it can also promote efficiency, as critical issues such as the location of new residential sites are discussed upfront once rather than each time an application is made.

---

[7] Department of the Environment, Planning Policy Guidance Note 1 (PPG1), 'General Policy and Principles' paragraph 5, 1988. This formulation is still contained within the current Planning Policy Guidance Note 4.
[8] Section 54A Town and Country Planning Act 1990, as amended by section 26 of the Planning and Compensation Act 1991.
[9] Friends of the Earth, *Listen Up: Community Involvement in the Planning Sstem – 7 Case Studies* (July 2006).

1.7   Of course if decisions are based primarily on development plans, it becomes critical to ensure those plans contain policies that help promote economic growth. And local development documents should be prepared with a view to contributing to the achievement of sustainable development. Planning Policy Statement 1 (PPS1) sets out that this involves: delivering social progress which recognises the needs of everyone; effective protection of the environment; the prudent use of natural resources, and – critically in this context – the maintenance of high and stable levels of economic growth and employment.[10]

1.8   There are some reservations about the plan-led system.[11] In an era of rapid economic and social change there are questions over whether plans could better be used as a guide to decision-making rather than a basis for it. There is also the potential for plan-making to be anti-competitive in that it is easier for firms with greater resources or close links to the authority to influence outcomes. These may often be larger firms. As the Country Land and Business Association has noted, 'SMEs simply do not have the time, personnel nor resources to continually lobby their Local Development Framework to influence the policies in their area',[12] particularly given the short time horizons under which many operate. Nor is it clear that plans necessarily deliver greater certainty. The evidence does not suggest that the plan-led system has ended 'planning by appeal': appeal rates averaged 4.57 per cent of decisions 1980-81–1990-91, and 4.18 per cent of decisions 1991-92–2000-01 (with the highest figures during the late 1980s boom).[13] And of course it is critical to the plan-led system that there are up-to-date and robust development plans, which local authorities often had difficulty delivering in the 1990s and early 2000s.

1.9   But no framework for determining the use and development of land is without drawbacks. The plan-led system commands widespread support, a testament to the benefits it can bring. The reforms set out in PCPA 2004 aimed at delivering a more effective system of spatial plans should also help ensure that the benefits of the plan-led system are fully captured, and it would be inappropriate to consider a fundamental reform to the planning system while these changes are still bedding-in. The further reforms set out in Chapter 5 of this Report aim to help deliver timely, robust and up-to-date development plan documents.

1.10   There is, however, a real issue about whether within the plan-led system there can be greater certainty in those instances when the plan is not up-to-date or determinate. It is clearly right that where the development plan is up-to-date and the relevant policies point in the same direction that this should provide a strong basis for decision-making. In this context it would be useful if it were made more explicit that where an application for development is in accordance with the relevant up-to-date development plan it should be approved unless material considerations indicate otherwise. But in many instances planning policies may pull in different directions (and in theory in some cases the plan could be silent). There may also be instances when the plans are not up-to-date, despite the recent reforms.

---

[10] Planning Policy Statements are issued by central government. They set out the Government's national policies on different aspects of land use planning in England. The policies should be taken into account by regional planning bodies in the preparation of Regional Spatial Strategies, by the Mayor of London in relation to the Spatial Development Strategy in London and by local planning authorities in preparation of local development documents. They may also be material to decisions on individual planning applications. Paragraph 3.14-3.15 of PPS1 outlines the objectives of sustainable development.

[11] The principles of the plan-led system have, for example, recently been strongly challenged by A. Evans and O. Hartwich in *Better Homes, Greener Cities,* Policy Exchange (2006).

[12] Country Land and Business Association, *Response to the Interim Report of the Barker Review of Land Use Planning* (2006) p. 1.

[13] PINS data, drawn in part from the DCLG Development Control Statistics in England series.

1.11   Applying the formulation that existed for much of the post-war period – that development should proceed unless there was demonstrable harm to interests of acknowledged importance – to these cases would not be satisfactory. It introduces uncertainty over whose interests are to be considered of acknowledged importance. It also suggests that there is an opportunity for all development causing demonstrable harm to be rejected, without acknowledging that in some instances the benefits of the development might outweigh any harm. Conversely, it could allow development to proceed when the environmental and social costs outweigh the economic benefits. This pre-1991 generalised presumption in favour of development would therefore not be appropriate.

1.12   Building on recent reforms aimed at supporting positive planning, a more helpful formulation would be to make clear that development should be allowed unless there is good reason to believe that the environmental, social and economic costs of the development outweigh the benefits. Decision-makers would still, as now, need to assess the likely environmental, social and economic impact of development and where there is good reason to believe that the costs outweigh the benefits then the application should be turned down. This approach supports the plan-led system by encouraging local authorities to maintain up to date local development documents in order to place-shape.[15] It also ensures that there is a positive approach taken to assessing applications when the plan is indeterminate. Where the benefits of development are often indirect, long-term and spread across a wide area, and the costs are often direct, short-term and localised, this will also help ensure a balanced approach to sustainable development. In this way the overall planning framework can help to support wider government initiatives promoting a system of culture change.

1.13   The principle that applications should be approved unless there is good reason to believe the costs exceed the benefits is a critical one and should be established as a matter of priority. One formulation would be to require a likelihood of the costs exceeding the benefits. Another would be to require clear evidence. A middle ground would be to require significant probability.

Recommendation 1

DCLG should revise the policy framework for decision-making, in the context of the plan-led system, to make clear that where plans are out-of-date or indeterminate applications should be approved unless there is good reason to believe the costs outweigh the benefits.

One way of implementing this would be to make clear that where an application for development is in accordance with the relevant up-to-date provisions of the development plan, it should be approved unless material considerations indicate otherwise. Where development plan provisions are indeterminate or where they are not up-to-date, the application should be approved unless there is a significant probability that the likely environmental, social and economic costs of the development will outweigh the respective benefits.

1.14   Alongside this change it would be desirable for other aspects of the planning system to support the principle that decision-makers should take full account of the potential benefits of development. These may be environmental or social as well as economic (new developments, for example, are likely to be more energy efficient than older stock).[16]

---

[15] Plan-making policy laid out in PPS12 and Schedule 8 of PCPA 2004 provides clear guidance on maintaining up-to-date development plan documents.

[16] Energy Saving Trust, *Response to the Barker Review of Land Use Planning Call for Evidence* (2006).

1.15   One option here would be to add this as a statutory requirement alongside other requirements, such as the need to pay special regard to the desirability of preserving a listed building (section 66 of the Listed Buildings Act 1990) or the need to have regard to the desirability of conserving the natural beauty and amenity of the countryside (section 11 of the Countryside Act 1968). But the same outcome could perhaps more readily be achieved through a revision to the Statement of General Principles (a supplement to PPS1), which does not currently make the point that due regard should be had to the economic, environmental and social benefits of development.

Recommendation 2

The Statement of General Principles should be revised to make clear that in determining planning applications, due regard should be paid to the economic, social and environmental benefits of development, such as the benefits new development can bring through low average energy consumption, alongside other material considerations.

A MORE SUPPORTIVE NATIONAL POLICY CONTEXT

1.16   National planning policy is a key material consideration used to determine planning applications. It therefore has an important role to play in ensuring a more positive approach to economic development by local planning authorities and a balance between the objectives of sustainable development. This section focuses on:

- a proposed new national policy statement on economic development;

- ensuring flexibility in future national policy revisions;

- reform to specific elements of planning policy; and

- the need to ensure a proactive approach to policies emanating from the EU.

Updating policy on economic development

1.17   There is a strong case for updating national policy on economic development and regeneration (currently Planning Policy Guidance 4: Industrial, Commercial Development and Small Firms). This has not been revised since 1992 and is widely considered to be out of date.[17] Failure to update this policy has led to some perceptions that the Government has prioritised other policy areas, such as transport or housing, over taking a balanced approach to the delivery of sustainable economic development.[18] Chart 1.1 below indicates how infrequently PPG4 is used when determining planning applications, suggesting the low influence it has. And as a recent report concluded:

> *'economic development applications are determined by planning departments on their own merits, although the development plan is the key consideration. Other important factors include the transport impacts of the proposal, access issues and the design. The economic benefit of the application tends to be a lesser consideration, although still important.'*[19]

---

[17] ODPM *Planning for Economic Development* (2004) p. 8.
[18] EMDA, Response to K. Barker, *Barker Review of Land Use Planning: Interim Report* (2006).
[19] ODPM *Planning for Economic Development* (2004) p. 11.

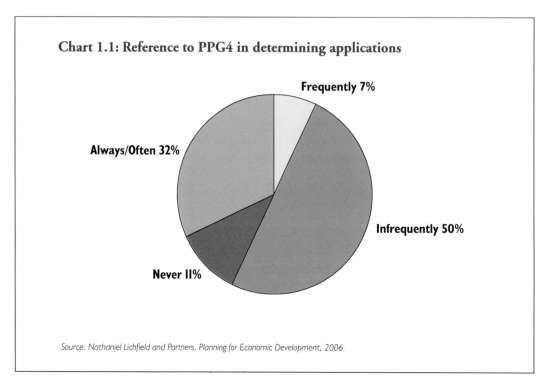

Chart 1.1: Reference to PPG4 in determining applications

Frequently 7%

Always/Often 32%

Infrequently 50%

Never 11%

Source: Nathaniel Lichfield and Partners, Planning for Economic Development, 2006.

1.18   The primary objective of this update should be to emphasise the importance of sustainable economic growth to individuals and communities and of the planning system seeking to enable such growth, in accordance with PPS1 principles. The productivity drivers of growth (investment, innovation, competition, enterprise and skills) should receive full attention in both plan-making and decision-making to allow a positive approach to new development which focuses on enabling proposals. By making explicit that sustainable economic growth is a necessary objective for all development plans, it should stress that planning must take full account of the direct and indirect benefits that may accrue from development, such as innovation, more employment opportunities, and a wider choice of retail and leisure services. Benefits and costs which fall beyond the boundaries of the determining authority still require factoring into decisions. It should also emphasise how development can promote wider social and environmental goals. Only one paragraph of current PPG4 is devoted to the need for a positive approach to development control and much of the rest of the document focuses on environmental and locational constraints now covered in other policy statements.

1.19   In addition, this national policy should reflect the need for planning to be more responsive to changing circumstances, due to an increased rate of economic change driven by technological innovation and globalisation. This implies including:

- an emphasis on the changing nature of the economy and employment. Planning needs to take better account of the changing economy. There has been substantial growth in the retail sector, for example, but the use class for allocating land for use as shops is different from the use class for businesses, meaning that the employment benefits of the retail sector may not be fully reflected in local development documents.[20] Equally, increased live–work uses mean that the boundaries between housing and employment use classes are now blurred, particularly for start-up firms. And the decline of the agricultural sector means that planning needs to play its role in supporting rural diversification to enhance the quality of life of those living in the countryside, rather than acting as an impediment to this change;

---

[20] Business in the Community, *Under-served Markets preliminary research findings* (2003).

- increased mixed use and faster speed of determining new uses. Preventing overly restrictive site allocations is a vital part of ensuring the planning system is responsive to changing conditions so that when demand for a certain type of land changes, the market can respond to that changing demand. In areas where mixed-use classifications are not possible, a change to a more productive use should not be disproportionately difficult, with a more positive approach taken to applications for change of use where there is no demonstrable harm. Currently a developer may have to spend up to two or three years proving that there is no demand for a site in its current use before it will be released: having a site lying derelict or vacant for a long time is unlikely to serve the public interest. However, there will be some circumstances when a local authority will want to discuss with developers the most appropriate use for sites, particularly large strategic windfall sites, and prepare masterplans. And if land use allocations are to have an impact there needs to be some restraint about allowing change of use, but this should be proportionate; and

- increased contingency planning in order to respond to the unpredictable. Planning now needs to focus more on contingencies in response to a range of potential scenarios, in order to deliver on meeting the needs of the economy. The Independent Examination for development plan documents recognises this by placing flexibility as one of the tests of soundness. The mechanism used in the application for development at Kings Cross in London is another way of achieving this for large-scale mixed-used development: the site has been divided into 20 zones, each of which has been allocated a maximum amount of floorspace for different uses.

1.20   A general tool in responding to changing economic circumstances is to ensure that better use is made of market signals. Where the price of land for industrial use is substantially below the price of similar land for commercial uses, this is a market signal that the industrial land could be more productively used for commercial purposes (see Box 1.1). Substantial price differentials between land allocated to different use classes provides important information that planners should take into account as a 'material consideration'. The higher the price differential, the less likely it is that other public interests will be of sufficient scale to justify not responding to that signal. Of course responding to these signals may mean, in certain circumstances, that land designated for employment use should be reclassified as residential. Where this is the case, it is of critical importance that the overall level of land supply is sufficient so that there is the right potential for both employment and residential use. This is particularly important given that sites currently used by smaller firms are more likely to be converted to residential units, resulting in difficulties for small businesses in accessing sites.

1.21   Price signals might also imply that a more positive approach might be needed to applications for tall commercial or mixed-use development in the right location where they are of high design quality, where the demand for space is high and where local transport hubs can accommodate them. As the recent experience of London demonstrates, a more proactive policy towards well-designed landmark buildings can enhance the skyline and create a sense of identity. Landmark buildings can also often enhance the setting of historic buildings and conservation areas, rather than detract from them – caution is therefore needed in suggesting that because a building affects a particular sight-line this should be regarded as sufficient reason to turn it down.[21]

Box 1.1: Planning and market signals

Market signals provide important information for planners in determining the most efficient use of land. Prices, for example, contain important information about demand for particular use classes. Where the price of land for industrial development is low relative to the price of residential land this contains important information about society's preferences. Of course, prices do not contain all the relevant information; in particular some costs and benefits are not factored into the market price, such as the recreational benefits of open space. But planning should take account of these market signals. These signals include information on:

- vacancies;
- take-up of newly built space;
- current construction rates;
- prime office rents;
- land values for different types of development; and
- trends in property choices.

This data must be treated with care. It can, for example, be difficult to distinguish cyclical from structural trends. The office market is more prone to cyclical changes than the industrial market. The residential market also has a different cyclical pattern, although in the long run the level around which it cycles may be of the same order of magnitude. If these trends are misinterpreted, a short-term housing price fluctuation could bring industrial sites into residential use, but the site cannot easily be transferred back if conditions reverse. But ignoring this type of data altogether runs the risk of serious distortions in land use allocations that work against the public interest.

There are a number of ways in which prices could be better reflected in plan-making and development control. One method is that planners could be required to take into account the price of land for different uses as a material consideration, and only reject a change of use when there is evidence that the social costs exceed this price discrepancy.[22] If a plot of agricultural land, for example, is worth £10,000 but the adjoining commercial land is worth £800,000 then after adjusting for infrastructure costs the change of use should occur unless the social value is over £790,000. In this way, where the amenity value is sufficient to override the price differential it should be allowed to do so.

---

[21] For further discussion see LSE for Development Securities, *Tall buildings: vision of the future or victims of the past* (2002); GLA *Interim Strategic Planning Guidance on tall buildings, strategic views and the skyline in London* (2001).

While this type of formal system has its drawbacks – in particular the difficulty determining the appropriate social value of land and the discount rate to be used – the insight that prices are important signals of demand is a critical one. The planning system is becoming more responsive to these signals. Housing land allocations will in future be influenced by price data, while at a regional level there are examples of best practice, as with the London Office Policy Review produced for the Greater London Authority (GLA), which provides consistent time-series data on performance indicators for the London office market, including permissions versus construction starts, and availability versus rents. The National Housing and Planning Advice Unit, which is developing methodology on how to judge housing affordability, is potentially well-placed to conduct further work here. There is also greater potential for less prescriptive use of different use classes, which will make it easier for plans to adjust to changing economic circumstances.

1.22   The new PPS4 should also comment on the approach to be used when sound development proposals are submitted to local planning authorities before development plan documents are completed. This is known as the issue of prematurity. There may be exceptional circumstances where the application cannot be assessed at the time of submission, or where a major scheme would have such significant effects on an area that full options for the site should be explored and decisions should therefore be deferred. However, in other cases there may be sufficient information with which to appraise the scheme and alternatives to it on the basis of the application together with other material considerations. This information would include national policy and the detailed information that is obtained from the masterplans for major schemes, particularly where these involve high levels of community involvement. The principle identified in draft PPS3 that local planning authorities should not refuse applications for planning permission simply on the grounds that the preparation or review of site allocation development plan documents would be prejudiced should also be adopted for commercial development. Responses to the Call for Evidence to this Review expressed concern that major regeneration schemes could be delayed for several years until not only the Core Strategy is developed (which is a reasonable requirement) but also until further development plan documents are completed.[22]

[22] P. Cheshire and S. Sheppard, *The Introduction of Price Signals into Land Use Planning Decision-making: A proposal* Research Papers in Environmental and Spatial Analysis, no. 89, London School of Economics (2004).
[23] Manchester City Council, *Response to the Barker Review of Land Use Planning Call for Evidence* (2006); Salford City Council, *Response to the Barker Review of Land Use Planning Call for Evidence* (2006).

> ### Recommendation 3
>
> DCLG should update its national planning policy on economic development by the end of 2007. This should include:
>
> - emphasising the critical role economic development often plays in support of wider social and environmental goals, such as regeneration;
>
> - strengthening the consideration given to economic factors in planning policy, so that the range of direct and indirect benefits of development are fully factored into plan-making and decision-making alongside consideration of any potential costs;
>
> - emphasising the role that market signals, including price signals, can play in ensuring an efficient use of land, both in plan-making and in development management;
>
> - requiring a positive approach to applications for changes to use class where there is no likelihood of demonstrable harm, to provide greater flexibility of use in the context of rapid changes in market conditions;
>
> - making clear that where a Core Strategy is in place, decisions on commercial development should not be delayed simply on the basis of prematurity;
>
> - ensuring that development in rural communities is not unduly restrained and allows for a wide range of economic activity; and
>
> - ensuring that in general a more positive approach is taken to applications for tall buildings where they are of very high design quality and appropriately located, and where there is the transport infrastructure to support them.

Ensuring wider policy supports sustainable economic development

1.23   Other Planning Policy Statements should also avoid unduly restricting responses to economic development. Environmental and social interests are rightly supported in national policy, but any further policies directed at these goals need to be able to demonstrate that planning policy is the best means to achieve the desired goals and to ensure that there is a strong evidence base supporting the policy – recent research into regional growth which analysed possible causes of regional disparities recommended that 'greater attention should be given both to developing evidence to support policy, and to developing an understanding of the impacts of policy once it has been implemented.'[24] National policy should also be strategic in nature so that the flexibility exists for local planning authorities to tailor outcomes that deliver the right investment in the right place having regard to local circumstances and conditions. The draft PPS3 on housing, which has a more flexible approach to density and use of previously developed land, is a good model here.

Heritage   1.24   As the Interim Report noted, progress has begun to be made in making heritage protection more proportionate, so that it enables the investment necessary to sustain heritage while protecting the assets of value to wider society. This is welcome, given that 30 per cent of planning applications have heritage implications.[25] Any future policy revision should ensure the continuation of this more proportionate approach, in particular:

---

[24] Frontier Economics, *Regional Growth: A report prepared for ODPM, HM Treasury and DTI* (2004) p. 2.

[25] English Heritage, *Heritage Under Pressure* available at www.english-heritage.org.uk/heritage/underpressure.

- delivering the recommendations of the Heritage Protection Review, in particular in terms of improved identification of what is significant about a building;

- making clearer in policy the importance of economic reality. For example, if a new doorway in an historic building could make a scheme that would rescue a building viable, this should be looked upon favourably. Keeping buildings in active use can be the best means of preservation;

- ensuring proportionality: planning controls that would be appropriate for a Grade 1 building should not be applied without discrimination to a Grade 2 building; controls should reflect the grading and importance of the building identified. Local conservation officers should adopt a response to proposals to change listed buildings that reflects the size of the change and the internal and external impact of the change;

- re-examining uniform coverage of tree preservation within conservation areas through active use of conservation area character studies;

- using Heritage Partnership Agreements more widely to protect national heritage by upfront agreement rather than individual applications; and

- considering the advantages of introducing partial or external listing in a way that does not add complexity so that only the part of the building that is of architectural and historic interest is protected.

Climate change – mitigation

1.25   There is no doubt that climate change is one of the greatest challenges facing public policy makers today. Ensuring that the planning system plays its role in helping with mitigation and adaptation is therefore an important priority. Given the nature and scale of the challenge, it is critical that the most effective and efficient policy levers are used in seeking to address climate change. In this context, it is important that the planning system is not asked to bear a disproportionate weight of the overall approach to this issue. In terms of transport emissions, for example, the evidence on the link between urban form and emissions is complex and contested, while planning often influences behaviour indirectly: requiring a site to be accessible by public transport does not mean that it will in fact be accessed in that way. Similarly, in terms of energy efficient building design, the planning system can only influence the small percentage (around 1 per cent for housing) of new stock each year and some renovations – though in the medium term this will impact on a sizeable proportion of total stock. Pricing mechanisms, on the other hand, could result in widespread behavioural change in even the short term and do so in a direct way by altering incentives. They may therefore be more efficient and effective tools for mitigating climate change impact.

1.26   Moving forward, the Government therefore needs to consider the right balance between these mechanisms. The Stern Review on *The Economics of Climate Change* points out that policies will be more efficient if they encourage private individuals and firms to take explicit account of the economic costs of climate change in their decision-making, rather than simply imposing prescriptive design standards.[26] Where there is a key role for carbon-efficient design of buildings it is also important to ensure that the relationship between building regulations and planning is firmly established, and that the tools for achieving desired outcomes are not overly prescribed: firms should be free to use whichever tool is most appropriate to deliver their desired outcome.

---

[26] Nicholas Stern, *Stern Review on the Economics of Climate Change* (2006) p. 420

1.27   A proportionate approach is also needed to development that may have transport implications, in particular by the Highways Agency taking a more balanced approach to implementing its responsibilities under its use of Article 14 powers, for development that increases trunk-road congestion. New draft guidance states that that 'under certain circumstances, Regional Spatial Strategies[27] (as approved and issued by the Secretary of State for Communities and Local Government) may include planning proposals which might increase traffic demands on the affected network above levels that would assure the efficient flow of traffic'. This more responsive approach is to be welcomed. Similarly, it would be helpful for a more flexible approach to be taken to the current national policy on the number of car-parking spaces allowed per square metre of office development, though it is important that green travel plans continue to be promoted.

Climate change – adaptation 1.28   Planning also has a clear role to play in adaptation. In particular, planning policy can and should ensure appropriate regulations against, for example, building on floodplains and protecting green space in cities – the latter not only helps adapt to long term consequences of flooding but also helps counteract 'heat island' effects (this issue is also explored in Chapter 2)[28]. Regional and local planning authorities are responsible for assessing flood risk as they prepare their development plans, and local planning authorities are responsible for ensuring that developers assess flood risk for their development proposals. Planning authorities and developers are advised by PPG25: 'Development and Flood Risk' to consult the Environment Agency on development proposals at risk of flooding.[29] The Secretary of State for Communities and Local Government will be announcing measures to tackle climate change through planning, building regulations and the Code for Sustainable Homes. This will not prescribe particular technologies but will set out the approach for delivering desired outcomes. It is an integral part of the strategy for delivering the Government's climate change targets to 2050.

Environmental policy 1.29   Policies which are prepared outside the planning system but implemented through the planning framework should be implemented in a proportionate way which reflects each of the objectives of sustainable development. Much environmental planning policy, including that derived from the Habitats and Birds Directive, stems from the EU. This limits the discretion of national policy and places a particular responsibility on Natural England to work with other stakeholders and advise local authorities on implementing these directives in a constructive manner so that within the policy framework sustainable economic development can be delivered where this is possible. There have been concerns that this has not always been the approach adopted, as with the initial approach to implementing the Habitats Directive in Thames Basin Heath.

Sequential and impact test guidance 1.30   Supporting guidance on delivering the town-centre first sequential and impact tests should be developed in a way that does not add to additional burdens in what is already a highly regulated policy. Under the sequential test, more accessible sites may be less economic to develop and the requirement that applicants be flexible in their business model may raise business costs. An overly prescriptive approach to the sequential test could therefore raise barriers to entry and limit scale economies. Similarly, there is the potential to reform impact tests with local authorities focusing on broad strategy rather than detailed but potentially inaccurate forecasting.

---

[27] A Regional Spatial Strategy articulates how a region should look in 15-20 years time and possibly longer. The Regional Spatial Strategy identifies the scale and distribution of new housing in the region, indicates area for regeneration, expansion or sub-regional planning and specifies priorities for the environment, transport, infrastructure, economic development, agriculture, minerals and waste treatment and disposal.

[28] Land Use Consultants in association with Oxford Brookes University, CAG Consultants and Gardiner & Theobald *Adapting to climate change impacts – A good practice guide for sustainable communities.* (2006) DEFRA, London.

[29] Environment Agency, *Development and Flood Risk Report 2004/05.* Since the guidance note's introduction in July 2001, the number of applications permitted by local planning authorities against Environment Agency advice because of flood risk has halved. Currently, some 8 per cent of decisions made by local planning authorities are not in line with Agency advice on flooding. Less than 4 per cent of appeal decisions were determined contrary to Environment Agency advice.

Focusing policy on market failure not 'need'

1.31   Policy revisions are also desirable to ensure that developments are not turned down on inappropriate grounds. It is not the role of local planning authorities to turn down development where they consider there to be a lack of market demand or need for the proposal. Investors who are risking their capital and whose business it is to assess likely customer demand are better placed than local authorities to determine the nature and scale of demand. Imposing requirements to demonstrate need in this development control context, as presently occurs in PPS6 is unnecessary, as well as adding to costs (needs tests can cost upwards of £50,000 each on top of planning fees and other documentation).

Planning for town centres   1.32   This is of relevance to town centre first policy. The town centre policy is – rightly – an important priority for Government. It helps to promote the vitality and viability of town centres, which brings a number of benefits. It is therefore important to assess the potential impact on the town centre of new development proposed beyond its borders. The sequential and impact tests have roles to play here and should be maintained. But while there is a role for local authorities in assessing the likely future requirements (market demand) for more floorspace when preparing their development plans, it is not appropriate to turn down applications on the basis of there being no need. This is simply likely to result in more limited choice and higher prices of goods in stores – it restricts the expansion of stores beyond the town centre that could enter the market without harming the town centre itself. Although consideration of the scale of demand may be of relevance in some planning contexts in order to assess the extent of the likely economic benefit, requiring the demonstration of need can therefore be removed without weakening the overall policy of seeking to promote the vitality and viability of town centres.

1.33   This is particularly important as the current system of needs tests in town centre first policy also can have perverse effects: it protects incumbents and gives preference to operators that have lower sales densities. These incumbents may be operating in out-of-town shopping centres, leading to the effect that if need is demonstrated and there is no impact on the town centre, an existing out-of-town shopping centre could expand while there is no application for a sequentially preferable site in the town centre. Furthermore, incumbents may find it easier to expand incrementally while prospective local entrants fail at any one time to demonstrate sufficient need for a one-off increase of space. The needs test should therefore be removed.

Supporting competition

1.34   Competitive markets can help drive efficiency in firms and deliver greater choice for consumers. Development plans and planning decisions often have effects on competition. It may be impeded in a number of ways: the complexity of the system, for example, may work to the advantage of large and experienced incumbent firms and against small businesses. In policy terms, it is arguable that market power may be inadvertently granted to certain participants in a market as a result of a lack of assessment of local market conditions in determining applications.

1.35   An example is the grocery retail sector, which has become increasingly concentrated in recent years (see Chart 1.2), with the market share of the four largest supermarket chains, according to one measure, increasing from 58 per cent in 2000 to 65 per cent in 2006.[30] The majority of the remainder is composed of convenience retailers, with traditional small retailers comprising about 7 per cent of sales.[31] This high concentration may simply reflect the superior performance of highly efficient and innovative companies. Nonetheless, it is important to maintain the dynamic competitive process so that the prospect of competition means that firms continue to strive to improve performance.

1.36   In a number of local areas there may be restricted competition due to the dominance of a particular market player. The Supermarkets Inquiry of 2000, for example, found 175 local monopoly and duopoly situations of concern,[32] while the 2003 Safeway Inquiry found that almost two-thirds of Safeway one-stop shops were located in areas of restricted choice.[33] The Office of Fair Trading (OFT) has cited data provided by CACI that out of 1,452 postal areas in Great Britain there are 104 where one retailer has more than a 50 per cent share by the number of stores.[34] More recently, evidence submitted to the Competition Commission suggested that 65 per cent of the urban population in Great Britain have fewer than four one-stop shop fascias, and hence restricted choice according to the Competition Commission's previous approach to assessing one-stop shop competition.[35] The planning regime potentially prevents entry in 72 per cent of these areas.[36] If any resulting market power is exploited, this may result in higher prices or lower quality of provision (for example, in terms of opening hours) than might otherwise be the case.[37] Others, however, suggest that local choice is extensive and competition at the national level secures benefits for consumers in each local market. Tesco reports high levels of consumer switching between fascias and that 94 per cent of customers have a local choice of three or more fascias.[38] The OFT, however, points out that these estimates are sensitive to the definition of store type and choice of shopping travel time.[39] The Competition Commission is currently exploring this issue in more detail.

---

[30] Office of Fair Trading, *Grocery Market: Proposed Decision to Make a Market Investigation Reference* (March 2006), p. 12.

[31] DEFRA, *Economic Note on UK Grocery Retailing*, May 2006, drawn from IGD Grocery Retailing 2005.

[32] Competition Commission *Supermarkets: A report on the supply of groceries from multiple stores in the United Kingdom* (2000), paragraph 2.71, p. 28.

[33] Competition Commission, *Safeway plc and Asda Group Limited (owned by Wal-Mart Stores Inc); Wm Morrison Supermarkets PLC; J Sainsbury plc; and Tesco plc: A report on the mergers in contemplation* (2003).

[34] Office of Fair Trading, *The Grocery Market: Proposed Decision to Make a Market Reference* (March 2006), paragraph 3.24, p. 19.

[35] Evidence submitted by Asda to the Competition Commission Groceries Inquiry, 10 August 2006, paragraph 1.8.

[36] In this context a 'fascia' is a particular multiple grocery retailer – ie. Asda and Tesco are both fascias. If a particular town had three stores all owned by the same retailer, only one fascia would be represented.

[37] See for example H. Smith, 'Supermarket Choice and Supermarket Competition in Market Equilibrium', *Review of Economic Studies*, vol. 71 (2004), pp. 235-263, p. 235. It was found that demerger of supermarket ownership would lead to an average price decrease of 1.67 per cent in the areas he models, and 2.69 per cent in Oxford.

[38] Evidence submitted by Tesco to the Competition Commission Groceries Inquiry, paragraph 4.19.

[39] Office of Fair Trading, *The Grocery Market: Proposed Decision to Make a Market Reference* (March 2006), paragraph 3.25-3.26, p. 19.

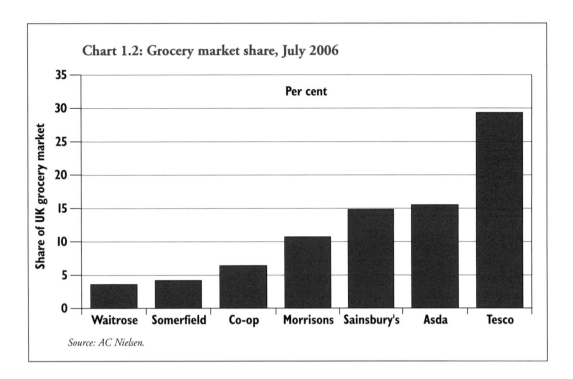

Chart 1.2: Grocery market share, July 2006

Source: AC Nielsen.

1.37   If local market power is indeed being exercised, one question is whether in determining applications there could be a means of taking into account the effect on competition of new development. There could be benefits from giving preference to a new entrant if there is a local monopolist and a further site becomes available. A simple mechanism aimed at measuring local market share or a simple test of local physical brand dominance through counting shop fascias could address this, though there are certain locations where the exact local geographical market may be difficult to define.[40] This could mean that local authorities presume against an incumbent in an area where isochrone analysis (which defines the number of stores within a 15 minute drivetime) reveals that there are currently three or fewer operators. The intention would be to promote entry at the local level so that consumers benefit from increased choice and, in some cases, lower prices.

1.38   The alternative would be to develop some form of competition assessment outside the planning system. The Competition Commission considered in its Supermarkets Inquiry whether the planning system could be refined to address the issue of choice in local areas and concluded that it was not best suited to achieving these outcomes, in part because the planning framework was undergoing significant change and would not respond well to further burdens.[41] It did, however, state:

> *'We recommend that in certain clearly defined circumstances, the Director General of Fair Trading's approval should be required for particular parties to be allowed to acquire or develop large new stores. These are that if Asda, Morrison, Safeway, Sainsbury or Tesco wish to acquire an existing store, or build a new store, having over 1,000 sq metres (about 11,000 sq feet) of grocery retail sales area within a 15-minute drive time of one of its existing stores, or significantly to extend the grocery retailing area of an existing store, it should be required to apply to the DGFT for consent'.*[42]

---

[40] Not all local markets are hermetically sealed. While a small and remote town clearly constitutes a distinct geographical market, a retail store in a location with strong and plentiful transport links may exert a wider competitive pressure that is difficult to define geographically.

[41] Competition Commission *Supermarkets: A report on the supply of groceries from multiple stores in the United Kingdom* (2000) paragraphs 2.604 and 2.606.

[42] Competition Commission *Supermarkets: A report on the supply of groceries from multiple stores in the United Kingdom* (2000) paragraph 1.15, p. 7.

1.39   The OFT did not explore the best location for implementation of such a competition test, and it did not prove practical for the OFT to examine all new site developments. Ahead of the Competition Commission's conclusions it is not appropriate here to make a firm recommendation. But, while it would represent a significant change, there is no in-principle objection to a test of this sort being delivered through planning if a simple yet robust tool kit could be designed: promoting competition is part of the PPS1[43] objective to promote sustainable economic growth. And there are a number of aspects of plans today which have an effect on competition as already indicated, for example maintaining a range of sizes of retail outlets in town centres. This approach would also sit well with wider government efforts to ensure positive planning. However, there could also be merit in maintaining the principle of planning being blind to the identity of the applicant and it is arguable that planners are not best suited to assessing competition effects.

Recommendation 4

Wider planning policy should be made more responsive to economic factors. This should include:

- building on the more flexible approach to car-parking spaces for housing, by applying this less prescriptive approach to commercial development in place of the current national maximum standards per square metre of floor space;

- ensuring that any review of heritage policy builds on the recent reforms of the Heritage Review, by emphasising the critical importance of viability and proportionality, and by facilitating modernisation that does not damage the historic or architectural significance of buildings;

- supporting the town centre first policy and the impact and sequential tests that help to deliver it, but removing the requirement to demonstrate need (the 'needs test') as part of the planning application process; and

- if the Competition Commission concludes that there is a problem relating to the exercise of local monopoly power as part of its current grocery inquiry, to establish how best to address these issues, either through planning or through other means.

In general, there is the need to establish a more robust evidence base for national policy, so that the costs and benefits of the policy can be better assessed. Furthermore, the Government should ensure that planning is used as a tool for delivering policy only when it is an appropriate lever and provides an efficient and effective means of delivering objectives.

Better forward negotiation of EU legislation

1.40   National planning policy does not only arise from UK regulation. There is now also a considerable body derived from EU legislation. Environmental requirements have in particular created a substantial additional load on the planning and development policy and process. The Habitats Directive, for example, introduces a network of Special Areas of Conservation and Special Protection Areas alongside the UK's Sites of Special Scientific Interest. The requirements of the recent Water Framework Directive for new river basin management plans will have implications for planners and developers.[44] Further regulations are likely to impose additional burdens in the coming years. Further areas of European regulation on soils and flood management are being prepared.

---

[43] DCLG *Planning Policy Statement 1: Delivering Sustainable Development* (2005).
[44] Directive 2000/60/EC of the European Parliament and the Council of 23 October 2000 establishing a framework for community action in the field of water policy. *Official Journal* L 327, 20 12 2000.

1.41   Additional EU environmental legislation raises the question of the balance of planning considerations in sustainable development between environmental and resource protection and social and economic needs: it is important to ensure that balance is retained. This is expressly the case in the protection of habitats, species and natural resources. The Department of Environment, Food and Rural Affairs (DEFRA), on behalf of the UK Government, must therefore be alert to this issue from the outset of its discussions with the European Commission and in negotiations with the European Parliament and in the Council of Ministers. The UK's negotiating remit should take full account of the costs to developers and the economy of the additional burden emerging proposals would place on the development process. Negotiators should also press the Commission for full assessments of the impacts of new proposals, in line with the Lisbon agenda, and of amendments proposed by the Parliament that would impose new burdens. Joined-up government in this area is of particular importance if desired outcomes are to be achieved.

Recommendation 5

The Government should engage more proactively at the policy development stage of European legislation with a potential planning impact. DCLG should resource and maintain close links with DEFRA, FCO and UKREP in particular, and other departments as necessary, in anticipating the domestic planning implications of emerging EU legislation. All departments should ensure that their negotiators fully take into account the implications of proposals for planning legislation, policy and the resulting outcomes for future development. Additions to existing domestic regulation should be avoided except where needed to address remaining areas of market failure. Where possible, transposition should use existing regulatory mechanisms.

PLAN-MAKING

1.42   New national policy on economic development will improve the context for the functioning of development plans. In addition to this, the framework and content of Regional Spatial Strategies (RSSs) and local development plan documents – the primary determinant for decision-making – need to enable the system to respond better to the needs of business.

Enhanced focus on economic development in plans

Supporting
productivity

1.43   The key conclusion of the Interim Report that this chapter seeks to address is the need for the planning system to be more responsive to changing economic circumstances and to balance each of the components of sustainable development. The following points should be considered in the preparation of development plan documents. Policies should consider how the drivers of productivity can be supported and core strategies should focus on sustainable development outcomes and not contain unnecessarily detailed policies – for example, in terms of energy efficiency, policies should aim to reduce the carbon footprint and leave the means of achieving this open. In addition, land uses should not be disproportionately restricted. Mixed-use development is increasingly appropriate in a country based on services rather than heavy industry, and rigid land use classifications can be unjustified.[45] It will be important to use the test of soundness to ensure plans are sufficiently flexible. Ensuring that there is a proportionate use of local protected area classifications is important in this context – there is a robust network of national protected areas, and excessive adoption of local classifications not only adds to complexity but also may unduly constrain the potential to deliver sustainable economic development.

1.44   Development plans do not impact on economic development only through land use designation. They should also highlight the benefits that employment and investment can bring to an area, and identify how these benefits can be realised in their region or locality. To do this successfully will mean taking business interests into account as development plan documents are prepared, though care needs to be taken to ensure that the policies do not simply reflect the views of large or incumbent firms over those of small to medium-sized enterprises (SMEs) or firms who are not currently represented in the area.

1.45   Current guidance on preparation of development plans already suggests engagement with businesses in preparing documents.[46] But further progress needs to be made. Current practice could be improved through:

- a stronger role for intermediary organisations, focus groups and business action groups;

- closer cooperation between planning departments and economic development units;

- increased importance of role for Local Strategic Partnerships (LSPs); and

- training planning officers and committee members to understand better the imperatives of business, particularly the locational needs of businesses and business planning.[47]

1.46   There is, in addition, a case for amending guidance to ensure that planning authorities are obliged to engage with the business community as a vital part of local communities, to balance the components of sustainable development and ensure that development plan documents focus on outcomes. This would make it clearer that one of the key aims of the new planning system is the delivery of outcomes that help to support economic growth.

---

[45] GLA Economics, *More residents, more jobs? The relationship between population, employment and accessibility in London* (2005); King Sturge, *The Contribution of the Retail Sector to the Economy, Employment and Regeneration* (2006).
[46] DCLG, *Creating Local Development Frameworks: A companion guide to PPS12* (2004).
[47] ODPM, *Planning for Economic Development* (2004), p. 12.

Site allocation 1.47　　Where it is important for economic development such as retail, storage or office space to be allocated separately, the priority is to ensure allocations are relevant and up to date. Despite the existence of best practice guidance, assessing the suitability of land allocations for employment use has in general had a low priority in terms of plan-making.[48] Indeed, as demand for housing rises, there is the danger that the employment land is being lost without suitable replacement sites being found – this may particularly affect SMEs.[49] Government research in 2004 found:

> 'some authorities are maintaining outdated, unrealistic lists of employment sites, effectively freezing sites from other land uses, particularly housing. Related to this, there is also evidence that:
>
> • current approaches to estimating the demand and supply of employment land can be fairly simplistic, often relying on past trends;
>
> • some planning authorities are placing too much emphasis on the overall quantity of employment land ahead of more qualitative considerations, such as the quality of the employment land supply; and
>
> • some planning departments have simply rolled forward employment land allocations between plans without significant review.'[50]

1.48　　The land allocated for industrial and commercial purposes needs to meet the requirements of firms of all sizes and within all sectors. Allocations should comprise a range of sites in terms of size, use class, accessibility and availability. Development plan documents should also make clear the role of market signals, such as the price of land for different uses in analysing the need for employment land.

1.49　　There is a particular issue relating to the identification of locationally specific areas in the RSSs. If provision of nationally or regionally important locations is not resolved in the RSS, or if decisions on them are delayed to a later stage, there is a lack of necessary direction on issues of strategic importance. At an early stage, panels need to identify which issues will cause most contentious debate and ensure that the plan-making process is robust enough to enable making difficult decisions with sufficient information.

1.50　　It is also important in regional and local planning to ensure a stronger link between plans and infrastructure provision, so that there is greater confidence that the infrastructure necessary to deliver large developments will be in place. Despite the more spatial approach to planning there is clearly some way to go before this issue is successfully resolved.

A better relationship between the Regional Spatial and Economic Strategies

1.51　　The PCPA 2004 gave the RSS development plan status. It is now a powerful tool for ensuring that decisions on major developments give proper weight to wider regional priorities. Each RSS is developed by the Regional Planning Bodies based within the Regional Assembly. Alongside the RSS is a Regional Economic Strategy (RES) prepared by Regional Development Agencies (RDAs), whose role is 'to provide a shared vision for the development of the region's economy, to improve economic performance and enhance the region's competitiveness'.[51]

---

[48] ODPM, *Planning for Economic Development* (2004), p. 37.

[49] Renaisi and ANCER SPA *Workspace supply and demand in the City fringe: A study for City Fringe Partnership Final Report* (2003).

[50] ODPM, *Planning for Economic Development: Study and Scoping Study* (May 2004).

[51] DTI, *Guidance to Regional Development Agencies on Regional Strategies* (2005).

1.52   The RSS should 'have regard to the Regional Economic Strategy'.[52] It is therefore important that the regional economic priorities of the RES are properly factored into the RSS so that the strategic vision it embodies is reflected in other regional strategies. It is clearly important that the preparation and content of an RES and an RSS are properly coordinated so that productivity issues, market signals, prices, and business needs are fully factored in. The joint Department of Trade and Industry (DTI) and DCLG *Guide to Improving the Economic Evidence Base* support *Regional Economic and Spatial Strategies*, published in September 2005, may help,[53] but concerns remain about the lack of integration between these two strategies, particularly in southern regions. There are a number of examples of this (see Box 1.2) with the RDAs concluding:

> *'It is critical to the successful delivery of both RES and RSS and to achieving more sustainable outcomes that they have a clear and consistent relationship. In some regions there is poor alignment of strategies ... while in other regions strong alignment exists .... Many regions have in the last 10 years witnessed the impact of planning strategy being poorly aligned with the economy. These have included:*

> - *under-provision of open market housing;*

> - *a lack of affordable housing;*

> - *poor locational choice of many employment sites;*

> - *increased long distance commuting; and*

> - *growing congestion causing unsustainable carbon footprints.'*[54]

1.53   In addition to the policy differences, there are timing differences between the two strategies. The RES sets out for the policies, aims and objectives for the regional economy for between 5 and 10 years,[55] while the RSS operates to a 15-20 year time horizon. Similarly they may be produced on different timeframes: it is hard to see how an RES can inform an RSS if the former is published after the latter. Where different evidence bases and sub-regional definitions are used, integration is also made harder.

---

[52] Regulation 10 of the Town and Country Planning (Regional Planning) (England) Regulations (2004).

[53] Office of the Deputy Prime Minister, *Guide to Improving the Economic Evidence Base supporting Regional Economic and Spatial Strategies* (September 2005).

[54] Regional Development Agencies, *Response to the Barker Review of Land Use Planning Call for Evidence* (2006).

[55] Department of Trade and Industry, *Guidance to Regional Development Agencies on Regional Strategies* (2005) paragraphs 25 and 33.

Box 1.2: RES and RSS alignment

- The South West draft RSS acknowledges that successful RES delivery is more likely to result in the continuation of strong growth. However, the draft RSS plans only for average economic growth at 2.8 per cent growth in Gross Value Added (GVA) p.a. rather than the 'strong' growth that the region has witnessed over the past 10 to 15 years. Therefore the RSS growth predictions imply that the RSS is not planning for successful RES delivery. This in turn is used to justify lower than necessary levels of housing provision. Evidence suggests that approximately 30,000 dwellings per annum are needed to support RES delivery whereas the draft RSS plans for only 23,000. The RDA has estimated that this contrast could have a large impact on delivery of the RES.

- The East Midlands Development Agency commissioned Experian to look at the impact of housing options to inform the development of the draft RSS in May 2006. Experian's report highlighted a significant concern that the RSS's preferred housing option would be likely to hold back employment and economic output in some parts of the region.[56]

- The East of England Regional Assembly prepared their draft RSS largely on the basis of the 2001 RES, which used a range of economic growth targets. The RDA has affirmed its support for the RSS through its continued engagement in the RSS process and joint research. The two strategies do have a major policy divergence in relation to the growth of airports, notably at Stansted. Although the Regional Assembly has acknowledged that airports are key economic drivers, it has consistently opposed a second runway. The RSS gives greater emphasis to retail than is supported in the RES. The review of the RES will begin before the publication of the RSS.

- GLA Economics provides a good example of a common economic information and research base which is used by both the London Development Agency and the GLA in preparing the RES and London Plan respectively.

1.54   While merging the RSS and RES into a single strategy would effectively overcome the problems of timing, evidence-base and organisational interaction (as well as potentially providing economies of scale) such a merger would have wider ramifications given the different statutory role of these two documents. There is more merit in tackling specific issues that are impeding integration. Ensuring that the sequencing of the RES with the RSS is such that updates of the former are produced at the right time to influence and be included in revisions to the latter will help remove one obstacle to integration. This will ensure that economic interests are better embedded within the statutory plan-making process. The Government's Sub-National Review of Economic Development may have further recommendations in this area when it reports in 2007.

---

[56] Experian, 'Impact of Housing Options to Inform the Development of the Regional Spatial Strategy. A report for East Midlands Development Agency' (August 2006).

Recommendation 6

Regional and local planning authorities should make planning for economic development a higher priority. To achieve this there should be:

- better integration of the Regional Economic Strategies (RES) and Regional Spatial Strategies (RSS), including enhanced alignment of timescales and compatibility of evidence bases, so that the RES can fulfil its role of informing the RSS. The Secretary of State should have regard to RES policies as part of her adoption procedures for the RSS;

- policies that set out how the drivers of productivity (competition, investment, skills, innovation and enterprise) will be supported. Care should be taken to ensure that plans represent the interests of small firms and potential new entrants to the market (who may not be in a position to engage with the plan);

- policies that focus, wherever possible, on desired outcomes rather than imposing the means of delivering those outcomes – for example in terms of climate change – the outcome should be to reduce the carbon footprint, with the best means being flexible;

- a stronger link between plans and infrastructure provision, so that there is greater confidence that the infrastructure necessary to deliver large development will be in place;

- a marked reduction in the extent to which sites are designated for single or restricted use classes – the need to ensure provision for live–work units is relevant in this context;

- where employment land needs to be separately designated, ensuring that employment land reviews are conducted regularly, making full use of market signals, so that there is a suitable range of quality sites which provide for all sectors and sizes of firm; and

- delivery of the Government's objective of avoiding rigid local landscape designations in the context of a robust network established at national level.

DECISION-MAKING: STRATEGIC DEVELOPMENT MANAGEMENT

1.55   Supportive national policy, together with development plans that take economic interests fully into account, should ensure that the outcomes of planning applications will better balance economic factors with environmental and social concerns. However, in addition, there are also important issues relating to the level at which planning applications are determined as part of development management. Many of the issues here relate to the need to foster a positive, collaborative approach to development management across local planning authorities and beyond. The need for this culture change cannot be overemphasised. This issue is explored more fully in Chapter 5. The remainder of this chapter explores a more structural feature of this issue – the level of decision-making.

1.56   The Interim Report identified the critical relationship between outcomes of the planning system and the level of government at which planning decisions are taken, building on the principle of subsidiarity in which government is devolved to the most effective level. Benefits of development such as employment opportunities and community facilities are felt across local-authority boundaries. But the costs of development, for example temporary traffic disruption or loss of amenity, can be locally concentrated. So, although local development documents must be in accordance with the RSS, there is still an inadequate incentive for local decision-makers to take this wider interest fully into account and decisions are not always made by those representing the full area in which the development impacts are experienced. This suggests it would be desirable to develop alternative models for decision-making on applications for strategically important developments which affect an area larger than a local planning authority (this principle is also developed in Chapter 3 on Delivering Major Projects).

1.57   Under the current system, there are national, regional and local plan-making bodies. But, with the exception of London, there are only local and national decision-making bodies, though regional planning bodies can outline the strategic developments on which they would like to be consulted when they come forward.[56] It can be argued that the benefits of more strategic decision-making could be felt in other areas.[57]

Economic area definitions   1.58   There is a range of suggestions for how administrative structures can better reflect functional economic areas and an increased interest in the role that cities play in driving growth.[58] Travel-to-work areas (sometimes referred to as city regions), which are relatively self-contained internally contiguous labour markets, are used as one type of functional economic area, though the catchment areas of different sections of the labour market will vary, with professional/managerial groups travelling further than others. Alternative methods for identifying functional economic areas include:[59]

- housing market definitions – measured by the area in which a household searches for a residential location. Assuming equal attraction of place, this implies house prices within such areas would move roughly in tandem;[60]

- economic activity based definitions – measured in terms of potential links between businesses and business services. Collecting data on this area is difficult, but there is an increasing recognition of the importance of flows of services and information;[61] and

- service district definitions – measured as the region from which users draw city-based goods and services.[62] Increased mobility complicates such patterns.

---

[56] Schedule 6 (16) (4) of the PCPA 2004.

[57] Steer Davies Gleave, *Northern Way and the Transport Strategic Direction* (forthcoming, 2006).

[58] Office of the Deputy Prime Minister, *The State of the English Cities*, Professor Michael Parkinson et al, (2006); HM Treasury, Department of Trade and Industry and Office of the Deputy Prime Minister *Devolving decision making: 3 – Meeting the regional economic challenge: The importance of cities to regional growth* (2006).

[59] Office of the Deputy Prime Minister, *A Framework for City-Regions: Working Paper 1 – Mapping City-Regions* (2006).

[60] In theory there is a close relationship between labour market and housing market areas since both will be affected by housing flows.

[61] This method together with analysis of information flows is explored in Peter Hall and Kathryn Pain's *The Polycentric Metropolis: Learning from Mega-city Regions in Europe* (2006).

[62] Central Place Theory proposes that customers use their nearest available service so that a large number of places offer a restricted array of frequently used services and fewer higher-order settlements offer increasingly wide arrays of more specialised services.

1.59   The significance of the sub-region is recognised in the planning system through RSSs. The approach taken in RSSs explicitly recognises the need to identify circumstances in which a sub-regional approach is required and is based on an assessment of functional relationships between settlements. There are also examples of local authorities working together to produce development plan documents (see Box 1.3). The issue is therefore addressed at the plan-making stage but not currently at the decision-making stage.

Box 1.3: Local authority joint working

North Northamptonshire

North Northamptonshire Joint Planning Unit (JPU) is a partnership between the Borough Council of Wellingborough, Corby Borough Council, East Northamptonshire District Council, Kettering Borough Council and Northamptonshire County Council. It was set up under Statutory Instrument 2005 No. 1552 made under section 29 of PCPA 2004. The JPU consists of planning officers seconded from the local planning authorities and a joint planning committee. The unit is funded through contributions from the local planning authorities and also partly resourced by the North Northamptonshire Development Company, which hosts the JPU and employs the planning manager.

The JPU has prepared a joint Local Development Scheme and a Statement of Community Involvement (SCI) and is currently preparing a joint Core Strategy for the area, programmed to be adopted by April 2008. The boroughs and districts that form the partnership are preparing site-specific and other appropriate development plan documents which are programmed for delivery shortly after the Core Strategy. The key benefit of the joint Core Strategy is that cross-boundary issues are addressed in a coordinated way, taking forward the sub-regional strategy at an appropriate level. There have been cost savings in procuring technical studies for the whole area and in producing joint documents (for example a single SCI rather than four separate consultations/examinations on district SCIs). There was a consensus among the district and borough councils that they would retain decision-making powers in order to ensure that decisions on the development plan were made at the local level.

Black Country

The four local planning authorities that make up the Black Country are preparing a joint Core Strategy under the leadership of a joint advisory group comprising the cabinet planning leads for each constituent local authority. There is an estimated programme date for adoption by each local authority in October 2009. Beginning in 2002 the Black Country Consortium (a voluntary public-private partnership which functions as the strategic body for the renaissance of this urban area of over 1 million people and 500,000 jobs) has led the preparation of the Black Country Study. This laid out a vision and strategy for the future of the Black Country to achieve urban renaissance in accordance with the adopted RSS. This Study has also formed the basis for a first phase revision of the RSS to provide a spatial and regeneration strategy specifically for the Black Country sub-region, as required by the Secretary of State. The joint Core Strategy will develop this vision and take forward proposals for a network of centres and corridors.

The decision to prepare a joint Core Strategy was made through local leadership, promoting the potential of the Black Country vision and regional recognition of the importance of local authorities working together in the sub-region.

The key benefit of the joint Core Strategy is that the full competitive potential of this sub-region can be articulated in the plan. There are also cost savings to joint working. However, the sequencing requirements of PPS11 and PPS12 and their separation of regulations between the RSS and the Core Strategy mean that some of those savings are not fully used as a result of a repetition.

1.60   Whatever model is used or definition taken there is the potential to consider whether more cross-boundary working could facilitate improved responsiveness to functional economic areas to take better account of costs and benefits of planning decisions for strategic applications. Different models have been implemented in France and Germany (see Box 1.4). There is already one successful example of this in England. The Mayor of London has had the power to direct a local authority to refuse a planning application that would have negative implications for the city more widely. The Government is proposing to extend the Mayor's powers so that for a limited number of strategic applications each year he can ensure the wider interests of London are taken into account. This is to be welcomed, provided it does not add excessive uncertainty or delay.

Box 1.4: International governance models

French Communite Urbaine

Lille Métropole Communite Urbaine (Lille Métropole) is designed to facilitate inter-commune cooperation. It gathers 85 communes (local authorities) and more than 1 million inhabitants from an area which contains both urban and rural settlements and has responsibility for town planning, public transport, water and sewerage, the collection of household refuse, the roadway system, car parks, the slaughter-houses and the market, and fire services. The smallest commune has 178 inhabitants, and four communes have more than 65,000 inhabitants and nearly 40 per cent of the area. The 170 elected members of Lille Métropole are chosen through indirect suffrage. The distribution of the seats between the communes is proportional and corrected to allow the presence of all the communes and to balance the representation of the territory. Thus, the number of elected officials per commune varies from one representative for the smallest to 24 for the largest. The elected members can gather and set up political groups – a group must have at least five elected officials. The Métropole currently has seven political groups. Elected members elect the President of Lille Métropole at the beginning of the mandate.

German Verband

In 2001 the Region Hanover was founded as a new regional government to serve as a county surrounding the city. In 2002, citizens from the entire metropolitan area directly elected not only the administrative head of the Region Hanover but also a regional parliament for this territorially consolidated and functionally strengthened urban county. State law in 1963 founded the first strong metropolitan institution in a German mono-centred city region: Verband Grossraum Hanover (VGH) which included the central city, three surrounding counties and 210 municipalities and had its own administration and parliament (indirectly elected and responsible for regional planning). The three administrative heads of the city, the county and the metropolitan association proposed a merger of the county and the metropolitan association in 1997.

1.61   The challenge for the future is to ensure that other areas of the country are in a position to benefit from this model, whether in the form of voluntary cooperative bodies such as the Association of Greater Manchester Authorities (comprising ten authorities surrounding Manchester City Council and three associate members) or through the establishment of alternative sub-national governance structures. A priority in the shorter term is to find mechanisms to encourage more joint decision-making across local authority boundaries, so that the benefits of joint working can be felt in development management as well as plan-making. Of course there are potential costs here, not least those associated with increased complexity, but the principle of better aligning spillovers with administrative boundaries is an important one.

Recommendation 7

Local authorities should be encouraged to work together in drawing up joint development plan documents and determining planning applications where there are significant spillovers which are likely to spread beyond the boundary of one authority. In the medium term, consideration should be given to how the London model, where strategic planning application powers are being granted to the Mayor, could be applied elsewhere.

2 More efficient use of land

INTRODUCTION

2.1   This chapter explores issues relating to the planning system's approach to providing the development land supply needed for economic growth and to meet our housing needs. It discusses:

- the difference between what proportion of land people believe is developed in England and the range of plausible estimates;

- the pressures which are resulting in higher demand for land; and

- the likelihood that over the next 20 years it will be increasingly difficult to meet a high proportion of these development requirements through land allocations in plans relating to existing urban envelopes.

2.2   It makes a range of recommendations aimed at ensuring an efficient use of urban land and that where new development cannot be accommodated within towns and cities the land that is identified for development is in the most sustainable location to achieve the maximum environmental and social benefit.

CONTAINMENT STRATEGY

The successful protection of open countryside and restraint on sprawl

2.3   While demand for land for development has been increasing due to rising population, changing household formation patterns and structural economic change, the English planning system over the past 60 years has been successful in protecting the countryside and curtailing the potential for urban 'sprawl', as characterised by interwar ribbon development. This has been achieved by a number of planning tools, including environmental designations such as Sites of Special Scientific Interest, and other policies that have aimed more strongly at concentrating development within urban areas. These include the setting of national targets for the percentage of development which should occur on brownfield land, the promotion of 'town-centre first' policies, the setting of national housing density targets and adopting a sequential approach to the allocation of land for development. Green belt designations (often wrongly thought of as an environmental designation) have also played an important role.

2.4   Despite this, there is a widespread perception that much of the country has already been built over. This has been widely reported anecdotally,[1] but has not been empirically tested recently. Research carried out by Ipsos MORI for this Review confirms that people have a marked tendency to overestimate the proportion of urban land in England. As Table 2.1 below shows, 54 per cent of respondents thought that around half or more of all land in England is developed, while only 13 per cent believed that less than a quarter is developed.[2]

---

[1] A. W. Evans and O. M. Hartwich, *Unaffordable Housing: Fables and Myths* (Policy Exchange, 2005), p. 26.

[2] Alan Evans points out that this misperception may be caused by most of the population living in towns; when people travel between towns they travel relatively rapidly, but they move more slowly within built-up areas and so perceive urban areas as being bigger. See A. W. Evans, 'Rabbit Hutches on Postage Stamps: Planning, Development and Political Economy', *Urban Studies,* vol. 28 (1991), pp. 853-870, p. 862.

Table 2.1: What proportion of land in England do you think is developed?[3]

	Per cent responding
Three-quarters or more	10
Between half and three-quarters	21
Around half	23
Between a quarter and a half	19
A quarter or less	13
Don't know	15

Source: Ipsos MORI poll for Barker Review of Land Use Planning.

2.5   In fact, as the Interim Report stated, the total area of England which has been developed is much lower. Although the exact figure is subject to some debate, the highest figure from all recent estimates is 13.5 per cent:

- using Department for Communities and Local Government (DCLG) guidance on the definition of urban areas based on 1991 urban settlement boundaries, the proportion of urban land in England is estimated at 8.3 per cent (referred to in the Interim Report[4]) and for 2001 urban settlement boundaries 8.9 per cent.[5] This is defined as land built on within settlements with a minimum population of 1,000 and a minimum land area of 20 hectares;

- the Countryside Survey 2000 estimated for England and Wales that the stock of developed land (including gardens) in both urban and rural areas was 13.5 per cent;[6]

- the Generalised Land Use Database (GLUD) provides an estimate of developed land in England for 2001 of 9.8 per cent, summarised in Table 2.2 below, a considerable proportion of which is formed of gardens;[7] and

- the EC-produced CORINE Land Cover 2000 survey reports that the percentage of England which is urbanised is 11.2 per cent.[8]

[3] 1,724 interviews with adults aged 15-plus were conducted face-to-face in homes across England, using the Ipsos MORI face-to-face Capibus survey, over 15-21 September 2006. Where figures do not add up to 100, this is due to multiple coding or computer rounding. The full question read: '"Developed land" (broadly, land which has been built upon) is defined as land in towns, cities and villages (including gardens but excluding parks) and all additional land used for infrastructure such as roads, paths and rail. What proportion of land in England do you think is developed?'

[4] K. Barker, *Review of Land Use Planning: Interim Report: Analysis* (2006), pp. 7, 33.

[5] The 8.9 per cent figure was calculated from data supplied by the Minister of State for Housing and Planning to the House of Commons on 13 January 2005, pending its publication. See Hansard, column 582W, http://www.publications.parliament.uk/pa/cm200405/cmhansrd/vo050113/text/50113w02.htm. For further details on how these estimates were created see DCLG, *Urban and Rural Definitions: A User Guide* at www.communities.gov.uk/index.asp?id=1147752. Urban land is defined as land built on with settlements with a minimum population of a 1,000 and a minimum land area of 20 hectares. All settlements of over 10,000 are treated as urban areas.

[6] R. H. Haines-Young et al., *Accounting for Nature: Assessing Habitats in the UK Countryside* (DETR, 2000), chapter 8, p. 109. This used data from the Land Cover Map 2000, which drew on satellite data.

[7] 42 per cent of developed land is garden space according to the GLUD. www.communities.gov.uk/pub/87/GLUDforLocalAuthoritiesExcel104Kb_id1146087.xls.

[8] The GLUD dataset is the most detailed available and is used in this chapter for regional comparisons, while the CORINE dataset is used for international comparisons. According to the CORINE dataset, the South West is the least urbanised at 6.7 per cent, while the South East is the most urbanised at 14.1 per cent (excluding London). The reason why GLUD estimates are preferred is that for the UK, the CORINE land cover map is based on a generalised version of the Centre for Ecology and Hydrology's Land Cover Map 2000 (LCM2000). This provides useful information at a national and regional level, but is too general at the urban level. It is based on a classified satellite image, picking up reflected light, generalised to approximately 1:1,000,000. GLUD statistics are based on Ordnance Survey products, at 1:1,250 or 1:10,000, based on real-world objects. This difference in methodology and scale may account for the divergence in estimates.

Table 2.2: Land developed in each English region

Region	Percentage of land developed, including gardens	Percentage of land as greenspace	Percenta... a...
North East	7.2	91.3	1.4
North West	10.9	84.0	5.1
Yorkshire and the Humber	8.6	89.7	1.7
East Midlands	8.2	89.9	1.9
West Midlands	11.0	88.0	1.0
East of England	8.7	88.9	2.4
Greater London	58.7	38.4	2.8
South East	12.2	85.7	2.1
South West	7.0	91.1	1.9
England	9.8	88.0	2.2

Source: Generalised Land Use Database.[11]

2.6   Looking at EU countries with similar population densities, these figures do not seem to be exceptional. The CORINE Land Cover 2000 study suggested that Belgium (20.4 per cent) and the Netherlands (11.4 per cent) have a higher proportion of land urbanised. Although the unified Germany (8 per cent) has a lower figure than that for England alone, the industrial states of the former West Germany – North Rhine-Westphalia (15.5 per cent) and the Saarland (14.6 per cent) – have more land urbanised than any region of England (excluding London).[9]

2.7   There is regional variation in the data. But even in the South East, often perceived as 'full up', only 12.2 per cent of land in the region is developed, according to the GLUD.[10] Taking London and the South East as a combined region, the figure is 17.9 per cent.

The benefits and costs of containment

2.8   This policy of containment has resulted in many beneficial outcomes. Green belts, for example, have aimed to achieve the following objectives:

- to check the unrestricted sprawl of large built-up areas;
- to prevent neighbouring towns from merging into one another;
- to assist in safeguarding the countryside from encroachment;
- to preserve the setting and special character of historic towns; and
- to assist in urban regeneration, by encouraging the recycling of derelict and other urban land.[12]

[9] EC, CORINE Land Cover 2000, http://dataservice.eea.europa.eu/dataservice/, and Campaign to Protect Rural England, *Policy-Based Evidence Making: The Policy Exchange's War Against Planning* (London, June 2006), pp. 3-8.
[10] Note that the South East as a region does not include Greater London.
[11] Office of the Deputy Prime Minister, *Generalised Land Use Database Statistics for England* (London, 2005). These estimates are for England as at 2001. The GLUD categorises land into: domestic buildings, non-domestic buildings, road, rail, path, gardens, greenspace, water and other (largely hardstanding). Table 2.2 defines 'developed land' as the first five categories plus 'other'. Where figures do not sum to 100 per cent this is due to rounding.
[12] DCLG, Planning Policy Guidance 2: Green Belts, paragraph 1.5.

ge of land
water
ient use of land 2

ecifically, restricting urban growth has meant that open space and the English been protected, generating social benefits of amenity, while some environmental have been generated through concentrating rather than scattering populations.[13] t urban sprawl and manage the release of land do have positive effects on quality ity value of open space at the edge of towns and cities is preserved, while vacant is are more likely to be redeveloped due to the constraint, thus driving urban is reduces transport costs, means that land take is lower than otherwise, and of providing and operating public services and utilities. The social benefits of containment are illustrated by an Eftec study, which estimated that the value to society of rural forest and natural wetlands reach £1.3 million per hectare.[14]

2.10   Tight containment policy has also contributed to a number of less desirable effects, which may be less well-recognised:[15]

- **environmental costs.** Although the growth of the largest towns and cities has been restricted, small towns and villages located beyond these areas have often been able to grow, and in the case of the New Towns, promoted as part of a decentralisation strategy. While it had been hoped that this development would result in self-contained towns, the increased availability of private cars and falling transport costs resulted in greater propensity to travel, so that commuting times increased, partly as new residential developments were often separated from new employment, leisure and retail activities. This has led to the 'jumping' of green belts, where commuters travel long distances over protected land in order to reach work, in part due to restrictions in the expansion of those towns and cities themselves.[16] There is also the risk that brownfield sites rich in biodiversity are developed while areas beyond the city of less environmental value remain protected.[17]

  In addition, while land at the urban fringe is protected from development, with agriculture often unviable there and a lack of alternative uses available to the landowner, land at the urban fringe has often become degraded. As the Bartlett School of Planning has suggested,

  farming in the countryside around towns – and within green belts – has only marginal viability (according to the RTPI, and this is despite proximity to urban markets) and may be one of the first activities to be abandoned in many

[13] In the economics literature, an urban growth boundary (UGB) is described as a 'second-best' policy: a direct control rather than a price- or quantity-based instrument, designed to reduce transport congestion, prevent excess development at the urban fringe and loss of open space amenity, and reduce excess infrastructure provision. A properly chosen UGB can be welfare-improving. However, emerging results from recent microsimulations suggests that UGBs can be hugely distortive. See J. Brueckner, 'Urban Growth Boundaries: An Effective Second-Best Remedy for Unpriced Traffic Congestion?', mimeo, University of California at Irvine, August 2006, and P. Cheshire and S. Sheppard, 'Taxes Versus Regulation: The Welfare Impacts of Policies for Containing Sprawl', Williams College, Department of Economics Working Paper 193, July 2002. For a guide to regulation and instrument choice, see C. Hepburn, 'Regulation by Prices, Quantities or Both: A Review of Instrument Choice', *Oxford Review of Economic Policy*, 22/2 (2006), pp. 226-247.
[14] Eftec and Entec, *Valuing the External Benefits of Undeveloped Land – A Review of the Economic Literature. A Report for the Office of the Deputy Prime Minister* (2002).
[15] P. Hall, R. Thomas, H. Gracey and R. Drewett, *The Containment of Urban England* (London, 1973); A. Gilg, *Planning in Britain: Understanding and Evaluating the Post-War System* (London, 2005).
[16] See Hall et al., *The Containment of Urban England*, vol. II, pp. 304-328, p. 380; A. Gilg, *Planning in Britain: Understanding and Evaluating the Post-War System* (London, 2005), pp. 116-119; D. A. Rodriguez, F. Targa and S. Aytur, 'Transport Implications of Urban Containment Policies: A Study of the Largest Twenty-five US Metropolitan Areas', *Urban Studies*, vol. 43 (2006), pp. 1879-1897 which finds a similar phenomenon in the US; M. Pennington, *Planning and the Political Market: Public Choice and the Politics of Government Failure* (London, 2002), p. 50.
[17] See Barker, *Review of Land Use Planning: Interim Report* (2006), pp. 18, 159-160.

fringe locations. Green belt designations place huge obstacles in the path of economic and land-use diversification; this means that as farming activity declines, it is very difficult to secure replacement activity and land formerly under agriculture may be abandoned and lose much of its previous quality. The green belt designation can drive or at least accentuate the degradation of urban fringe land.[18]

- **social costs.** With land supply limited, developers have responded to growing demand by building houses at greater density. While higher-income groups have been able to afford to buy houses in protected areas with access to open spaces nearby, lower-income groups in cities have tended to enjoy increasingly little green space in their area due to infill development.[19] They have also had to pay higher prices for housing than would otherwise have been the case, as land supply restrictions contributed to land and property value increases well in excess of inflation, as Chart 2.1 below illustrates.[20]

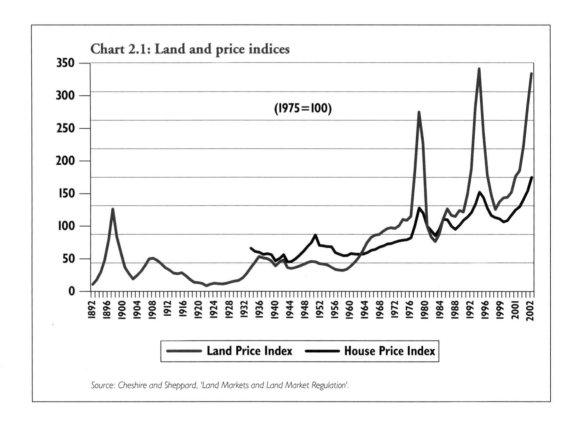

Chart 2.1: Land and price indices

(1975=100)

Land Price Index   House Price Index

Source: Cheshire and Sheppard, 'Land Markets and Land Market Regulation'.

---

[18] J. Andersson, N. Gallent, R. Oades and M. Shoard, 'Urban Fringe – Policy, Regulatory and Literature Research. Report 2.3: Green Belts', Bartlett School of Planning Report for the Countryside Agency, June 2003, p. 13.

[19] See case studies provided by the Greater London Authority and London Assembly, 'Green Spaces Investigative Committee: Scrutiny of Green Spaces in London' (November 2001), p. 50, which illustrate the linkage between social deprivation and absense of green space. See also Pennington, *Planning and the Political Market*, pp. 83-85.

[20] See K. Barker, *Review of Housing Supply. Securing our Future Housing Needs. Interim Report: Analysis* (2003), pp. 15-46, and K. Barker, *Review of Housing Supply. Securing our Future Housing Needs. Final Report: Recommendations* (2004), pp. 13-14, 40. Also see P. Cheshire and S. Sheppard, 'Land Markets and Land Market Regulation: progress towards understanding', *Regional Science and Urban Economics*, 34/6 (2004), pp. 619-637. Gilg's, *Planning in Britain*, while concluding that the planning system has been generally effective, concurs that '[planning] has had a number of side effects, the most serious of which has been inflationary land values and related house price inflation and shortages, notably in the South East' (p. 195).

This inflationary effect was noted as far back as 1973 in Peter Hall et al.'s evaluation of the impact of the Town and Country Planning Act since its inception in 1947.[21] While land prices are driven largely by house prices – demand for land is a 'derived demand' – house prices are themselves also driven to some extent by a shortage of land available for development; and[22]

- **economic costs.** Land use restrictions limit the potential for investment beyond urban areas, and therefore they hinder the ability of the rural economy to diversify beyond agriculture as the sector has declined.[23] In addition, the increasing cost of land through supply restrictions has a number of economic effects as well as social ones, as outlined in the Interim Report:

  - they may contribute to high office occupation costs, which are 40 per cent higher in Manchester and Birmingham than in Mid-town Manhattan;[24]

  - reduced efficiency and competition, by limiting the potential for scale and scope economies due to site-specific restrictions; and by raising the cost of entry for new firms. For example, existing firms who own the freehold of their property do not have to face the high rents charged to new entrants;

  - an adverse impact on labour market flexibility; by reducing the movement of labour between regions, as some workers are priced out of the local market for housing;[25]

  - hampering innovation; as clusters near university towns face impediments to expansion. The growth of the Cambridge and Oxford clusters may have been slowed by containment policies, while some universities, such as Bath, Surrey and York, have had their expansions delayed by many years; and

  - insufficient agglomeration economies; as towns and cities may themselves end up below the size that is most efficient for economic growth.[26]

2.11   There are therefore a number of economic, environmental and social costs and benefits associated with containing towns and cities. When the Government sets out one of the goals of sustainable development as being to ensure 'efficient use of land' it therefore needs to be clear that this does not imply minimal use of land but rather the best use of limited land resources, taking all factors into account.

---

[21] Hall et al, *The Containment of Urban England*, pp. 197-245.

[22] Barker, *Review of Housing Supply: Final Report*, p. 12.

[22] See, for example, the identification of 'planning constraints for on-farm diversification enterprises' as a weakness for future economic development in SWOT analyses conducted by the Regional Planning Boards of the North East, North West, Yorkshire and Humber, West Midlands and East of England regions. For London, 'the large area of Green Belt restrict[ing] rural diversification' was identified as a regional weakness. For the South East, 'nimby culture limiting change', 'green belt/planning restricting diversification' and 'urban fringe problems' were identified as weaknesses, and 'Planning/environmental restrictions ossifying rural economy' identified as a threat to the region, together with 'fragmentation and neglect of agricultural land'. However, in the South West, 'community planning' was identified as providing an opportunity for regional development. See DEFRA, England Rural Development Programme 2000-2006, Appendices: Regional Chapters, www.defra.gov.uk/erdp/docs/national/. However, also see Land Use Consultants, 'Planning for Sustainable Rural Economic Development: Part A Final Report, Findings from the Case Studies' (April 2003), which identified a range of opportunities for rural diversification together with a number of constraints, and concluded that 'Although planning has not been a major barrier in the majority of cases the culture of planning, and its largely reactive response to applicants, can be off putting' (p. 29).

[23] CB Richard Ellis, *Global Market Rents*, January 2006.

[24] P. Cheshire and S. Sheppard, 'The Introduction of Price Signals into Land Use Planning Decision-making: A Proposal', mimeo, London School of Economics, June 2004, p. 13.

[25] See P. P. Combes, G. Duranton and H. Overman, 'Agglomeration and the Adjustment of the Spatial Economy', CEP Discussion Paper no. 689, Centre for Economic Performance, London School of Economics, May 2005.

RESPONDING TO THE CHALLENGE OF FUTURE HIGH DEMAND FOR SPACE WITHIN URBAN ENVELOPES

2.12   What is the context for decisions about where to site new development over the next few decades, to be reflected in Regional Spatial Strategies and Local Development Frameworks? Demand for land will clearly continue to grow. The pressures of globalisation mean that businesses require access to high-quality commercial space in a variety of locations and in increasing quantities; in London, for example, it is estimated that an additional 6.6-8.9 million square metres of additional office space will be needed by 2026, on top of the 2005 stock of 28.5 million square metres.[27] While buildings can go 'up' as well as 'out', the need for associated transport and other infrastructure will mean that a minimal land take is not always feasible. The evidence for this is clearest for housing development, where land for related types of development such as transport infrastructure, schools, hospitals and other services will also be required. The population of England is projected to rise to 55 million by 2026, up from 46.4 million in 1971, with population growth accelerating from an average increase of 108,000 per year for 1971-2003, to 225,000 per year for 2003-26.[28] Household numbers have also grown significantly, from 16 million in 1971 to 21.5 million in 2006 (with an average increase of 153,000 per year over 1971-2003) and are projected to reach 25.7 million by 2026 (an average increase of 209,000 per year for 2003-26).[29] This means that an additional 4.8 million households are likely to be formed over the period 2003-2026.[30] This pressure is a consequence of the long-term trends described in the Interim Report: changing social trends such as people increasingly living alone, reducing the average household size to 2.1 by 2026; demographic trends relating to increasing longevity; and higher migration.[31] Over 2.3 million households are projected for Greater London, the South East and the East of England (see Table 2.3 below – although it should be noted that these figures provide a central estimate within a wide range).

---

[27] See Mayor of London, *Draft Further Alterations to the London Plan: Spatial Development Strategy for Greater London* (September 2006), p. 101, using estimates based on Mayor of London, *London Office Policy Review 2006* (August 2006), p. 78, Table 17: Office Capacity versus Potential Need in London by Borough 2006-2026.

[28] Note that these population estimates and projections are 2003-based (rather than using more recent estimates) in order to compare like-for-like with the official estimates of household projections, which are also 2003-based. The 2003-based population estimates are available at DCLG, Table 422: Live tables on household and population estimates and projections, http://www.communities.gov.uk/pub/107/Table422_id1156107.xls. Data for 1971-80 are added from table 421 and the 2003-based population projection for 2026 has been added from C. Shaw, Government Actuary's Department, *Interim 2003-based National Population Projections for the United Kingdom and Constituent Countries* (2004).

[29] The average increase was 135,000 per year 1971-81, 180,400 per year 1981-91, 135,700 per year 1991-2001, projected to reach 204,300 over 2001-11, and 221,500 2011-21. The average rates of growth for 1971-2003 and 2003-26 are given here – rather than using 2006 as a cut-off – because the official estimates use 2003-based projections and are familiar to commentators.

[30] DCLG, Table 401: Household estimates and projections: Great Britain, 1961-2026. Live table accessed 7 November 2006. Note that these figures are subject to change; much depends on the assumptions made by the Government Actuary's Department as to mortality, fertility and migration trends. The household estimates are based on updated projections of household formation taking account of the 2001 Census and on the Office for National Statistics' sub-national population projections and the Government Actuary's Department's national population projections (2003 based). For more detail on how the estimates are created, see DCLG, Communities and Local Government 2003 based Household Projections: Methodology and Sources of Data (October 2006), www.communities.gov.uk/index.asp?id=1156096.

[31] Household size estimate for 2026 available from DCLG, Table 401: Household estimates and projections: Great Britain, 1961-2026.

Table 2.3: Projected household growth by region[32]

	Number of households			Annual increase
	2003	2021	2026	2003-26
North East	1,088,000	1,194,000	1,211,000	5,300
North West	2,847,000	3,290,000	3,378,000	21,900
Yorkshire and Humberside	2,104,000	2,437,000	2,511,000	17,700
East Midlands	1,782,000	2,146,000	2,230,000	19,500
West Midlands	2,193,000	2,526,000	2,602,000	17,800
East of England	2,286,000	2,797,000	2,926,000	27,800
London	3,093,000	3,756,000	3,926,000	36,200
South East	3,348,000	4,013,000	4,184,000	36,300
South West	2,137,000	2,622,000	2,745,000	26,400
England	20,904,000	24,781,000	25,713,000	209,000

Source: DCLG, Household Estimates and Projections.[33]

More efficient use of urban land – planning tools

2.13   Some of this new development will be able to take place on previously developed land. This often makes good sense – other things being equal, it is preferable to recycle derelict land than to develop agricultural land, although as the analysis above suggested, containment brings costs as well as benefits. Policies such as the national target that 60 per cent of residential development should occur on previously developed land help to facilitate this. In London, for example, there is a target to achieve 457,950 new homes over the 1997-2016 period, all to be accommodated within the city boundaries without encroaching on open space, through development of areas near train stations, development of infill sites, building on derelict land, development of airspace and from reuse of sites originally developed for commercial purposes, as with the Docklands.[34] The London Plan has set an ambitious target to increase the proportion of development on previously developed land by 5 per cent per 5-year period; in 2005 the provisional figure reached 98 per cent.[35]

2.14   However, there is only a limited supply of previously developed land. Even with 'windfall sites' coming forward, this supply will be insufficient to meet anticipated demand. Furthermore, not all of the previously developed land that physically exists is suitable for redevelopment: some previously developed sites are too complex to develop economically, have 're-greened', or are located where people simply do not wish to live or where firms do not wish to locate. In addition, it is extremely important that the social and environmental value of open urban land such as parks, playing fields and other recreation areas – land which is highly valued by the community – should be factored in to decision-making, so that it is not subject to development pressure. DCLG annual statistics show that in 2005 a stock of 63,500 hectares of previously developed land was available

[32] DCLG, New Projections of Households for England and the Regions to 2026, DCLG Statistical Release 2006/0042, 14 March 2006. These projections were drawn up by Professor Dave King and a team at Anglia Ruskin University. Note that these figures are subject to change; much depends on the assumptions made by the Government Actuary's Department as to mortality, fertility and migration trends. Projected population trends are sensitive to these assumptions while the household estimates draw on population estimates.

[33] DCLG, Communities and Local Government Statistical Release 2006/0042: New Projections of Households for England and the Regions to 2026, 14 March 2006, http://www.communities.gov.uk/index.asp?id=1002882&PressNoticeID=2097.

[34] See Mayor of London, Housing in London: The London Housing Strategy Evidence Base 2005 (June 2005), and Mayor of London, The London Plan, Housing: Supplementary Planning Guidance (November 2005), p. 6.

[35] DCLG, 'Land Use Change in England: Residential Development to 2005', Update, July 2006, pp. 4-5.

for development, of which 44 per cent (27,600 hectares) was judged to be suitable for housing.[36] Not all previously developed land is available for housing as some needs to be reserved to secure a sufficient stock of high-quality employment sites. Based on current permissions and density targets, currently vacant and derelict land and buildings could yield 436,720 dwellings, while property currently in use with known redevelopment potential could yield a further 543,950. On this basis, DCLG predicts that this would yield 980,700 new dwellings,[37] far short of what is needed over the next 20 years.[38] However, the gap will probably be reduced in practice by windfall sites, and possibly by higher average densities. Recent evidence shows that in England there is only a certain proportion of land with known development potential not in plans (see Table 2.4).

Table 2.4: Percentage of previously developed land in use

Region	Vacant land	Derelict land and buildings	Vacant buildings	All vacant and derelict land	Percentage allocated in plans or with planning permission	Known redevelopment potential but not in plan	All in use	All previously developed land
North East	35	30	4	69	18	13	31	100
North West	23	45	5	73	19	8	27	100
Yorkshire & Humber	28	33	10	71	18	11	29	100
East Midlands	20	31	11	62	22	15	38	100
West Midlands	25	30	6	61	30	10	40	100
East of England	18	31	5	54	30	16	46	100
London	12	7	7	26	67	7	74	100
South East	18	13	5	36	49	15	64	100
South West	17	28	5	50	30	20	50	100
England	22	29	6	58	30	13	42	100

Source: DCLG, National Land Use Database. [49]

2.15   Ensuring appropriate density levels will also ensure that urban land is used efficiently. A total of 82 per cent of households live in houses rather than flats, with only 2.4 per cent of all UK households living in flats higher than four storeys.[39] The Government's target of a minimum density of 30 dwellings per hectare is needed to ensure that densities do not fall too low – a certain level of density enables residents and workers to have a choice of access to public transport, shops, health services and schools. As household size continues to fall, physical densities may need to increase to ensure viability of such services. There is a range of estimates for the level of housing density necessary to ensure the viability of public transport, with a definitive figure difficult to

---

[36] DCLG, 'One million new homes could be built on brownfield land', News Release 2006/0086, 29 August 2006.
[37] DCLG, *Results from the National Land Use Database of Previously-Developed Land* (August 2006), p. 9, www.communities.gov.uk/pub/313/PreviouslyDevelopedLandthatmaybeavailableforDevelopmentEngland2005_i d1502313.pdf.
[38] Indeed, many London boroughs are actively identifying possible windfall and infill sites which are too small to be captured by the NLUD.
[39] DCLG, live tables on housing stock, Table 117, www.communities.gov.uk/pub/23/Table117_id1156023.xls, accessed 07 November 2006, section on housing statistics; National Board of Housing, Building and Planning, Sweden, and Ministry for Regional Development of the Czech Republic, *Housing Statistics in the European Union 2004*, p. 43.

provide given that employment density, population density, accessibility and congestion are other important variables.[40] One estimate is that public transport may need a minimum density of 25 dwellings per hectare to make a bus service viable, and 60 dwellings per hectare to make a light transit rail system viable.[41] Anne Power et al. suggest that 50 dwellings per hectare is the minimum viable density for provision of community services, including public transport, schools, shops and banks.[42] URBED cites a simple and similar heuristic: 100 persons per hectare to support a good bus service.[43]

2.16   However, even if average densities are maintained at the 41 dwellings per hectare achieved in 2005,[44] there will be a limit on the ability to site the majority of necessary development on previously developed land. This is partly because while the move from low to medium densities saves a lot of land, the move from medium to high density saves less: the marginal impact of an extra dwelling per hectare on land saved decreases with higher density. At a density of 10 dwellings per hectare, 40 hectares of land are needed to deliver 400 housing units; this falls to 10 hectares at a density of 40 per hectare. However increasing densities to 60 per hectare still requires 6.6 hectares. The benefits of density appear to be most apparent at 30-40 dwellings per hectare.[45] Such a level of density does not necessarily imply high-rise development; a study by the LSE noted that most 1960s tower-block estates surrounded by disused open space were built at considerably lower densities than streets of traditional two-storey terraced housing, which can reach a density of over 60 dwellings per hectare.[46]

---

[40] Overly prescriptive standards to ensure specific transport patterns may not have the desired results – the resident population may choose large-scale, more remote facilities rather than small-scale local facilities despite the presence of excellent public transport links. However, where public transport is valued, it will generate greater site value than the costs of installation and operation. Each unique configuration of services, population, commerce and public transport will give rise to differing increases in site values, the aggregated value of which may indicate whether the public transport system is viable. Source: information provided by Professor Chris Webster, University of Cardiff.

[41] D. Rudlin and N. Falk (URBED), *Building the 21st Century Home. The sustainable urban neighbourhood* (Oxford, 1999), and DETR, 'The Use of Density in Urban Planning' (1998), pp. 61-62. Note that while compact cities are the aim of many planning policies, there is little quantitative evidence to support the claims made in their favour, partly because there are no agreed methods to measure compactness or how it would reduce traffic. Work by M. Breheny and D. Stead suggests that there is not a strong relationship between land use patterns and transport patterns. Stead has calculated that socio-economic characteristics explain two-thirds of travel behaviour, with land use patterns accounting for the other third. The challenge for planners is to produce a land use pattern that provides mobility without sacrificing too much land and creating too much noise and pollution. See A. Gilg, *Planning in Britain*, p. 119; M. Breheny, 'The Compact City and Transport Energy Consumption', *New Transactions of the Institute of British Geographers*, vol. 20 (1995), pp. 81-101; E. Burton, 'Measuring Urban Compactness in UK Towns and Cities', *Environment and Planning B*, vol. 29 (2002), pp. 219-250; D. Stead, 'Relationships between Land Use, Socio-Economic Factors, and Travel Patterns in Britain', *Environment and Planning B*, vol. 28 (2001), pp. 499-528. However, recent work by L. Newman suggests that a density of 35 people and jobs per hectare of urbanised land will reduce car dependence, while a density of over 100 people and jobs can ensure a walking-oriented centre. See P. Newman, 'How dense and mixed do centres have to be before you reduce auto dependence?', mimeo, Institute for Sustainability and Technology Policy, Murdoch University, Western Australia, September 2006, presented to European Transport Conference 2006, 18-20 September.

[42] A. Power, L. Richardson, K. Seshimo and K. Firth, *A Framework for Housing in the London Thames Gateway* (London 2004); also see Proceedings of the LSE London Density Debate, 19 June 2006, www.lse.edu/collections/londonDevelopmentWorkshops/density%20debate/report.doc.

[43] P. Hall, *The Land Fetish* (2005), p. 16.

[44] DCLG, 'Land Use Change in England: Residential Development to 2005' Update, July 2006.

[45] P. Hall, *The Land Fetish* (2005) p. 16. Hall points out that this will not yield the population density which was achieved in the past, due to changes in household formation.

[46] R. Burdett, T. Travers, D. Czischke, P. Rode and B. Moser, *Density and Urban Neighbourhoods in London: Summary Report* (Enterprise LSE Cities, 2004), pp. 13-14. In Clissold, Stoke Newington, two-storey terraced housing reaches a density of 148.1 persons per hectare or 66.8 dwellings per hectare (p. 13).

2.17   It should also be recognised that the UK does not in general currently have low density levels, contrary to common assumptions. Data for the densities of cities needs to be interpreted with care. For example, if administrative boundaries are used, much will depend on how far this boundary encompasses the suburbs. But on the data provided by the EC-sponsored Urban Audit, UK cities are around the European average in terms of density, though by world-city standards London has a relatively low density (see Chart 2.2).[47] Of the 252 cities in the Urban Audit survey for which density data are available, the mean for Europe is 2,243 per square kilometre (and the median 1,649 per square kilometre), while the mean for UK cities is 2,609 per square kilometre.[48]

---

[47] www.urbanaudit.org. The Urban Audit data suggests that Inner London has a population density of 8,671 people per square kilometre while la Ville de Paris has a density of 20,248, although an official estimate which includes the Greater Paris area is not available. The problems caused by the spatial definition chosen are particularly relevant when comparing London with Paris. The administrative level for which there is a mayor, i.e. Greater London and la Ville de Paris, yields different spatial units: Greater London has a population of 7.2 million and la Ville de Paris 2.1 million. Urban Audit created an additional city level for both cities. 'Inner London' comprises the City of London and the twelve most central boroughs: Camden, Hackney, Hammersmith & Fulham, Haringey, Islington, Kensington & Chelsea, Lambeth, Lewisham, Newham, Southwark, Tower Hamlets and Westminster. For Paris, a larger city level, called 'Paris et petite couronne', was constructed which is roughly comparable to Greater London: the city of Paris itself plus Hauts-de-Seine, Seine-Saint-Denis and Val-de-Marne. Nevertheless, there are no Urban Audit population density data for Paris et petite couronne or for the Parisian Larger Urban Zone to compare with Greater London and the Greater London Larger Urban Zone, although it is generally known that the Greater Paris region has low residential density. For example, see European Commission, Urban Transport Benchmarking Initiative, which reports that 'Greater Paris' (Ile de France) has a density of 937 people per square kilometre. (See www.transportbenchmarks.org/pdf/final/Paris-Isabelle-Bachmann-RATP.ppt). This compares with the 1,303 people per square kilometre for the Greater London Larger Urban Zone reported by Urban Audit. An alternative measure estimated that London has a density of 5,045 people per square kilometre, lower than Milan (5,825 per square kilometre), Paris (6,413 per square kilometre) and Madrid (12,407 per square kilometre). See S. Angel, D. Civco and S. Sheppard, *The Dynamics of Global Urban Expansion* (World Bank, 2005). The authors used a sample of 90 cities across the globe and the subset for Western Europe was small in number. The LSE points out that by worldcity standards, London has a relatively low residential density level; the lowest density levels in Manhattan equate to the highest in Central London. Furthermore, while Central London supports 1.4 million workplaces, Manhattan sustains 2 million workplaces over a similar area. See R. Burdett, T. Travers, D. Czischke, P. Rode and B. Moser, *Density and Urban Neighbourhoods in London: Summary Report* (Enterprise LSE Cities, 2004), pp. 20-21. Central London equates with zone 1.

[48] Inner London is excluded from the calculation of the average of UK cities since London is also included. The figures are rounded. The Urban Audit aims at a balanced and representative sample of cities in Europe. Note that of the Urban Audit sample of 258 cities, approximately 20 per cent of the national populations were covered by the sample, including all capital cities, most regional capitals, as well as a variety of medium-sized cities geographically dispersed within each Member State.

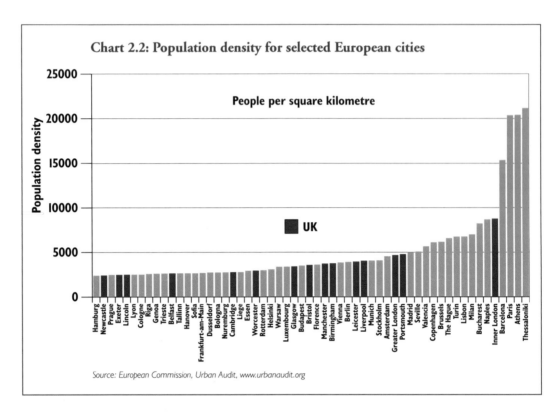

Chart 2.2: Population density for selected European cities

Source: European Commission, Urban Audit, www.urbanaudit.org

2.18   There are also limits to how high densities can reasonably be taken throughout the whole of England, particularly once people's preferences are taken into account. One survey shows that only 2 per cent of people, for example, would choose to live in a low-rise flat and less than 1 per cent in a high-rise block, while 52 per cent of the population would ideally live in a detached house.[50] But in 2004 34 per cent of new completions were flats, up from 16 per cent in 1999.[51]

Fiscal incentives for using urban space efficiently

2.19   One potential means of encouraging a greater proportion of new development to take place in urban areas is the application of active fiscal policies, so that tax on land and property is raised with as few distortions and as equitably as possible. One much-discussed proposal is the equalisation of VAT for renovation and new build. At present, VAT is payable on the renovation and repair of existing homes, but not on the building of new dwellings. This creates a distortion; it may, at the margin, be cheaper to build new houses than to renovate existing homes, with consequent inefficient use of the existing stock. Since EC law prevents the extension of the zero-VAT rate, this implies applying VAT to new housing. While this has attractions, there are also a number of disadvantages. In particular, under EC rules, VAT can only legally be levied at the same rate throughout a territory: either 5 per cent or 17.5 per cent in the UK. The variability of land values across the UK is such that VAT charged on the value of a house, the incidence of which would tend to fall on the landowner rather than the home buyer, would mean that (for a 17.5 per cent tax rate) land would effectively be taxed at a very high rate in the North East and a much lower rate in the South East.[52]

---

[49]DCLG, Results from the National Land Use Database of Previously-Developed Land (August 2006), p. 10, www.communities.gov.uk/pub/313/PreviouslyDevelopedLandthatmaybeavailableforDevelopmentEngland2005_i d1502313.pdf.

[50]CABE, 'Public Attitudes to Architecture and Public Space: Transforming Neighbourhoods: Final Report. Research Study Conducted for the Commission for Architecture and the Built Environment' (November 2004), p. 30.

[51]CABE, 'Public Attitudes to Architecture and Public Space', p. 33.

[52]K. Barker, *Review of Housing Supply: Final Report,* pp. 79-83.

2.20   There are, however, other options available. One would be to consider changes to the relief from national non-domestic rates (NNDR), commonly known as 'business rates' currently available on empty property. NNDR is calculated by applying a standard multiplier to the rateable value of the property, as assessed by the Valuation Office Agency. Various analyses have shown that NNDR is highly – if not completely – capitalised, and therefore that the economic incidence of the tax falls primarily and perhaps exclusively on property owners.[53] In this respect NNDR has some of the characteristics of a tax on land values, often described (from Adam Smith and David Ricardo to Kay and King)[54] as one of the least distortive ways of raising tax revenue.

2.21   Reliefs currently available when property falls empty differ according to the 'bulk class', or type, of property. All properties receive 100 per cent relief for the first three months of their being left vacant, regardless of bulk class. After three months, only those properties assessed as belonging to 'industrial' or 'warehouse' bulk classes receive 100 per cent relief; all other premises (offices, commercial property and retail space) receive 50 per cent relief.[55]

2.22   The principle behind this relief is to create a broadly symmetrical tax, given uncertainty: when property earns a positive revenue, it is taxed; when it does not, relief is granted. This helps remove what would otherwise be a distortion and helps to share risk between property owners and the government.[56] There is, therefore, a sound a priori economic case for saying that some relief should be available to rateable property that has been vacant for some period, and that a natural rate of turnover of property exists.

2.23   One justification for the variation in relief payments by bulk class might be that office and retail space is of lower market risk than industrial property. In fact, comparing annual volatility of property values in the different sectors over 1981-96,[57] we find that while retail properties display the lowest volatility, the office sector has the highest.[58] On this basis alone it would be difficult to justify offices receiving the least relief. Conversely, some industrial property may be so specific to its current use that the scope for immediate sale or re-letting is lower than, say, for a relatively standard office or retail unit. Assessed from this point of view, there may be a case for some sectoral differences in the form of the relief.

2.24   However, risk is not always of this simple, external nature. The value of a property will be significantly determined by its owners in addition to external factors. Owners may perhaps allow property to fall into disrepair; they may be uninformed about better uses to which it could be put; and they may be keeping a property empty for speculative reasons. While these behaviours are clearly not the norm, and most commercial property is actively employed, there may be a particular concern about this speculative effect to the extent it is caused by interaction between the planning and the local taxation systems.

---

[53]IFF Research Ltd, 'The Impact of Rates on Businesses', Report for Department of the Environment (1995); Institute for Fiscal Studies, 'The Relationship Between Rates and Rents: An Analysis of the Relationship Between Non-Domestic Rates and Commercial Rents', Report for the Department of the Environment (1995), N. Mehdi, 'The Capitalisation of Business Rates: An Empirical Study of Tax Incidence in Six London Boroughs', Ph.D. thesis, London School of Economics, 2003; S. Bond, K. Denny, J. Hall and W. McCluskey, 'Who Pays Business Rates', *Fiscal Studies* (1996), 17/1, pp. 19-36, p. 21.

[54] J. A. Kay and M. A. King, *The British Tax System* (Oxford, 5th edition, 1990).

[55] Details from DCLG website at www.neighbourhood.statistics.gov.uk/dissemination/MetadataDownloadPDF.do;jsessionid=ac1f930dce67b8afff69 a234158a15891e7131c8d80.e38OaNuRbNuSbi0Nbh0LbhyRaxb0n6jAmljGr5XDqQLvpAe?downloadId=18166 &bhcp=1.

[56] See, for details, A. B. Atkinson and J. E. Stiglitz, *Lectures in Public Economics* (New York, 1980), chapter 4, for details on tax systems and risk.

[57] Calculated from the IPD database.

[58] Measured by standard deviation of a price index over the years stated for each property sector.

2.25   A closer look at where empty property is found suggests that vacancies are not only found in former industrial areas (see Table 2.5). Accepting that there is a natural rate of vacancy,[59] these data nonetheless suggest that there are parts of the country where significant amounts of land and property are not in use. This seems at odds with the joint environmental and economic objectives of efficient use of developed land and efficient markets for commercial property.

Table 2.5: Highest-ranked local authorities by rate of vacancy (percentage of property vacant), 2002-03 to 2004-05

	2002-03	2003-04	2004-05
Hackney	22	20	28
Slough	17	18	20
Birmingham	14	15	19
Ealing	18	18	18
Manchester	16	17	18
Hyndburn	12	13	17
City of London	9	14	16
Brent	19	16	16
Sandwell	13	14	16
Wolverhampton	12	14	13

Source: DCLG, Commercial and Industrial Estimated Vacancy Statistics. [60]

2.26   In addition, vacant previously developed land exists which has not yet been brought forward for redevelopment, as mentioned above. Clearly some of this land may be affected by contamination, and some of it lies in areas with very low demand. These characteristics should be captured in the land values. However, where land is scarce and suitable for development, prices will be high. Given the economic and environmental benefits from reusing previously developed land for new developments, it seems sensible for these sites to be developed as soon as possible. As discussed in the *Barker Review of Housing Supply*, there is a case for a charge on some forms of previously developed land to raise the opportunity cost of holding them unused at times of high demand.[61] In the case of low-demand areas or contaminated sites, the low value of the site will mean that there is little by way of charge to be paid.

2.27   Following this analysis, there is good reason for reform of Empty Property Relief. Any such change could be supported with measures to encourage renovation of existing property and to ensure that the existing property stock is not subject to acts of deliberate dereliction. This reform could be considered in the context of the Lyons Inquiry into Local Government.

2.28   Consideration should also be given to considering how best to extend a charge to vacant and derelict previously-developed land and buildings, based on the existing methods of capturing returns to non-domestic land and property through business rates.

2.29   Allied to these incentives for increased recycling of previously developed land, the Government should consider reform of the existing Corporation Tax relief for remediating contaminated land to focus additional support on developers who wish to bring forward hard-to-remediate previously developed sites. This would be particularly important in the context of the proposed Planning-gain Supplement, as identified in the *Barker Review of Housing Supply*.

---

[59] S. Titman, 'Urban Land Prices under Uncertainty', *American Economic Review*, vol. 75 (1985), pp. 505-514.
[60] DCLG, Commercial and Industrial Property Estimated Vacancy Statistics: England, 2004-05 (July 2006), p. 7.
[61] K. Barker, *Barker Review of Housing Supply: Recommendations* (2004), p. 73.

2.30   While any reform to Empty Property Relief and a future charge on previously developed land will involve some impact on certain sectors, and there are certain legal circumstances and cases of reserved strategic capacity where these new incentives should not apply, these changes would have a number of beneficial effects:

- when there is the prospect of continued vacancy, landlords are more likely to reduce rents in order to encourage occupation. This is beneficial for both new and existing business tenants;

- landowners have less of an incentive to hold back land in the expectation that property values will continue to rise or to secure a change of use. This will increase the supply of land for development; and

- development is encouraged on sites which have already been developed, which reduces the need to build on greenfield sites and improves environmental outcomes.

Recommendation 8

The Government should make better use of fiscal interventions to encourage an efficient use of urban land. In particular, it should reform business rate relief for empty property and consider introducing a charge on vacant and derelict brownfield land. This reform could be considered in the context of the broader set of issues in relation to local government finance being examined by the Lyons Inquiry.

In parallel with the introduction of the proposed Planning-gain Supplement, the Government should consult on reforms to Land Remediation Relief to help developers bring forward hard-to-remediate brownfield sites.

RESPONDING TO INCREASED DEMAND FOR LAND BEYOND CURRENT URBAN ENVELOPES

2.31   Ensuring a more efficient use of urban land via planning and fiscal means will help to reduce the need to develop open land. But it will not eliminate it. The analysis above indicates that there will need to be a continued, and probably higher, use of presently undeveloped land beyond towns and cities in coming decades, though the scale of this should not be exaggerated. There is already clear evidence of supply constraints: in 2005 the value of land for residential use in England and Wales was £2.6 million per hectare and £779,000 per hectare for business class B1.[62] A sustainability study conducted as part of the Government's response to the *Barker Review of Housing Supply* estimated that compared to the existing urbanised land of 2.6 million hectares, the baseline planned growth 2001-31 would occupy an additional 85,800 hectares or 3.3 per cent of the current total urbanised area, whilst the high additional growth scenario in the south could require an additional 38,000 hectares of land, or a further 1.46 per cent of the current total urbanised area.[63]

---

[62] Valuation Office Agency, *Property Market Report* 2006.
[63] ODPM, 'A Sustainability Impact Study of Additional Housing Scenarios in England' (December 2005), pp. 61-62.

Protecting the land that matters most

2.32   It is crucial that environmentally sensitive land or land with high scenic value is protected properly, and the various criteria-based environment and landscape designations do this extremely well. They include National Parks, Sites of Special Scientific Interest, Areas of Outstanding Natural Beauty, Special Areas of Conservation and Special Protection Areas. Many of these areas overlap, but they still protect a sizeable area of England from development, as illustrated in the Interim Report.[64] Of course, even within these areas there will be planning applications that should be accepted, but these are generally not appropriate areas for substantial levels of new development. Many of these areas are designated on intrinsic scientific or technical grounds rather than attempting to take economic and social concerns into account, in order to maintain high environmental and landscape standards. DEFRA's work with DCLG to ensure that consideration is given to sustainable use and protection of soil during planning and development is also of value here. The Stern Review has also noted that future species migration patterns must be anticipated:

> 'Policies for nature protection should be sufficiently flexible to allow for species' movement across the landscape, through a variety of measures to reduce the fragmentation of the landscape and make the intervening countryside more permeable to wildlife, for example use of wildlife corridors or "biodiversity islands".'[65]

2.33   At the same time, land at risk of flooding needs protection. The risk associated with developing on flood plains, where many previously developed sites are located, may in some cases only be alleviated by extremely costly methods, such as construct new flood defences. Approximately 10 per cent of homes, housing 5 million people, are located in areas at substantial risk of flooding.[66] The Office of Science and Technology predicts that increased flood risk is among the likely effects of climate change, suggesting that annual average damage claims would increase between two- to twentyfold by the end of the century.[67]

2.34   There may be market failures in the provision of insurance against flood risk, where developers cannot assess potential flood risk accurately, or where individual insurers cannot cover widespread risk. By forcing developers to account for risk before building, planning can address these problems. A study by the Association of British Insurers suggested that planned development in four Thames Gateway designated growth areas would increase national flood risk by 5 per cent, but would add less than 1 per cent additional housing capacity and that using existing planning guidelines 'would almost completely eliminate' the flood risk.[68] Land use planning and performance standards, in encouraging private and public investment towards locations that are less vulnerable to climate risks and flooding, are important elements for managing flood risk in the long term.[69]

[64] K. Barker, *Review of Land Use Planning: Interim Report* provides a map on page 34.

[65] N. Stern, *Stern Review on the Economics of Climate Change* (2006), p. 422.

[66] Association of British Insurers, 'Flooding and insurance' at www.abi.org.uk/flooding.

[67] Office of Science and Technology, 'Future Foresight: flood and coastal defence' (2004) at www.foresight.gov.uk/previous_projects/flood_and_coastal_defence/index.html.

[68] Association of British Insurers, Submission to the Barker Review of Land Use Planning, www.hm-treasury.gov.uk/media/15E/89/barker2_2006_associationofbritishinsurers_72kb.pdf.

[69] N. Stern, *Stern Review on the Economics of Climate Change* (2006), pp. 419-422.

Making green belt policy work better

2.35   In many instances, land that is suitable for development in sustainable development terms is likely to be that found within or near to large towns and cities. Land close to transport nodes is less likely to require the construction of extensive additional infrastructure. It also enables development to take place relatively close to current employment and leisure centres, rather than encouraging lengthy commuting patterns. This limits the 'leap-frogging' that otherwise takes place.[70] Lengthy commuting patterns are already apparent in the South East due to the 'pull' of London as an employment centre.[71] The Royal Town Planning Institute (RTPI) notes that 'there is a super-London functional labour market area with a 60 km radius ... [with] a clear commuter ring embracing the London urban area in a shape that resembles a symmetrical eye'.[72] The locational choices of dual-income households where earners work in different areas, or a genuine desire to live in the countryside, may also lead to this outcome.

---

[70] M. J. Elson, 'Green Belts: The Need for Re-Appraisal', *Town & Country Planning*, 68/5, pp. 156-158; E. Glaeser and M. E. Kahn, 'Sprawl and Urban Growth', NBER Working Paper No. 9733, May 2003, p. 4.
[71] Maps provided by the RTPI are particularly illustrative. See RTPI, *Uniting Britain: The Evidence Base – Spatial Structure and Key Drivers* (July 2006), p. 25. Department for Transport data shows that mean commuting times increased from 23.6 minutes to 25.9 minutes a day over 1994-2004 (Transport Statistics Great Britain 2005) while Evans and Oswald report that full-time workers in London lost 70 minutes a week of leisure time to commuting during the course of the 1990s. See S. Evans and A. Oswald, 'The Price of Freedom: A Non-Technical Explanation of the Case for Road Pricing', *Transport Review* (Winter 1999-2000), pp. 28-29.
[72] RTPI, *Uniting Britain*, p. 23.

2.36   It is also likely that this is the land that people would be, relatively, the most comfortable about seeing developed. A survey commissioned for the Review asked respondents to choose the three categories of land they would most like to see protected from development.[73] The results, summarised in Chart 2.3 below, were that 71 per cent of respondents chose land with endangered wildlife as one of their three categories, with 54 per cent choosing land with scenic value, and 47 per cent choosing green spaces in towns and cities. Only 17 per cent cited land on the edge of towns and cities as being among the most important to protect, indicating that such land did not have the greatest priority for respondents.[74] This is as suggested by the analysis of the social benefits of different types of open space previously referred to – for example, the social value per hectare of natural and semi-natural wetlands is on average over £1.3 million, while the value of urban fringe green belt is around £180,000.[75]

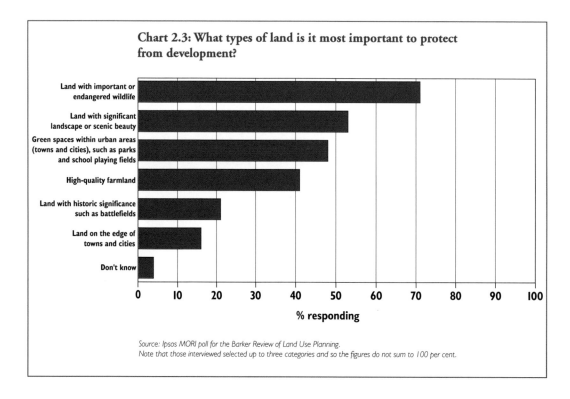

Chart 2.3: What types of land is it most important to protect from development?

Source: Ipsos MORI poll for the Barker Review of Land Use Planning.
Note that those interviewed selected up to three categories and so the figures do not sum to 100 per cent.

---

[73] Respondents were offered three categories to capture the fact that people may have multiple preferences.

[74] The question put to survey respondents was: 'It is very likely that with a growing population, increasing wealth and changing household structure, more land will be required for development such as housing, infrastructure, schools, hospitals and commercial development. With this in mind, what type of land is it most important to protect from development? Please choose three from the following list: land with important or endangered wildlife; land with significant landscape or scenic beauty; green spaces within urban areas (towns and cities), such as parks and school playing fields; high-quality farmland; land with historic significance such as battlefields; land on the edge of towns and cities'.

[75] See K. Barker, *Barker Review of Land Use Planning: Interim Report* (2006), chapter 8, p. 155. Note the detail on methodology in the appendix to that chapter; the composition of benefits estimated for each land type differ slightly.

2.37   At present, a large proportion of land near many of England's large towns and cities is classified in regional and local plans as green belt. The concept of a green belt being used to separate a major metropolis from satellite towns and to act as a locus for agriculture and institutions such as hospitals was popularised by the Garden City movement and by the work of Ebenezer Howard.[76] The designation has been in use for over 50 years. It was originally designed 'to provide a reserve supply of public open spaces and of recreational areas and to establish a green belt or girdle of open space';[77] when introduced as a national policy in 1955, green belt objectives expanded to check the further growth of a large built-up area, to prevent neighbouring towns from merging into one another, and to preserve the special character of a town.[78] More recently, the objectives of regeneration and safeguarding the countryside have been added. The major success of green belt policy over the past two decades has been in driving regeneration and urban renaissance, in conjunction with policies to encourage the use of underused urban land.[79]

Success of green belts

2.38   There is little doubt that green belt policy has played a major role in checking the unrestricted sprawl of large built-up areas and safeguarding the countryside from encroachment. Without the green belt, the benefits of containment would have been much harder to achieve. This remains the case today. The key principles of green belt policy remain valid. It should also be noted that despite widespread perceptions that the green belts are under threat, the area under green belt designation has grown markedly over the past 50 years, including in the past ten years, as illustrated in Table 2.6 below. At present, green belts cover almost 13 per cent, or 16,768 square kilometres, of England – an area only a little less than the highest estimate of all developed land cited earlier in this chapter (13.5 per cent). In the South East alone there are over 600,000 hectares of green belt land. Besides this, it is estimated that an additional 13,000 hectares (130 square kilometres) are earmarked in provisional local development plans for future designation.

2.39   Green belts also appear to be popular. In a recent survey, respondents were given a brief explanation of green belts – including key arguments for and against – and asked for their view on the idea that such land should remain undeveloped. Six in ten respondents were strongly in agreement, while just 6 per cent disagreed to any extent. People feared the biggest threats facing green belts were house building, road building and other kinds of built development, including airport expansion.[80] But as the analysis set out below suggests, it is not clear that people understand the function of green belts, and it is also unlikely that many appreciate its extent or indirect costs.

---

[76] E. Howard, *Garden Cities of Tomorrow* (London, 1902).

[77] Greater London Regional Planning Committee (1935).

[78] M. Elson, *Green Belts: Conflict Mediation In the Urban Fringe* (London, 1986), p. 14.

[79] M. Elson et al, *The Effectiveness of Green Belts. A Report for the Department of the Environment* (1993).

[80] MORI survey for the Campaign to Protect Rural England, conducted 30 June-4 July 2005. Results available at http://www.cpre.org.uk/news-releases/news-rel-2005/49a-05.htm.

Table 2.6: Area of green belt land by region, 1997 and 2004

Region or area of England	Area of green belt 1997, hectares	Area of green belt 2004, hectares
North East	53,410	71,900
North West	255,760	260,600
Yorkshire and Humber	261,350	262,600
East Midlands	79,710	79,500
West Midlands	269,170	269,500
East Anglia	26,690	26,800
London and South East	600,320	601,400
South West	105,900	106,000
England	1,652,310	1,678,200[81]

Source: DCLG.[82]

Need for boundary reviews

2.40   In the context of the pressures for more land to be developed, and the reality that it is desirable that some of this should, for environmental and economic reasons, be provided in areas currently near towns and cities, there is already pressure on green belts in a number of locations. Different areas have different needs and the green belt policy should be sensitive to the impacts in each specific case. A number of locations are sensibly adjusting their green belt boundaries in the context of growing pressure for development. Cambridge provides a notable example, where a balanced approach was pursued to accommodate growth pressures. This is welcome. There is likely to be increased need for green belt reviews, both to ensure that the integrity of green belts is maintained where necessary and to ensure that the development that takes place in England is genuinely sustainable (with careful evaluation of the different environmental impacts of different patterns of development). The requirements of sustainable development suggest that some urban extensions and new settlements should take place clustered around transport corridors, or at the edge of urban areas. The policy framework should clearly allow for this. Given the high proportion of land that is green belt, limited and properly justified change of classification could be allowed without jeopardising the overall goals for which green belts are designed. As the Town and Country Planning Association (TCPA) argues, 'green belt in some areas, especially in the south east, have become 'green blankets' stretching 20-30 miles around cities. Their role should be refocused as an effective means of achieving sustainable development'.[83] But in other areas, such as the North West, the green belt has played, and should still play, a vital role in securing regeneration and efficient use of urban infrastructure – it is less likely that significant alterations to green belt boundaries would be justified here.

---

[81] This is the published total and reflects rounding of regional figures.
[82] ODPM News Release 2005/237:http://www.communities.gov.uk/index.asp?id=1002882&PressNoticeID=2002 for 2004 data and ODPM News Release 2004/1655 at http://www.communities.gov.uk/index.asp?id=1002882&PressNoticeID=1655 for 1997 data. Previous estimates were compiled from local and regional reports, reflecting different levels of local knowledge of the status and detail of the green belt, derived from different scales of maps and plans, using different area measurement techniques, and with some reporting out-of-date data. Since 1999 areas are calculated from digitised Green Belt boundaries shown in proposals maps from adopted or deposited area-wide local plans and unitary development plans.
[83] TCPA Policy Statement: *Green Belts* (accompanying press release), May 2002.

Enhancing quality of green belts

2.41 A further issue which should be addressed is how the quality of the green belts can be enhanced. This is particularly the case given that the great majority of green belt land is not available for recreation, and a large proportion of it is low-value agricultural land, or previously developed land, such as airfields, with little social value. In a small, densely populated island, it is necessary to ensure that the maximum environmental and social value is being obtained from the available open space. Contrary to popular belief, green belts are not an environmental designation. A survey conducted for the Review, summarised in Table 2.7 below, shows that 60 per cent of respondents thought that one of the main functions of the green belt is to protect wildlife and the environment, with 46 per cent believing that it is to protect and enhance landscape and scenic beauty, while 24 per cent believed one of its functions is to protect high-value farmland. Less than half correctly identified a primary purpose of green belt policy as being the prevention of unrestricted spread of towns and cities.[83] The MORI survey for the Campaign to Protect Rural England (CPRE), cited earlier, found that a quarter of the public (27 per cent) claimed to be well-informed about green belts, while a similar proportion (25 per cent) said that they knew nothing. The remaining 47 per cent knew 'just a little'. These figures provide some justification for the RTPI's suggestion that green belt policy 'is probably also the policy that is most familiar to, but most often misinterpreted and misunderstood by, the public at large'.[84]

Table 2.7: What, if any, are the functions of the green belt?

	Percentage responding
Protecting wildlife and the environment	60
Protecting and enhancing the landscape and scenic beauty	46
Preventing spread of urban areas (towns and cities) into the countryside	45
Protecting high-value farmland	24
Protecting the setting of historic towns	22
Encouraging regeneration of urban areas (towns and cities) through re-using previously developed land	21
Don't know	7
None of these	1

Source: Ipsos MORI poll for the Barker Review of Land Use Planning.

Note that those interviewed provided multiple responses and so the figures do not sum to 100 per cent.

2.42 This raises the question of how green belts can be enhanced so that their potential benefits are maximised.[85] This is likely to involve a more positive approach than is currently in place. As the RTPI has expressed more forcibly:

'There is a need for a much more pragmatic approach to the control of development in green belts, with a lot more flexibility and realism than the PPG suggests. New policies must recognize the need to protect green belts from inappropriate development, but not to the extent that the land becomes a museum of inactivity ... the present unimaginative view of development that is "appropriate" in green belts is damaging to environmental

[83] The question put to respondents was: 'Green belts surround some of our towns and cities. Which of the following, if any, are the main functions of the green belts?' The 'true' functions of the green belt are the third, fifth and sixth in the list – see paragraph 2.8 above.

[84] RTPI, 'Green Belt Policy: A Discussion Paper' (2000), p. 1.

[85] Annex A of PPG 2: Green Belts gives short guidance on how this might be achieved: namely, working together with landowners and advising voluntary organisations such as Groundwork Trusts and statutory bodies such as the Countryside Commission, the Forestry Commission and English Partnerships. The annex advises that where existing boundaries have been determined they should be protected, but where they have not been established in detail, to consider whether land should be reserved for development, to ease pressure elsewhere and thus 'develop and maintain a positive approach to land management which both makes adequate provision for necessary development and ensures that the Green Belt serves its proper purpose'.

quality in just the areas where amenity demands are highest. Agriculture is experiencing a hard time generally. Farming on the urban fringe – which is where most green belts are found – has long been only marginally viable and is now increasingly so. Where restrictive development control policies prevent its diversification, much land becomes effective incapable of any beneficial use, and its environmental quality declines accordingly. This is unacceptable in the areas that many urban dwellers look to for fresh air and recreation.[86]

2.43   The most practical means of achieving this may be to provide a more positive approach to applications for development in green belts *where they will contribute to the delivery of green belt objectives*. At present, these positive objectives for land in the green belt comprise the following:

- to provide opportunities for access to the open countryside for the urban population;

- to provide opportunities for outdoor sport and outdoor recreation near urban areas;

- to retain attractive landscapes, and enhance landscapes, near to where people live;

- to improve damaged and derelict land around towns;

- to secure nature conservation interest; and

- to retain land in agricultural, forestry and related uses.[87]

2.44   If development clearly delivers social and environmental benefits of this kind there is the potential for all to gain. This model has in fact been applied in the past, where a derelict landfill site close to Heathrow Airport, which happened to lie within the green belt was approved for redevelopment on condition that the site was successfully landscaped (see Box 2.1). The same concept was set out in a recent study which called for the 're-greening of England' through allowing development such as affordable housing in areas, including green belts, where there was the potential for environmental gain through the provision of additional areas of woodland.[88] The Report suggested that 3 per cent of agricultural land – 143,000 hectares – could be converted into 90 per cent woodland, 5 per cent new housing and 5 per cent supporting infrastructure. Not only could this result in around 950,000 new homes and so increase housing affordability for first time buyers but it would also create areas rich in insect, bird and animal life, and, by adding around 11 per cent to the stock of woodland, help combat climate change. The scale of this proposal may be too large, and the costs of managing the woodland may be high, but in some areas this approach may be appropriate.

---

[86] RTPI, 'Green Belt Policy: A Discussion Paper' (2000), p. 10.
[87] See Planning Policy Guidance 2: Green Belts, paragraph 1.6. These objectives are considered, in current policy, to be 'second-order' and the purposes of including land in the green belt, described in paragraph 2.8 above, take priority.
[88] M. Balen, *Land Economy* (2006).

Box 2.1: Stockley Park: Enhancing landscape at the urban fringe

Stockley Park was built on a derelict landfill site close to Heathrow Airport where London's bricks had once been made. Following increased planning flexibility in the early 1980s, due to the merging of industry and office classes under B1 use, developers had the opportunity to creative an innovative business park together and undertake major landscaping of the adjoining derelict land, which involved massive landfill and soil transfer. Although a costly project, the developers and investors were confident that the quality of the resulting development would draw in tenants and make it viable. The developers approached Hillingdon Borough Council with a masterplan. Development began in 1985 and the park was opened in 1986. The result was an environmental and economic win—win.

Stockley Park comprises 168 hectares, with the business park itself covering 57 hectares. The park is one of the largest man-made parks in London. Over 30 companies are currently located there, in high-quality office buildings spread out with green spaces between each. The park includes a lake, a golf course and a public park, which is extensively used by walkers. Around 140,000 trees and shrubs were planted in the public park by 1993, and 47 species of birds are permanently or occasionally resident. The business park works to an environmental management plan, which includes a travel plan run by the resident companies to encourage green travel and cut car use, with high-quality bus and rail links, a car-sharing scheme and provision of cycling facilities.

Other patterns of green space provision

2.45   For the longer term, there is also a question about the most appropriate pattern of protecting open space. The general model in England of a relatively dense city surrounded by an open belt is only one of a number of possibilities. The model of green wedges – providing recreational space to the public near built-up areas rather than on the edge of cities – is a concept that has been used to great effect abroad (see Box 2.2) and at the discretion of some local authorities in England.[90] Allowing towns and cities to have a greater overall geographic footprint but more open urban space and parkland within the urban boundary might be a preferable model for future development. A survey conducted for the Commission for Architecture and the Built Environment (CABE), illustrated in Chart 2.4 below, found that the vast majority (91 per cent) of the public believes that public parks and public open spaces improve people's quality of life. In this context, and given the need to adapt to the 'heat island' effects caused by climate change, there would be value from research into the effectiveness of different models of green space provision.[91] As the Urban Task Force pointed out,

> 'there is a need for a more sophisticated approach in protecting and designating urban green space. There are important green buffer zones and strategic gaps both within and between our urban areas which could be given the same weight in development control terms as the Green Belt designation. This would help to protect urban biodiversity and ensure strong urban green space networks'.[92]

[90] Strategic gaps and green wedges were first referred to in policy guidance in PPG7: The Countryside, in 1997. These are local tools, which currently impose a lesser degree of restraint than green belts, and appear to have been in use for many decades. The designations have been used extensively by towns such as Salisbury to protect setting and retain open land. For example, in the former West Sussex Structure Plan, strategic gaps were designated to separate Chichester, Bognor Regis, Selsey, Littlehampton, Worthing, Lancing and Shoreham. The 1980 Structure Plan introduced large strategic gaps separating Horsham, Crawley and East Grinstead, bordering the Metropolitan Green Belt and the Surrey county boundary in the vicinity of Gatwick Airport. Strategic gaps also separate Haywards Heath, Burgess Hill and Hassocks, located in the London-Brighton corridor. See DETR, Strategic Gap and Green Wedge Policies in Structure Plans, January 2001, paragraph 2.3. Leicestershire County Council also adopted a green wedge policy in its structure plan in the 1980s, to protect valued green space along its river valleys and to link the town and countryside.

[91] Note that a previous DEFRA study into the environmental impacts of increasing the supply of housing called for a review of the role and function of green belts. See Entec, Eftec and Richard Hodkinson Consultancy, 'Study into the Environmental Impacts of Increasing the Supply of Housing in the UK. A Report to DEFRA' (2004), Recommendation 12, p. 72.

[92] Lord Rodgers and Urban Task Force, *Towards an Urban Renaissance* (London, 1999), p. 219.

2.46   Reviewing the merits of different models of green space provision, combined with a proactive approach to protecting urban green space – as, for example, has been achieved in terms of tightening the regulation on the sale of school playing fields – is therefore of importance.[93]

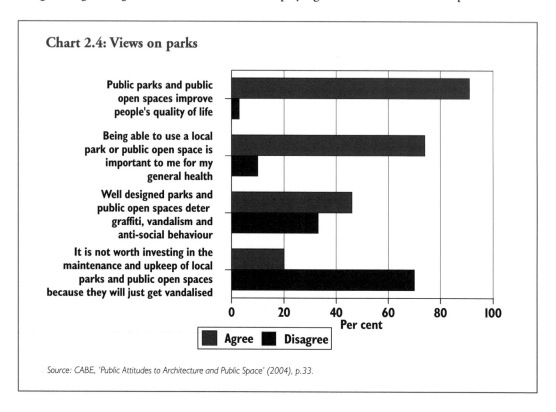

Chart 2.4: Views on parks

Source: CABE, 'Public Attitudes to Architecture and Public Space' (2004), p.33.

Box 2.2: Green hearts and green fingers

The Netherlands – the Randstad: This area of the Netherlands is an area that houses half the population and containing many of its largest cities, including Amsterdam, The Hague, Rotterdam and Utrecht. The area enclosed by these largest cities is described as the 'Green Heart'. The open land that remained was of little landscape or biodiversity value. The Dutch government therefore developed a 'Randstad Green Structure' strategy, which aims to provide more green areas around the towns and cities along a 'green hearts' model between the built-up areas. The Green Space Structure Plan aims to acquire 13,300 hectares by 2013.[94]

Denmark – Copenhagen: A 'finger plan', or starfish model, was drawn up in 1947 to facilitate growth along radial suburban train lines travelling into central Copenhagen, 'the palm of the hand', where growth had historically been concentric. Large service and production centres were planned in the junctions between the 'fingers', with housing built around suburban railway stations. The space between the fingers was to remain undeveloped in favour of green space. This largely defined the spatial pattern for Copenhagen, although urban growth was concentrated in the three northern 'fingers' while significant suburban development also occured outside the pre-planned 'fingers' in the 1960s. Successes of the strategy included the facilitation of an extensive public transport system, protection of green zones and extensive areas of forests, together with the addition of artificial lakes and hills.[95]

---

[93] See the protection currently provided via DCLG, Planning Policy Guidance 17: Planning for Open Space, Sport and Recreation (2002).

[94] Environmental Data Compendium, www.mnp.nl/mnc/i-en-1336.html.

[95] J. Hermansson, 'Greater Copenhagen: The Finger Plan', Report for TRANSLAND (2000), www.inro.tno.nl/transland/cases_nonprio/COPENHAGUE.PDF.

Recommendation 9

In the light of growing demand for land and the need to ensure that areas of high public value (such as sites with important or endangered wildlife) or areas at higher risk from flooding due to climate change are adequately protected:

- regional planning bodies and local planning authorities should review green belt boundaries as part of their Regional Spatial Strategy/Local Development Framework processes to ensure that they remain relevant and appropriate, given the need to ensure that any planned development takes place in the most sustainable location;

- local planning authorities should ensure that the quality of the green belts is enhanced through adopting a more positive approach towards applications that can be shown to enhance the surrounding areas through, for example, the creation of open access woodland or public parks in place of low-grade agricultural land; and

- the Government should consider how best to protect and enhance valued green space in towns and cities. In this context, the Government should review the merits of different models of protecting valued open space, including the 'green wedge' approach.

3 Delivering major projects

INTRODUCTION

3.1   Ensuring the delivery of important major infrastructure projects is of critical importance for the UK economy. Benefits include energy security (through securing increased energy supply in the context of rising demand), more flexible labour markets (through delivery of transport infrastructure) and limiting environmental harm (through supply of waste facilities). There are a number of issues that affect the provision of infrastructure, but, as the Interim Report made clear, planning often has an important role to play. The main problems that need to be addressed are:

- the **length of time** it takes to make a decision on projects that are outside the statutory timetabling framework. Taking a major infrastructure project through to planning inquiry and eventual decision can be a very lengthy process. Over 50 per cent of power station applications that have gone to inquiry since 1990 have taken at least two and a half years to gain approval,[1] while large transport cases can take several years;

- the **uncertainty** that this brings for developers as well as local communities involved in the delivery of national infrastructure. As the recent Energy Review stated, there is a need across the UK to 'reduce risk and uncertainty for developers and others, while maintaining the openness, fairness and accountability of the current system';[2]

- the **increased costs** to both the public and the developer which delay and complexity bring. It is estimated, for example, that the application for a recent proposed port in Dibden Bay cost in the region of £45 million.[3] The costs to communities of postponing major development, such as delaying new employment and regeneration and, more generally, increasing uncertainty about the future of a local area can also be significant; and

- the **lost investment** if schemes are not brought forward because of the perceived difficulties in obtaining consents.

3.2   It is vital that major infrastructure schemes are subject to the right amount of scrutiny and that appropriate public participation and consultation is carried out, given the controversy that often surrounds them and the complexity of the issues that need to be examined. However, there needs to be a more effective way of both meeting these goals and delivering infrastructure and other major schemes in a timely fashion, to bring wider social and (in the case of renewable energy) environmental benefits, alongside the positive spillover effects for the local, regional and national economy.

---

[1] K. Barker, *Review of Land Use Planning. Interim Report*, (July 2006), p. 63.
[2] Department for Trade and Industry, *The Energy Challenge*, (July 2006), p. 137.
[3] The Associated British Ports estimate that the application for a Harbour Revision Order, planning permission and other associated consents and subsequent inquiry cost in the region of £45million.

3.3   This is not the only Review that is concerned with the relationship between planning and the consenting regimes for major infrastructure. These proposals have been developed in consultation with the recent Energy Review, which concluded that there was a need for fundamental change to the planning system in England and Wales for major energy projects. The Department of Trade and Industry has recently issued a consultation document which sets out a number of proposed streamlining measures in advance of wider energy planning reforms. These include improved pre-inquiry and inquiry procedures and better use of e-planning.[4] This Review has been developed in consultation with the Eddington Transport Study which will also bring forward recommendations in this area as part of a wider analysis of the economic impact of transport.

3.4   This chapter sets out a package of reforms for planning for major infrastructure, specifically:

- the need for clearer statements of national policy by Government. This will provide greater certainty for developers and a robust framework within which planning decisions for major projects can be made;

- the case for a new independent Planning Commission to determine planning applications for major projects, as a result of the front-end loading of the democratic mandate, and the scope of decision-making for this new body; and

- the implications this new model will have for other aspects of the planning system, in particular the role of the Secretary of State in Town and Country Planning applications and appeals.

DELIVERING A NEW NATIONAL DECISION-MAKING FRAMEWORK

The importance of clear national policy

3.5   A critical component of ensuring timely decision-making is that the strategic framework for decisions is clearly set out by central government. Among the principles that apply to decision-making at either national or local level (see Box 3.1) is that decisions should be made at the spatial level that best reflects the spillover effects. The vast majority of planning applications have only a local impact and should be determined at the local level by local planning authorities. But projects that are of national significance should be determined at the national level, while preserving the democratic mandate given to local authorities (and recently reinforced by the Local Government White Paper).[5] These national decisions need to take account of wider factors. They must be made fairly and even-handedly and be taken following public consultation and full consideration of all the issues. This will allow local communities to express their views.

---

[4] Department of Trade and Industry, *Updating the Electricity Generating Stations and Overhead Lines Inquiry Procedure Rules in England and Wales* (November 2006).
[5] Department for Communities and Local Government, Strong and Prosperous Communities: *The Local Government White Paper* (26 October 2006).

Box 3.1: Principles for decision-making

- Decisions must be made at the appropriate level;

- Decisions should only be taken out of local decision-makers' hands in circumstances where there are wider spillovers;

- Decision-makers must act, and be seen to act, fairly and even-handedly;

- All decisions must be taken in the light of full public consultation and consideration of local as well as regional and national issues and any other material considerations;

- All decisions should be open to scrutiny through the courts; and

- Decisions must be taken by a democratically accountable body or in circumstances where such a body has established a clear framework for decision-making.

A framework for
decision-making

3.6   Setting out a clear framework for decision-making at the national level has three principal additional benefits:

- **greater certainty and reduced time spent debating need.** Clearer national policy here would reduce the time spent at inquiry debating whether there is national need for a project. It would provide greater clarity and certainty and reduce both delay and costs to the developer, the local authority and other parties. At the inquiry into the application for a new container port at Dibden Bay, for example, although the range of issues debated was very wide (see Box 3.2), one of the main issues was the 'need' for the proposed development, including forecast demand for UK container port capacity. Clear national policy on the need for major infrastructure would be an important material consideration to be factored into decision-making on planning applications although they would not, of course, obviate the requirement for detailed examination of local issues. BAA, in their response to the Call for Evidence to this Review, stated:

  '*The causes of much of the delay in the T5 Inquiry related to the lack of strategic framework for development. The Airports White Paper now provides that guidance. As long as this is carried through to the decision-making process, the length of any inquiry should be significantly reduced.*'[6]

- **reduced time spent debating alternative locations.** Clearer national policy, if it were more spatially specific, could also reduce the time spent discussing whether there is a need for the development in a broad location. Local opposition to major infrastructure projects can often focus on whether or not there is a more suitable 'alternative site' and local plans, by their nature, rarely plan for new developments that are in the national or regional interest. This is perhaps particularly true of large-scale infrastructure projects. Electricity generated from a new power station, for example, feeds into the National Grid so that there is no clear local benefit other than the additional employment created and the contribution to the local economy. However, this should improve as the changes in the Planning and Compulsory Purchase Act (PCPA) 2004 come into effect. The 2004 Act includes the requirement that local development documents be in general conformity with the Regional Spatial Strategy (RSS) and the RSS should include assessments of infrastructure requirements and proposals for how they will be met.

---

[6] BAA submission to the Barker Review of Land Use Planning, March 2006.

Box 3.2: Dibden Bay Terminal Inquiry

Second revised list of topics (26 July 2001):[7]

1. **The Proposals:** Scope and objectives of the applications and draft Orders.

2. **Planning Background and Overview:** Relevant policies – extent to which proposals are consistent with national, regional and local transport and planning policy.

3. **Need for the Proposed Development:** Current throughput, capacity and limitations of UK container ports. Forecast demand for UK port capacity. Need for further capacity in the Port of Southampton for containers, ro-ro, aggregates. Economic need for port development and employment implications.

4. **Alternative Solutions:** Potential for providing additional capacity (both by increased efficiency of use and by development) within the existing Port of Southampton and at other locations (e.g. Shell Haven, Felixstowe, Bathside Bay, Tilbury, Thamesport/Isle of Grain).

5. **Erosion and Deposition of Sediment:** Effect of works, dredging and wave action on erosion and deposition processes. Likely stability of existing features (including sea defences) and of the proposed Cadland/Hythe Recharge.

6. **Nature Conservation:** Likely effect on the flora and fauna of the relevant SPAs, cSACs and Ramsar Sites. Effectiveness of proposed habitat creation/improvement measures (short and long-term) at Dibden Creek, Church Farm and Hythe/Cadland Recharge; maintenance of coherence of the Natura 2000 network.

7. **Fisheries:** Salmonid migration. Commercial fishing, including shellfish.

8. **Navigation:** Effect of increased use of deep-water channel on shipping movements and safety; need for further capital dredging. Effect of development on recreational sailing.

9. **Land Access to Dibden Bay:** Potential traffic – including volume, modal split and distribution of port traffic and other demands on the network. Capacity of road network. Effectiveness and viability of proposed 'park and ride' service – future of existing ferry. Rail capacity and operational implications. Consequences of the removal of the designation of Totton Goods Yard as a strategic freight site.

Other important inquiry topics were: Noise and Vibration; Visual Impact; Air Quality and Climatic factors; Countryside Issues; Effect on Public Rights of Way; Effect on Tourism and Recreation; Flooding and Drainage; Archaeology and Architecture; Contaminated Land; Effect on Marchwood Military Port Safeguarded Area; Effect on Sea-water Abstraction by Local Industries; Effect on Outfalls, Pipelines and Other Apparatus; Compulsory Purchase Issues; and Human Rights Issues (including effect on property values).

[7] Taken from the planning Inspectorate's list of Public Inquiries, available at http://www.planning-inspectorate.gov.uk/dibden/topics.htm. Note that 'ro-ro' is the acronym for Roll On/Roll Off vessels. SPAs are Special Protected Areas, primarily areas of importance for birds designated under the EU Birds Directive (79/409/EEC). SACs are Special Areas of Conservation and cSACs are candidate Special Areas of Conservation, prime wildlife conservation areas designated, or proposed to be designated, under the EU Habitats Directive (92/43/EEC). Ramsar sites are wetlands designated under the Convention on Wetlands, signed in Ramsar, Iran, in 1971. This is an intergovernmental treaty to frame national action and international cooperation in the conservation wetlands.

- **a more joined-up framework for the provision of infrastructure nationally.** Clearer policy could also provide a more integrated framework for infrastructure provision, alongside other forms of development, in England. It is in this context that discussions about a national spatial strategy are often placed. There is an increasing focus on spatial planning which has been reinforced in the new planning system at the regional level through Regional Spatial Strategies. Local planning authorities must have regard to the Regional Spatial Strategy in preparing their local development documents. The Government is committed to devolving and decentralising responsibilities wherever possible, whether this is at the regional level, across regions, sub-regionally or locally. It also wants the regions to be able to take a strategic long-term approach to matters such as planning, housing and economic development. However, it is arguably the role of central government to support economic growth by setting out national statements of need for development, with spatial specificity where relevant.

3.7   There is an increasing interest in having a clear spatial policy, although only a small selection of the range of views on this issue is mentioned here. For example, the *State of the Cities* report suggested that the Government should provide greater clarity and a national spatial strategy, noting 'there is still a need for government to provide greater clarity about what it wants to do, how, where and when. It would be better to have greater clarity in a national strategy which specified some clear spatial goals and some simple policy instruments.'[8] A large number of responses to the Call for Evidence to this Review and through the Review's field research also supported the view that a clearer national policy framework, perhaps in the form of a national spatial strategy, could help with the delivery of major infrastructure projects. The Town and Country Planning Association (TCPA) has argued that, 'the lack of an overall national planning framework for England obstructs good planning for economic growth'[9] and has called for a bottom-up participative model of developing a national framework. And the Royal Town Planning Institute (RTPI), noting the presence of national frameworks in countries such as the Netherlands (see Box 3.3) has argued:

> *'All regions depend upon core national infrastructure networks, which involve long-term national commitment to capital spending and impact on the nation's economic competitiveness. A national spatial planning framework is essential to achieve an integrated approach to the future of airports, ports, and major road and rail projects. Other essential national infrastructure networks and supplies, including those for energy, IT and water cut across the boundaries of established administrative regions and cannot be planned on a local, or even regional, basis.'*[10]

---

[8] Office of the Deputy Prime Minister, *The State of the Cities Report*, vol. II, (March 2006), p. 149.

[9] The Town and Country Planning Association, submission to the Barker Review of Land Use Planning, 2006.

[10] The Royal Town Planning Institute, *Uniting Britain. The Evidence Base – Spatial Structure and Key Drivers* (June 2006).

> **Box 3.3: Netherlands National Spatial Strategy**[11]
>
> The Dutch Government has adopted a National Spatial Strategy that it is based on earlier spatial planning documents. Within the context of a framework that decentralises non-strategic responsibilities to other tiers of government, the central government now gives a greater lead on issues of national importance. Matters of national importance are included in the National Spatial Strategy. As well as Amsterdam Schiphol Airport and the Port of Rotterdam, and the infrastructure linking these mainports (and mainport regions) with the metropolitan areas in the Netherlands and abroad, the Dutch Government has also designated a number of greenports (agricultural production and trading centres) and one brainport, the Eindhoven/Zuidoost-Brabant region – which is of considerable economic importance due to the concentration of research and development activities. The National Spatial Strategy also identifies the important nature areas, world heritage sites and landscapes the Government wants to preserve for future generations.

The potential models for clearer national policy

3.8   There are three main models that could be used to deliver greater clarity of national policy for major infrastructure in England. Each would involve looking at demand and capacity projections in relevant sectors and would also have to ensure that the policy being advocated was compatible with the overall principle of delivering sustainable development. The models are:

- **Assessments of Need.** This would involve the Government drawing up a set of assessments of need for major transport infrastructure developments as well as for sectors such as energy, strategic waste and water. These would provide a framework for decision-making on individual projects and indicate the principle of the need for each particular type of development. There would be no requirement for coordination between different types of infrastructure. An example here could be the statement made recently to the House of Commons by the Secretary of State for Trade and Industry on the need for additional gas supply infrastructure.[12] This statement set out the context and economic case for the growing need for new gas supply infrastructure and was intended to provide assistance to planners making development management decisions on energy infrastructure;

- **Statements of Strategic Objectives.** An alternative model would be to have Statements of Strategic Objectives (Statements). These would be similar to assessments but would, where appropriate and possible, be spatially specific, and would provide a clearer spatial framework to aid decision-making for major infrastructure. They would also assess the environmental, social and economic impact of the different options needed to meet likely future requirements and so go beyond mere expressions of need. A possible model to follow is the Air Transport White Paper[13] which looked at the future needs of the UK's air transport

---

[11] Dutch National Spatial Strategy, 'Creating Space for Development'.

[12] Energy statement on need for additional gas supply infrastructure made by the Secretary of State for Trade and Industry to the House of Commons, 16 May 2006, at http://www.dti.gov.uk/files/file28954.pdf.

[13] Department for Transport, *The Future of Air Transport* (16 December 2003).

market to 2030 and identified new capacity requirements, setting out where these were likely to be needed. Statements would be drawn up following full public consultation and would have to be developed with regard to other Statements to ensure policies were consistent. These Statements would have to be kept up to date as necessary. The Government would also have the option to include geographically specific government priorities, similar to the approach taken in the Government's Sustainable Communities Plan.[14] Statements of Strategic Objectives would have to be taken into account by the Regional Planning Bodies to ensure that policies contained within them were factored into the development of Regional Spatial Strategies; and

- **A National Spatial Strategy.** A third option would be a broader and fully integrated national spatial strategy. This would set out social and economic trends such as changing demographics and household structure, globalisation, increased mobility and technological change and the likely impact on the way in which land is used and needed. It would be at a local level, within and across regions, and in certain circumstances at a national level. The Strategy would have to include, in spatial form, the major centres of population within each region and a discussion about changing demographics within each area. It could include policy on the relationship between regional housing markets, labour markets, travel patterns and supporting infrastructure, such as the need for more house-building in the South and the need to revitalise areas of low demand in the Midlands and Northern Regions as set out in the Sustainable Communities Plan.

3.9 A wider set of issues would need to be considered before any of the three models were adopted:

- the legal status of the Statements. In most countries national spatial strategies are not binding plans but are instead mechanisms for dialogue and gaining a better understanding of the relative importance of issues for different tiers of government. Crucially, for the policy to be effective however, due weight must be placed on it at the decision-making phase;

- mechanisms for delivery (some plans, such as the Dutch, include a vehicle for delivery);

- period of reference (most continental strategies typically have a time frame of between 15 and 20 years); and

- whether Statements would be subject to the regulations that transcribe the Strategic Environmental Assessment Directive into UK law. It is clear that the more specific the strategy with regard to locations, the greater the likelihood that it will be subject to Strategic Environmental Assessment.

[14] ODPM, *Sustainable Communities: Building for the Future* (2003).

3.10   There are strengths and weaknesses attached to each of the three possible approaches. Having separate assessments of need would give greater flexibility, allowing Secretaries of State to produce them or update them, as they were required. They would be more responsive to change – politically, economically, socially and environmentally. However, as they would primarily explore issues of economic need they would be less able to fulfil the role of broad government strategy, balancing environmental and social factors alongside economic ones. At the other end of the spectrum, a full national spatial strategy would be extremely resource-intensive, and the complexity of the issues involved could lead to substantial delay in the production of such a strategy. It could also be inflexible. It is notable that the countries that have adopted this path – including Scotland, Ireland and the Netherlands – have much smaller populations and it could be argued that Regional Spatial Strategies are in some respects the equivalents of national spatial strategies for some countries. There is therefore merit in the middle approach of drawing up Statements of Strategic Objectives with a degree of spatial specificity where this is possible and appropriate. These would have to be drawn up with regard to the operational requirements of the different sectors to which they refer, while ensuring that they do not attempt a level of specificity that would unduly constrain the market. They would also have to have regard to other such statements. Importantly they would have to be reviewed regularly to ensure that assumptions within them remained up to date.

3.11   It would also be critical for these Statements to be subject to full and wide-ranging public consultation. This would not only help to elicit a wide range of views concerning need, impact and options, but it would also play an important role in legitimising the framework and securing public buy-in for the need for the infrastructure in question. These Statements would, as with plans at the local and regional level, be subject to challenge through the courts.

THE CASE FOR A NEW DECISION-MAKING BODY

3.12   Introducing clearer national policy for major infrastructure raises the possibility of introducing a new planning body – an independent Planning Commission – to determine applications for major infrastructure in the context of the Government's established strategic priorities, thereby removing the need for Ministers to be involved at the end of the decision-making process.

Rationale for an Independent Planning Commission

3.13   There are a number of benefits of this model:

- **Quicker decisions.** There are a number of stages to planning applications for major infrastructure that are decided by Ministers: information gathering, submitting applications, consultation, inquiry, the writing of the Inspector's report and the Ministerial decision following receipt of that report. The additional time taken in this final stage can be considerable. The London International Freight Exchange, for example, took 15 months between receipt of report and Ministerial decision. Despite a lengthy inquiry of 11 months, resolution of a number of outstanding matters meant that it took Ministers eight months to determine the application for an upgrade of the West Coast mainline.[15] There are particular issues in terms of joint and linked decisions, where more than one Minister determines cases. The problem is exacerbated by major infrastructure decisions not being subject to the targets, and more recently, from 2005, statutory timetabling, which applies to decisions made by the Secretary of State for Communities and Local Government. The benefits to be derived from quicker decision-making for major infrastructure projects is one of the main arguments in favour of removal of Ministers in decision-making in favour of a new Planning Commission. As Transport 2000 has noted:

> '*Where delays occur [to transport projects] they are often blamed on involvement of the public or the planning system per se... [However] most of the time taken to approve and build transport schemes is not in fact taken up by public consultation or inquiries, but in decisions by Ministers. This is particularly true of schemes involving public funding, notably road, rail, and light rail schemes.*'[16]

- **Professional input into decision-making.** Ensuring that Ministers set clear policy up front and give a context for national decision-making means there is no requirement for them to be involved in the often complex detail of decision-making. There could be significant gains from having a team of independent professionals who understand the wide range of issues at play in complex applications, including major infrastructure projects. The Planning Commission, if involved from an early point in the planning process, could ensure that a decision was taken in full consideration of all the material factors, including clearly articulated Statements of Strategic Objectives;

- **Providing clarity of role and function.** Establishing a Planning Commission for major cases would ensure that individual planning decisions were not used as a vehicle for setting policy. Ministers would focus on setting clear policy up front and the Commission on determining applications; and

- **Removing suggestions of bias.** Taking Ministers out of the decision-making process would also remove from the planning process any suggestion of bias and unfairness. There could, for example, be concerns about particular political interests or high-profile interest groups influencing decision-making under the current system, from which an independent Planning Commission would be comparatively free. However, this argument needs to be treated with care and is probably more an issue of perception than reality. When making planning decisions Ministers act in a quasi-judicial capacity and may not take into account privately-made representations, or take decisions in which they may have a constituency interest or any other personal interest. Ministers also have to produce a decision that is capable of withstanding challenge in the courts.

---

[15] K. Barker, *Review of Land Use Planning: Interim Report*, Table 3.2.
[16] Transport 2000 Response to the Barker Review of Land Use Planning: Interim Report, July 2006, p. 1.

3.14   It should also be noted that, currently, many planning decisions are taken without input from politicians. Where there are clearly-expressed policies and plans, it is possible for decisions to be delegated – indeed some 90 per cent of decisions made by local authorities (over 500,000 cases a year, although many of these will relate solely to householder development) are delegated to officers. The vast majority of appeals to the Secretary of State for Communities and Local Government are transferred to the Planning Inspectorate to be determined on her behalf (out of about 23,000 appeals she recovers only about 100-120 appeals each year).

Operational issues

Constitution of the
Commission

3.15   For an independent Planning Commission to be effective, it would require a panel of well-respected experts of considerable standing in their fields. Given the range of issues that are commonly at play in major infrastructure cases, this could include expertise in the fields of law, economics, engineering, environmental science and planning. Operating on a similar basis to other independent bodies such as the Competition Commission, Ministers would have no day-to-day involvement in the operations of the Commission. The role of Ministers would be limited to establishing the legal framework under which the new Commission would operate and they would also appoint members to it. Monitoring and auditing arrangements would also have to be established to ensure there was appropriate accountability and probity. Ministers would also need to establish clearly the relationship between the Planning Inspectorate, which currently manages inquiries on major infrastructure projects on behalf of the Secretaries of State and makes recommendations to them, and the new Commission.

3.16   The Commission would assess applications as they came forward, in the context of declared national policy. It could engage in pre-application discussions with developers, as local planning authorities do, to ensure that the range of consents needed had been applied for, and to ensure that developers had carried out the appropriate consultations with local communities as well as statutory consultees. It would be critical that the Commission took appropriate account of local interests in its decision-making. Even where national need was clearly established, local considerations would have to be taken into account and local communities given the opportunity to express their views and concerns. The European Convention on Human Rights, which is incorporated into UK law by the Human Rights Act 1998, has enshrined the principle that everyone should have the right to a fair hearing. In making decisions on planning, whether at a local or a national level, this means that the principles of natural justice must be applied, and that parties to planning applications should be treated fairly and even-handedly. It would also be important to ensure that the reasons for the final decisions were properly explained to those affected at the local level.

3.17   It would also clearly be the case that other principles that apply to making planning decisions (see box 3.1) would apply to an independent Planning Commission. In making decisions the Commission would also be acting in a quasi-judicial capacity and its decisions would be open to scrutiny and legal challenge. The Commission would have to act, and be seen to act, in a way that demonstrated that it had not prejudged the application it was considering. It would have to determine applications in full consideration of all the relevant issues, including all relevant environmental issues. Even where national need was clearly established, local circumstances might indicate that the costs of granting planning permission outweighed the benefits. In that case the Commission would have the powers to refuse the application it was determining.

Additional process 3.18   An independent Planning Commission would work most effectively in combination with
improvements further process efficiencies. In addition to the reduction of time spent discussing the need for
development as outlined above, these would include:

- **a clear timetable** with key milestones for delivery of the decision to be agreed
  between the Commission and the developer – this could be subject to a statutory
  time-limit for decisions taken by the Commission;

- **improvements to the inquiry process,** including a less adversarial approach and
  a greater use of written representations, although inquiries are likely to be needed
  for the most complex or controversial cases. This should substantially increase the
  timeliness of decision-making by ensuring better day-to-day management of the
  inquiry process; and

- **provisions to allow the Commission to determine the range of consents**
  (Transport and Works Act, Planning Permission, Harbour Order, Listed Building
  consents, etc.), in place of current procedures that result in multiple decision-
  makers, which adds to uncertainty and delay. For example, an application for a
  new gas-storage scheme which involved works to a listed building and needed a
  footpath diversion order, would need only one consent and not three. This would
  ensure that developers of large schemes do not have to submit numerous different
  applications under many different consent regimes, with different statutory
  processes for consultation or the need for an inquiry.

3.19   There are, however, a number of additional issues that will need to be resolved if major
infrastructure decisions are to be made by an independent Planning Commission, including:

- **the scope of the decision-making powers.** There are a large variety of cases that
  could potentially be handled by an independent Planning Commission.
  Determining the categories and thresholds for these cases will therefore be critical;

- **handling legal implications.** Transferring decision-making to an independent
  Planning Commission would require potentially complex legislative changes.
  These might include: powers to allow the Commission to determine applications
  currently determined by Secretaries of State; unifying consent regimes for major
  infrastructure; and ending joint and linked decisions. Under the current system,
  some proposals may require the separate decisions of two or more different
  Secretaries of State and, in certain circumstances, two Secretaries of State may take
  a decision jointly; and

- **wider implications for Ministerial involvement.** There are a large number of
  complex 'planning' consent regimes beyond national infrastructure where there is
  currently some Ministerial role (see Table 3.1). However, in many policy areas, for
  example retail, leisure or commercial warehousing, up-front Statements of
  Strategic Objectives are less appropriate. In these instances retaining decision-
  making by the local authority, with the potential for Ministerial call-in where there
  were wider implications – social, economic and/or environmental – may still be
  the right approach.

Table 3.1: Summary of the primary consent regimes

Project	Permission/regulation	Authority
Onshore power stations >50MW and offshore power stations >1MW (territorial waters) and >50MW (REZ)	Electricity Act 1989	Secretary of State for Trade and Industry
Overhead power lines	Electricity Act 1989	Secretary of State for Trade and Industry
All other electricity infrastructure (e.g. small power stations, substations)	Town and Country Planning Act 1990	Initial applications by local authorities. Appeals and call-ins by Secretary of State for Communities and Local Government. Substations jointly determined with Secretary of State for Trade and Industry
Associated Compulsory Purchases of Land and Necessary Wayleave (granting access to land for developers of overhead lines)	Electricity Act 1989	Secretary of State for Trade and Industry
Gas or oil-fired power stations proposal of >10MW	Energy Act 1976	Secretary of State for Trade and Industry
Gas supply arrangements for gas-fired power station	Energy Act 1976	Secretary of State for Trade and Industry
Underground gas storage facilities (including surface infrastructure) for non-licensed gas transporters	Town and Country Planning Act 1990	Initial applications by local authorities. Appeals and call-ins by Secretary of State for Communities and Local Government
		If applications by a licensed gas transporter jointly determined with Secretary of State for Trade and Industry
	The Planning (Hazardous Substances) Act 1990	Initial applications by local authorities. Appeals and call-ins by Secretary of State for Communities and Local Government
LNG import terminals	Town and Country Planning Act 1990	Initial applications by local authorities. Appeals and call-ins by Secretary of State for Communities and Local Government
Underground gas storage facilities (including surface infrastructure) but only for licensed gas transporters	Gas Act 1965	Secretary of State for Trade and Industry
Gas transporter pipelines (pipelines that form the National Transmission System)	Gas Transporter Pipeline Works (Environmental Impact Assessment) Regulations 1999	Secretary of State for Trade and Industry
	Town and Country Planning (General Permitted Development) Order 1998	Local planning authority can make request of Secretary of State for Communities and Local Government that permitted development rights should not apply (which would force a separate planning application)
Commercial pipelines >16.093km	Pipelines Act 1962	Secretary of State for Trade and Industry
Commercial pipelines <16.093km	Town and Country Planning Act 1990	Initial applications by local authorities. Appeals and call-ins by Secretary of State for Communities and Local Government
Harbour Revision Orders	Harbours Act 1964	Secretary of State for Transport
Construction works, dredging or depositing in coastal waters	Coast Protection Act 1949; Food and Environment Protection Act 1985	Secretary of State for Environment, Food and Rural Affairs

Table 3.1: Summary of the primary consent regimes (continued)

Project	Permission/regulation	Authority
New slip roads, highways, trunk roads, etc.	Highways Act 1980	Secretary of State for Transport
		Associated planning applications would be determined by the Secretary of State for Communities and Local Government
Orders relating to inland waterways, navigation works, railways, trams, etc.	Transport and Works Act 1992	Secretary of State for Transport for transport projects; Secretary of State for Environment, Food and Rural Affairs for inland waterways
New reservoirs	Water Industry Act 1991 (power not yet used)	Secretary of State for Environment, Food and Rural Affairs
Footpaths, hedgerows, bridleways, etc.	Highways Act 1980; The Hedgerows Regulations 1997	Initial applications by local authorities. Appeals by Secretary of State for Environmental, Food and Rural Affairs
Applications for planning permission	Town and Country Planning Act 1990	Initial applications by local authorities. Appeals and call-ins by Secretary of State for Communities and Local Government
Enforcement notices against unauthorised development	Town and Country Planning Act 1990	Notices are served by a local authority. Where appeals are lodged they are determined by Secretary of State for Communities and Local Government
Listed building and conservation area consent	Planning (Listed Building and Conservation Areas) Act 1990	Initial applications by local authorities. Appeals and call-ins by Secretary of State for Communities and Local Government
Scheduled monument consent	Ancient Monuments and Archaeological Areas Act 1979 (as amended)	Secretary of State for Culture Media and Sport

SCOPE AND IMPLICATIONS FOR THE CURRENT CONSENT REGIMES

3.20   A critical issue in establishing an independent Planning Commission would be determining the scope of its decision-making powers. In addition to major infrastructure projects, such as transport and energy projects, there is also a range of other schemes which could potentially be brought within the remit of the Commission. These could include water projects such as new reservoirs or treatment plants and waste projects such as incinerators as well as disposal schemes, and other schemes such as large housing and commercial schemes. For each sector it would be necessary to determine which cases fell to the Commission, and what would happen to those that did not.

Energy proposals   3.21   For major energy applications that are currently determined nationally – such as large onshore power stations that generate over 50 megawatts of electricity (the Electricity Act 1989) – it might be more appropriate for those to be determined by an independent Planning Commission. Given the complex array of consent regimes in this area which can, for example, mean that some major energy schemes are actually made to local authorities despite their national significance (e.g. gas storage facilities) a decision would have to be made about whether any of these could usefully be raised up to be considered by the Commission. Commercial pipelines of over 16.093 km, for example, are determined nationally under the Pipelines Act 1962 while local authorities under the Town and Country Planning Act 1990 determine shorter pipeline schemes.

3.22   Conversely, while the Secretary of State for Trade and Industry currently decides the majority of major energy infrastructure cases, following a public inquiry, it is also notable that a large number of relatively small-scale planning applications in this area are made to central government. For example, while the Secretary of State expects to decide around six applications for onshore windfarms in 2006-07 he also expects to handle around 400 applications for overhead power lines and around 400 applications[17] for compulsory wayleaves, although these figures will vary year on year. Although most wayleave cases are resolved privately between the landowner and the power company, for other cases DTI officials carry out the functions of local authorities, such as arranging inquiries. There may be some scope here for referring some of those applications to local authorities to determine, or the Planning Inspectorate where an appeal is lodged, rather than having all these transferred to the Commission.

3.23   There is also scope for rationalising consent regimes on energy schemes to ensure that they provide some consistency of approach and give developers greater clarity and certainty that the right decisions are taken at the right level and to ensure that they are taken more quickly.

Transport proposals   3.24   The Eddington Transport Study has been looking at the current system of transport planning, alongside other issues, and will bring forward recommendations in this area. This Review has looked at the planning system as a whole, including the provision of transport infrastructure. There are a number of transport consent regimes that are currently operated at the national level. For example, new highways or trunk roads are determined under the Highways Act 1980 by the Secretary of State for Transport. For ports applications, an order is made under the Harbours Act 1964 and the Secretary of State will determine applications for railways or trams or inland waterways schemes under the Transport and Works Act 1992.

3.25   Large new transport schemes can be controversial as well as very complex and, as noted above, can take Ministers considerable time to determine. Statements of Strategic Objectives for projects such as airports, ports or major new road networks would give a stronger framework for decision-making and should reduce the amount of time spent at inquiry debating need. Statements could also, in these areas, potentially incorporate a degree of spatial specificity. This would also reduce some of the debate at inquiry, were one to be held, about alternative locations, although full consideration would have to be given to site-specific matters.

Waste proposals   3.26   Applications for waste management proposals – landfill, recycling, incineration and many other forms – are primarily determined by unitary authorities and in two-tier areas at the county level under Town and Country Planning legislation. The majority of waste applications, some 1,198 in 2005-06,[18] are relatively small-scale but there are a minority of proposals which, either because of their likely throughput or the specialist waste management need being addressed, are critical to the delivery of waste management needs identified nationally. A body other than the local authority could determine these proposals. The decision to grant planning permission to Riverside Resource Recovery Ltd's application for an energy from waste power station at Belvedere in south-east London, for example, was determined at a national level by the Secretary of State for Trade and Industry under the current legislation in the Electricity Act because of the scale of the electricity generation involved.

---

[17] Information from the Department of Trade and Industry.
[18] DCLG, *Development Control Statistics: England: 2005-06* (October 2006), Table 3.5.

3.27   Although DCLG's development control statistics indicate that some 90 per cent of waste applications are granted there is some anecdotal evidence that a number of applications for waste disposal or recovery do not come forward at all. It is not possible to be clear about the reasons for this, but factors such as failure of the planning system to bring forward suitable sites, local communities' concerns about the possible health implications of waste schemes, and insufficient thought on the part of developers regarding how to engage positively with the planning system may all play a part. A national Statement of Strategic Objectives for waste projects, such as the national waste strategy currently being updated by DEFRA will clarify current Government policy on waste management technologies, identify the additional waste management capacity to move away from the current reliance on landfill, and identify the facilities that are required nationally. In line with current Government policy in PPS10[19] Regional Planning Bodies and planning authorities will need to reflect this when drawing up their Regional Spatial Strategies and waste plans, which should include identifying new sites for waste facilities to complement existing provision. The waste strategy will be a material consideration of some weight to be taken into account in determining planning applications.[20]

3.28   Applications for waste management facilities, the need for which has not been identified nationally, could remain with the local planning authority although this should be kept under review. Applications for energy from waste proposals, which are currently dealt with under the Electricity Act, could be referred to the Commission. The current threshold is >50 MW for onward referral to Ministers and this Review does not recommend changing this.

Water proposals   3.29   Applications for water and wastewater infrastructure can, at present, be dealt with via an application under the Town and Country Planning Act 1990, or through a Compulsory Works Order (CWO) under the Water Industry Act 1991 (section 167). The CWO is a one-stop-shop whereby the water company can apply to the Secretary of State and then, if the Order is made, can also deem planning permission, provide compulsory purchase powers, and grant any other necessary consents (other than abstraction and impounding licences). This potentially reduces substantially the number of applications that might otherwise be needed under the TCPA route. However, this power is still untested. Nevertheless, following a number of dry summers and winters, new reservoirs are being actively considered, especially in the south-east of England, to meet expected future demand for water. Establishing Statements of Strategic Objectives drawn up with full consultation, including with the water companies who are responsible for identifying the need for, and development of, new infrastructure, and a Commission to manage and determine large-scale reservoir applications, could prove helpful. The Statement should reflect the need identified by water companies for new infrastructure. It could therefore be spatially specific and indicate, at least to the regional level, where new proposals are needed.

Major commercial   3.30   In 2005-06 about 3,500 planning applications for major commercial development were
development   made and 22,000 minor ones. Permission for about 85-90 per cent of those is granted by local planning authorities. Very few schemes will be of national economic significance – most cases will be local or perhaps regional in importance only. There are also only a very small number of commercial applications called-in – for example about 2 per cent of major retail cases each year.

---

[19] DCLG, Planning Policy Statement 10, *Planning for Sustainable Waste Management* (July 2005).
[20] Planning Policy Statement 10, Waste Strategy 2000 (as amended) and the development plan for the area form part of the Waste Management Plan for the purpose of Article 7 of the Waste Framework Directive (Directive 75/442/EEC). The new national waste strategy will similarly form part of the Article 7 Plan and be a weighty material consideration in decision-making.

3.31   Unlike applications for major infrastructure, it would not be appropriate for the Government to establish national Statements of Strategic Objectives for development such as retail, offices or warehousing. National planning policy does, however, set out the Government's approach more generally towards economic development. The vast majority of commercial applications that come forward are minor applications and even for those that have a wider significance, it is not the role of central government to determine, at a national level, where individual developments, such as new supermarkets or warehouses, should come forward. It is the responsibility of regional planning bodies and local planning authorities to plan for new commercial development in their areas.

3.32   Where unanticipated commercial development is processed, which may have regional or even national implications, it would seem less appropriate for an independent Planning Commission to decide the planning application in the absence of a national framework which had been set by Government following full consultation. Without this up-front Ministerial involvement the case for major commercial cases being determined by the Commission is weaker. Indeed, it could be argued that it is difficult for central government, regional planning bodies or local planning authorities to anticipate significant changes in the commercial sector. Cases of such significance will be few, perhaps particularly once the new local development frameworks are fully in place. It is recommended that applications for commercial development, which are currently made to local authorities, remain in their hands. One option here would be to expand the role of Advisory Team for Large Applications (ATLAS) to remove bottlenecks in the delivery of commercial development (see Chapter 5) by supporting local authorities in determining large or complex applications that they receive only infrequently. Only in exceptional circumstances might Ministers intervene through the existing call-in procedures, where there were implications that warranted a decision being taken at a higher level.

Major housing development 3.33   Planning for housing is one of the most important areas of work for a local authority and can be an effective lever for social and economic change in many areas. Other than the large volume of householder applications – discussed elsewhere in this Report – residential development is the largest area of work for most local authority planning departments. In 2005-06, for example, some 81,000 planning applications were made for residential development and, of those, 10,900 were classed as major applications. As a core function of local authorities, intervention in planning applications for housing should take place in exceptional circumstances only. This should remain a fundamental responsibility of local government.

3.34   Furthermore, given the volume of residential planning applications made, it is difficult to consider how even applications for large-scale residential development could be transferred to an independent Planning Commission. Thresholds would have to be set at a very high level to ensure that any intervention happened at an early enough stage to be meaningful. There were, in 2005-06, about 11,000 applications classed as major residential developments. This is defined as an application for ten houses or more. The Commission would not be able to determine 11,000 applications per annum, and nor should it. Instead, the thresholds would have to be set at a much higher level – perhaps 500 or 1,000 houses – and even then would involve a very large number of applications. Furthermore, an application for 500, or even 1,000, houses would not necessarily be an application of national significance, indicating that intervention by Ministers or the Commission was warranted and that the decision should not be taken by the local planning authority.

3.35   However, at a national level, the delivery of housing to meet rising demand for new homes in the context of changing demographics and a shortage of affordable housing in some areas is very important. The Government has recognised the important role that housing and planning play and has brought them together at the regional level, with the Regional Assemblies and the Mayor in London taking on the responsibility for delivering integrated strategic plans. The Government has set out its plans for housing numbers and has established strategic growth corridors. Development

Corporations, such as the London Thames Gateway Urban Development Corporation, have been established which have had planning powers transferred to enable them to drive forward development, including housing development and employment opportunities. Urban Development Corporations (UDCs) are typically established in key growth areas, or for new towns, where these cut across local authorities boundaries. UDCs have a limited lifespan of no more than ten years, but do have planning powers which enable them to take on the development management function from a local authority for strategic and significant applications which are in support of its objectives. While UDCs have planning powers, these are limited to the development management function – they cannot, for example, set the overall level of housing provision or infrastructure requirements – these are set at the plan-making level, through the Regional Spatial Strategy and new Local Development Frameworks. UDCs also have powers to acquire, manage and dispose of land or property, and ensure the provision of essential infrastructure alongside broad powers to facilitate development.

Box 3.4: The purposes of Urban Development Corporations

- To bring land and buildings back into use;
- To encourage the development of existing and new industry and commerce;
- To create an attractive environment; and
- To ensure that housing and social facilities are available to encourage people to live and work in the area.

3.36   UDCs are one vehicle for delivering schemes of regional or sub-regional importance, although it is essential that, where it is clear that such a body is needed to deliver new development, they are established quickly so that they can shape outcomes from an early stage. There are also mechanisms for local authorities to work across boundaries. In particular, local authorities can work together to develop plans. Chapter 1 discussed this in more detail.

3.37   For other large-scale applications the issue is perhaps whether local authorities have the capacity to cope with unexpected applications for major development. One option here, as for commercial developments above, would be to expand the role of ATLAS to remove bottlenecks in the delivery of new housing (see Chapter 5 of this Report) to help local authorities determine large or complex applications that they receive only infrequently. Statistics from DCLG (see Chart 3.1) indicate that call-in, where housing is concerned, is used more frequently for smaller cases – these are more likely to be due to breaches of other policies such as permitting development on green belt land.

Recommendation 10

To improve the framework for decision-making for major infrastructure to support a range of objectives, including the timely delivery of renewable energy:

- Statements of Strategic Objectives for energy, transport, waste proposals (including energy from waste) and strategic water proposals (such as new reservoirs) should be drawn up where they are not in place presently. These should, where possible, be spatially specific to give greater certainty and reduce the time taken at inquiry discussing alternative sites. Regional Spatial Strategies and local plans should reflect these national Statements and indicate, in particular, where regional facilities are needed;

- a new independent Planning Commission should be established which would take decisions on major infrastructure applications in the above areas. Decisions would be based on the national Statements of Strategic Objectives and policies set in the Regional Spatial Strategy, local development documents and other relevant considerations, including local economic, environmental and social impacts;

- the Planning Commission would be comprised of leading experts in their respective fields. Proceedings would be based on a streamlined public inquiry model, using timetabling to ensure timely decision-making. Full community consultation would be carried out and decisions would be taken in a fair, transparent and even-handed manner; and

- decisions which are of local importance only, including housing and commercial applications made under Town and Country Planning legislation, should continue to be made by the local planning authority. Where appropriate, and in order to ensure successful delivery of major commercial and housing development with national or regional spillovers, Government should consider the scope for greater use of delivery bodies such as Urban Development Corporations.

TRANSITIONAL ARRANGEMENTS

3.38   Establishing an independent Planning Commission would be a major reform to the planning system as a whole. While there are a number of potential benefits to be derived from it, it may take some time to put in place and there are some improvements that could be actioned immediately now to improve the process in the meantime. In particular, Ministers could commit to timetabling for all major infrastructure decisions, to help give greater certainty to developers regarding the time taken to make decisions.

3.39   Unlike Secretary of State decisions on planning applications under Town and Country Planning legislation, decisions taken on energy and transport applications are not subject to statutory timetables. Ministers do not have to inform developers and interested parties when they will receive a decision and there is no incentive to address the amount of time taken to reach a decision. For example, the average time taken to decide the more complex call-in or appeal cases determined solely by the Secretary of State for Communities and Local Government from the close of the inquiry is approximately 29 weeks.[21] For applications made under other consent regimes the time taken can be much longer: Dibden Bay (an application for a Harbour Revision Order as well as planning permission and other consents) took 66 weeks and the Midlands Metro (an application for a Transport and Works Act Order) 67 weeks.

3.40   Ensuring all Ministers are subject to timetabling would be a valuable reform independently of, or in anticipation of, the creation of an independent Planning Commission. Equally, even in the absence of a Commission there is a strong case for placing planning powers in only one Secretary of State and ending joint and linked decision-making. Large and complex cases, which would formerly have been dealt with by one or more Secretaries of State, would typically be identified at an early stage and be determined by the Planning Commission. Less complex and controversial cases could be determined by the local planning authority or on appeal by an Inspector on the Secretary of State's behalf.

Recommendation 11

In order to ensure that this new decision-making model is effective the Government should:

- rationalise consent regimes to ensure that infrastructure projects of major significance can be treated holistically and that the independent Planning Commission can take all the necessary planning decisions (if more than one is still required) on a particular scheme. Environmental consents would, however, remain separate from planning consents and be the responsibility of the Environment Agency;

- critically examine whether there are smaller infrastructure decisions currently made at the national level that should instead be determined by the local planning authority, or by the Planning Inspectorate on appeal;

- end joint and linked decision-making so that large infrastructure applications, or applications made by statutory undertakers, which would previously have been decided by two or more Secretaries of State will be transferred to the independent Planning Commission for decision. Non-strategic applications will be determined by local planning authorities or by the Planning Inspectorate on appeal; and

- as an interim measure, all Government departments with responsibilities for planning decisions should draw up timetables based on the DCLG model, for major applications decided by Ministers before the introduction of the independent Planning Commission and to ensure that decision-making is expedited in the short term.

---

[21] Information from DCLG indicates that in the six months from 1 April 2006, 92 per cent of decisions were made within 16 weeks from the close of the inquiry, with the remaining 8 per cent taking on average 29 weeks.

WIDER IMPLICATIONS FOR MINISTERIAL INVOLVEMENT

Town and Country Planning call-in powers

3.41   In terms of decisions made under the Town and Country Planning Act, the Secretary of State can currently 'call-in' a planning application that she wishes to determine. There is no necessary conflict between having an independent Commission determine large-scale cases subject to up-front Ministerial involvement through a national Statement of Strategic Objectives, and having Ministers involved in decisions that have not been subject to such a process. Indeed, there may be a number of reasons why it could be important to retain the involvement of Ministers in certain decisions. A small number of planning applications will come forward which have regional or national implications – social, economic and/or environmental – and in some circumstances it will be difficult for a local authority to make a decision because it does not have an appropriate framework for making decisions which have regional or national spillovers. Additionally, there may be a small number of cases where exceptional circumstances necessitate a decision being taken by Government Ministers – for example on matters of national security.

3.42   This Review does not recommend that there should be a change to Ministerial decision-making under the Town and Country Planning legislation. In the future, it may be appropriate for the Government to look again at the need for Ministerial involvement in decision-making on planning applications made under the Town and Country Planning legislation.

3.43   However, there is a case for keeping the Ministerial role to a minimum. This involves further progress being made in reducing the volume of cases determined by the Secretary of State in Town and Country Planning call-ins. This would mean a rethink of the current call-in policy that Ministers apply to planning applications referred to them. A more rigorous approach should be applied to establish whether the planning application has spillovers of such importance that it warrants the intervention of Ministers.

> **Box 3.5: Call-in Policy**
>
> The call-in policy[22] states that the Secretary of State will be 'very selective about calling in planning applications. She will, in general, only take this step if planning issues of more than local importance are involved.' A number of examples are given to illustrate how the policy may operate:
>
> - may conflict with national policies on important matters;
>
> - could have significant effects beyond their immediate locality;
>
> - give rise to substantial regional or national controversy;
>
> - raise significant architectural and urban design issues; or
>
> - may involve the interests of national security or of foreign Governments.
>
> However, each case will continue to be considered on its individual merits.

---

[22]This extract on the call-in policy is taken from the Official Report, Col 138, c. 333, 16 June 1999.

Reforming call-in
directions

3.44   Additionally, a reform of the number of directions (see Box 3.6) that spark Government Office involvement would reduce complexity and aid certainty. There are six current directions that lead to certain types of cases being referred to the Secretary of State via Government Offices. The Government has also consulted on proposals to produce a new direction on flooding because of existing concerns about planning permissions given by local authorities, despite objections being lodged by the Environment Agency. The proposed new Flooding Direction is part of a package of measures being introduced by the Government in connection with climate change adaptation.

3.45   Although only about 70 planning applications were called-in by the Secretary of State in 2004-05, a far greater number, over 1,300, were referred to Government Offices acting on behalf of the Secretary of State for consideration. Cases are referred under a number of directions with the greatest number being referred under the Departures Direction because they depart from 'one or more provisions' of the development plan, and are potentially significant because of their scale and nature, or because they are on land belonging to the local authority. It seems disproportionate, however, to refer 1,300 cases when only five per cent or so are actually called-in given the length of time it takes – up to seven weeks – to determine whether or not to call-in and the additional costs the developer may have to incur as a result of this. One reason why such a large number of applications may be referred under the Departures Direction is because of the number of out-of-date plans. This should decrease once new Local Development Frameworks are in place. Nevertheless, the Government should take steps now to reduce the delay and uncertainty associated with the call-in process.

Reducing the
number of
directions

3.46   Although directions, such as the recent Density Direction, give an indication to local authorities and developers of the importance the Government places on certain matters, it is by no means clear that this is an adequate justification for having a wide range of directions. As mentioned above, the majority of applications are referred to the Secretary of State (via the Government Offices) under the Departures Direction and on one level this seems the right approach. Under a plan-led system where local government is accountable for planning decisions, there seems little justification for central government intervening unless what is proposed involves a significant breach of the plan. One way of achieving a reduction in delay and uncertainty would be to reduce significantly the number of existing call-in directions, particularly where they duplicate the content of other directions or are no longer required for policy reasons. In particular the Density Direction, the Greenfield Direction and the Shopping Direction should be reviewed with an eye to withdrawing them in the near future.

3.47   An option here would therefore be to rethink the Departures Direction. Applications to which the local authority propose to grant consent should be assessed to establish not just the degree to which they are a departure from one or more provisions of the plan, but to the extent to which they are in general conformity with it. A 'general conformity' direction would mean that a local authority would have to assess how significant the proposal was in terms of its lack of conformity with the local development documents and the Regional Spatial Strategy. The fact that the proposed development would contravene one or more core policies would not of itself indicate that it should be referred to the Secretary of State.

Box 3.6: Call-in directions

The Department for Communities and Local Government (and its predecessors) have issued a number of drections through which applications are brought to the Secretary of State's attention:

Green Belt Direction: relates to development on green belt land which would involve the construction of building(s) with a floorspace of more than 1,000 square metres or any other development which would have a significant impact on the openness of the green belt;

Density Direction: (applies to London, the South-East, the South-West and East England and Northamptonshire) relates to applications where (a) it is proposed that there will be the provision of houses or flats on sites of 1 hectare or more; and where (b) the residential density is either not provided in the application for planning permission or will be less than 30 dwellings per hectare;

Greenfield Direction: relates to applications for 150 or more houses or flats, or residential development on sites of five or more hectares on greenfield land (not previously developed);

Departures Direction: relates to development that is contrary to one or more provisions of the development plan and which consists of, or includes the provision of more than, 150 houses or flats, or more than 5,000 square metres of gross retail, leisure, office or mixed commercial floorspace, is development of land belonging to the local authority, or is development of such a scale, nature or location that it would jeopardise the development plan;

Playing Fields Direction: relates to planning applications that have been objected to by Sport England on the grounds that a shortage of playing field provision would result, or that the replacement is not of matching quality, quantity or accessibility to that lost, but the local authority proposes to grant permission; and

Shopping Direction: relates to proposed developments for more than 20,000 square metres gross shopping floorspace, or to those between 2,500 and 20,000 square metres that will exceed 20,000 square metres when aggregated with other shopping floorspace within a radius of 10 miles from any part of the development.

3.48   An alternative approach would be to keep the Departures Direction but revise it to clearly state the types of schemes to which it would apply, including specific criteria or the scale of development. For example, although the Departures Direction includes a threshold of 150 houses, Chart 3.1 indicates that only five applications for between 150 and 250 houses were called in and decided by the Secretary of State between 2002 and 2006. Raising the thresholds for housing, retail, leisure, office or commercial would ensure that Ministers focus their attention on cases of national significance or where there are wider spillovers. The aim is to cut radically the number of cases that are referred unnecessarily to the Secretary of State for possible call-in.

Reforming
call-in policy

3.49   The current call-in policy states that applications will only be called-in if planning issues of more than local importance are involved. There has been welcome progress by DCLG here, with numbers called-in reduced from 128 cases in 1999-00 to 75 in 2005-06.[23] Despite this, the statistics suggest that a number of cases, which are quite small-scale, are called-in to be determined by the Secretary of State. For example, over the period 1 April 2002 to July 2006 the Secretary of State issued some 109 planning decisions on residential development. Of those 109 cases, 60 were applications for 25 houses or fewer. Of course, factors other than just the number of housing units have to be taken into account when determining whether or not to call-in an application, but the extent to which housing applications for 25 units or fewer raise issues of more than local significance is perhaps unclear.

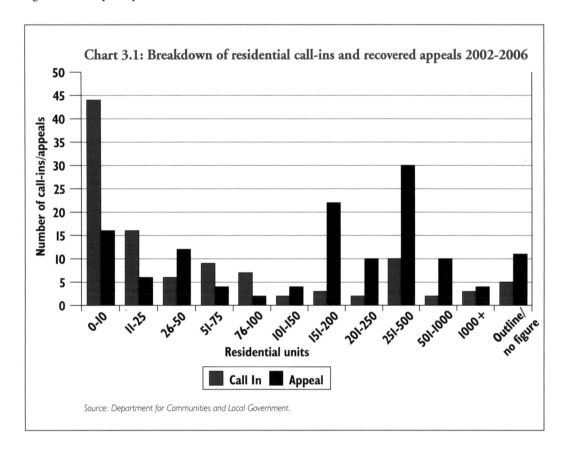

Chart 3.1: Breakdown of residential call-ins and recovered appeals 2002-2006

Source: Department for Communities and Local Government.

Quicker
decisions
to call-in

3.50   It is also important to ensure that, as well as reducing the overall number of planning applications called-in, the actual decision to call-in should be taken more quickly. Under the terms of the Departure Direction, the Secretary of State (via the Government Office) has a statutory 21-day period for reaching a decision on a departure application starting from the day that all the relevant documents have been received. If further time is required to decide whether or not to call-in, the Government Office has to issue an Article 14 direction.

3.51   Government Offices, if they miss the 21-day period for decision, operate a secondary target of seven weeks. In 2005-06, only 5 per cent of those cases that were called-in met the 21-day target and then 29 per cent the seven-week target. Some 71 per cent failed to meet the target.[24] Performance here should be improved. If local planning authorities have nine weeks to determine an application from receipt of the papers, it must be possible to improve on the time taken to

---

[23] Information from the Department of Communities and Local Government.
[24] Information from the Department of Communities and Local Government.

decide whether or not to call-in an application. In the context of far fewer applications being referred to the Secretary of State, more stretching targets must be applied. Time taken to call-in should be no longer than five weeks from receipt of the relevant documents. The average time taken to decide to call-in a case must be reduced from its present average of 86 days for those cases that are called-in to no more than 35 days.

3.52   It is acknowledged that 79 per cent of those cases referred to the Government Offices that are not called-in ('non-intervention cases') are sent back to the local planning authority within 21 days and a total of 90 per cent within the seven weeks. Nevertheless, given the costs to the developer it is essential that when decisions are taken to call-in planning applications they are made much more quickly. Efforts should also be made to reduce the amount of time taken to determine call-ins themselves from the close of the inquiry, in the context of the most complex cases taking a number of months.

Town and Country Planning recovered appeals

3.53   Another area where there may be too much ministerial intervention in Town and Country Planning issues is 'recovered' and transfer excepted appeals. All applicants for planning permission have a right of appeal to the Secretary of State if the local planning authority refuses or fails to determine their application within a given period. The Secretary of State delegates the powers to determine these appeals, currently about 23,000 per annum, to Planning Inspectors. However, she can 'recover' appeals for her own determination. This power is generally used quite sparingly and appeals are recovered in accordance with published criteria.

3.54   There are also some classes of appeals that must be determined by the Secretary of State – transfer excepted appeals – because Planning Inspectors have no powers under the existing legislation to determine them. One example of this is applications or appeals made by statutory undertakers.[25] The Town and Country Planning Act 1990, section 266 states that where an application for planning permission or an appeal is made by a statutory undertaker, the application or appeal 'shall be dealt with by the Secretary of State (for Communities and Local Government) and the appropriate Minister'. A small number of these applications come forward each year and, despite being relatively minor applications, for the most part have to be referred to the Secretary of State and the appropriate Minister to determine the application jointly. Recent examples include a car park extension application by Railtrack; a footbridge over a level crossing application by Network Rail and an application by the Environment Agency to vary the conditions of a flood alleviation scheme.

3.55   There is little added value in having national government – and indeed more than one government Minister – determine applications or appeals that are essentially local in their nature despite the status of the applicant. It would therefore be appropriate to devolve these decisions to the local planning authority or to the Planning Inspector if there is an appeal. Where there are very large and complex decisions that currently come forward as joint or linked decisions these are more likely to be infrastructure projects which should be referred at an early stage to the independent Planning Commission to decide.

---

[25] These are defined as 'persons authorised by any enactment to carry on any railway, light railway, tramway, road transport, water transport, canal, inland navigation, dock, harbour, pier or lighthouse undertaking or any undertaking for the supply of hydraulic power and a relevant airport operator' (TCPA 1990,s.262(1)) and also 'any public gas supplier, water or sewerage undertakers, the National Rivers Authority, the Post Office and the Civil Aviation Authority' (TCPA 1990, s.262(3)).

3.56   The remaining categories of transfer excepted appeals should also be removed: Listed Buildings in receipt of Grant Aid, Enforcement appeals accompanied by Environmental statements, Tree Preservation Order appeals and Hazardous Substances appeals. Amending secondary legislation in this area would enable Planning Inspectors to decide these appeals and end mandatory Ministerial involvement in minor matters.

Recommendation 12

Measures should be taken to limit Ministerial decision-making to only those cases where there are national or wider than local spillover effects and to reduce the time taken to decide planning applications made under the Town and Country Planning legislation. The Government should:

- review the Town and Country Planning call-in directions. This should involve:
    - revising the Departures Directions so that it more clearly indicates that only those proposals that are at significant odds with the core strategy of a new Local Development Framework, or similarly significant provisions of the Regional Spatial Strategy, could be considered a departure. The departures thresholds should also be tightened so that only those schemes of national and strategic significance which are at odds with the development plan could lead to notification to the Secretary of State; and
    - reviewing other directions, in particular the Density, Greenfield and Shopping Directions and withdrawing them if no longer necessary. The overall aim should be to reduce significantly the number of cases referred to the Secretary of State for possible call-in;
- review the Town and Country Planning call-in policy by the end of 2007-08 and implement tighter criteria to the cases that are subsequently called-in following referral. Call-in should be used only in exceptional circumstances for those cases where significant national or wider than local issues are raised (particularly where there is no clear framework at the regional and local level to enable appropriate decision-making to be made). The aim should be to reduce the numbers called-in by 50 per cent by 2008-09;
- review the recovered appeals policy by the end of 2007-08 and so govern more strictly the appeals that are recovered, with the result that only those cases where significant national or wider than local issues are raised, are recovered for Ministerial decision;
- reduce the amount of time it takes to decide whether or not to call-in an application. In particular the Government Office's secondary target of seven weeks should be reduced to no more than five weeks; and
- amend secondary legislation to remove the remaining categories of transfer excepted appeals: Listed Buildings in receipt of Grant Aid, Enforcement appeals accompanied by Environmental Statements, Tree Preservation Order appeals and Hazardous Substances appeals.

This Review does not recommend that there should be a change to Ministerial decision-making under the Town and Country Planning legislation. In the future, it may be appropriate for the Government to look again at the need for Ministerial involvement in decision-making on planning applications made under the Town and Country Planning legislation.

4 Streamlining the planning system

INTRODUCTION

4.1   The English planning system has become increasingly complex over recent decades. As the Interim Report made clear, much complexity is inevitable in a system that governs the use and development of land in a small, densely populated island. In addition, European law has added substantially to planning regulation. Some steps towards simplification have been taken in recent years including, for example, moving from three tiers of plans to two as a result of the Planning and Compulsory Purchase Act 2004 (PCPA 2004). But there are still widespread concerns about unnecessary levels of complexity. This:

- adds to uncertainty as applicants find it difficult to negotiate their way through numerous layers of regulation;

- adds to delay and the wide range of associated costs, including missed market opportunities;

- increases resource pressures on private sector applicants and on public sector service providers. According to DCLG figures, in 2004-05 the top 44 highest earning planning consultancies earned £39 million from government departments, £33 million from local government and £28 million from other public bodies; and

- makes planners' jobs harder as they struggle to plan effectively in the context of extensive bureaucratic demands. This can result in adverse effects for the quality of the natural and built environment.

4.2   This chapter considers how the planning system could be simplified and unnecessary complexity removed to tackle the issues listed above. It covers the three main components of the planning system: national policy, plans and development management.

NATIONAL POLICY

4.3   The principal components of national policy are primary legislation, secondary legislation, national policy and ministerial statements, guidance and supporting documentation including best practice guidance, and ministerial speeches.

Primary and secondary legislation

4.4   The primary legislation relating to planning has grown in complexity in recent years. In 1990 the main planning legislation was consolidated into four acts – the Town and Country Planning Act; the Planning (Listed Buildings and Conservation Areas) Act; the Planning (Hazardous Substances) Act; and the Planning (Consequential Provisions) Act. Since then there has been the Planning and Compensation Act of 1991, which introduced substantial amendments to this consolidated legislation, and the Planning and Compulsory Purchase Act of 2004, which made further amendments. On top of these six core statutes are a wider series of around 30 statutes that contain provisions closely related to planning, including the Wildlife and Countryside Act 1981, the Compulsory Purchase legislation and heritage legislation.

4.5   In addition to this large body of primary legislation, there is a growing body of complex secondary legislation related to planning. The Planning Encyclopaedia (itself now over 12,000 pages and comprising eight volumes) contains 201 statutory instruments, of which around 100 are of direct relevance and a further half of indirect relevance. Much of this complexity relates to revisions to previous regulations. The General Development Procedure Order (GDPO) for example, has had extensive sets of revisions in the past two years alone. In addition to the GDPO and all its amendments, there are the Applications Regulations, the Fees Regulations and all the regulations relating to the other types of consent. There are also various court procedures such as statutory challenge under section 288 of the 1990 Act (six weeks, no permission needed from the court); appeal under section 289 (four weeks, needs permission), and challenge by way of judicial review (three-month time limit, needs permission). Where planning applications are called-in by the Secretary of State, or appealed if the application is refused, there are further sets of regulations and a further four sets of regulations for enforcement.

4.6   This complexity can greatly impede the transparency of the system, and means that legal advice must often be sought when interpreting and applying the law (though of course much legal advice would still be needed under a simplified system). Moving towards a much more streamlined legislative framework would therefore be desirable (Box 4.1 provides an ideal model). This issue is one of prioritisation, so that activity is focused on where there would be the greatest returns relative to cost. In general, secondary legislation is more easily consolidated than primary and efforts should focus here in the short term. A priority is the consolidation of the GDPO, so that the substantive amendments are all brought together into one document. A replacement of the GDPO and Fees Regulations into one statutory instrument determining how planning permission is sought would also be valuable. This would present one set of rules, following the procedure through from pre-application discussions, through to application, fee, notifications, publicity, request for further information and, finally, the decision.

Box 4.1: Model for primary and secondary planning legislation[1]

Primary legislation. In place of the current 30 Acts have:

- Countryside and Biodiversity Act defining special areas in relation to countryside and the natural heritage, and identifying species for general protective measures;

- Historic Environment Act defining special areas in relation to the built heritage;

- Planning (Hazardous Substances) Act;

- Spatial Planning Procedures Act providing for plan-making and the control of development, including the policy basis, applications and appeals, and enforcement;

- Rights of Way Act providing for rights of access to land, including rights of way, commons and village greens, and access land; and

- Compulsory Purchase Act dealing with compulsory purchase and compensation.

Secondary legislation. In place of the current 201 statutory instruments have:

- Permitted Development Rules setting out when planning permissions are required;

- Spatial Planning Application Rules, replacing the GDPO, the Applications Regulations, the Fees Regulations and unifying consent regimes (this last would also require primary legislation);

- Spatial Planning Policy Rules, setting out the policy basis for planning decisions in terms of national guidance and regional and local plans;

- Enforcement Rules to determine the course of action for what happens in the event of proceeding without planning permission when it was needed;

- Planning Appeal Rules replacing all of the Appeals and Inquiries Regulations and Rules; and

- Additional Planning Regulations picking up miscellaneous matters beyond the above five!

4.7   There are costs associated with rationalising secondary legislation, but it is possible to overestimate these. The cost of a small team of lawyers could be relatively modest and potentially substantially less than the litigation costs associated with court cases instigated by the lack of clarity in the statutory framework that are part funded by the taxpayer. It would also save private sector costs, both directly and in savings on indirect costs of, for example, the added delays associated with increased complexity. International experience also shows that this can be possible – New Zealand, for example, introduced a single legislative structure in the form of the Resource Management Act which has substantially simplified the system. As an interim measure, the Government should also develop the Planning Portal to provide an effective electronic guide to all relevant national planning policy and procedures that would help people navigate through the rules, regulations and best practice.

Recommendation 13

The Government should consolidate the secondary legislation related to planning. A priority is to consolidate the General Development Procedure Order and its subsequent amendments – this should be undertaken in 2007.

---

[1] Based on Charles Mynors, Planning Law and the Need for Reform, paper presented to the Planning Summer School (September 2006).

National policy guidance

4.8   A second area of complexity relates to the volume of national policy guidance. National government has a role in setting policy guidance on issues of national importance and where the planning system is required to implement Government priorities at the local level. Local authorities tasked with implementing national policy through the planning system often welcome the weight that such guidance carries in the decision-making process. There can also be benefits from having ready-made processes and methodologies that save local authorities the effort of producing their own and can also provide a consistent approach for applicants.

4.9   The Government itself recognised in its 2002 Green Paper Planning: *Delivering a Fundamental Change*,[2] that the level of complexity had grown too great. Some progress has been made through the move to new Planning Policy Statements. However, there are still over 830 pages of guidance, with a wide array of best practice documentation and other supporting literature; and several years after the reform process began, there are still a number of Planning Policy Guidance notes that sometimes blend policy with guidance in an unhelpful and often duplicative manner. And while there continues to be a range of forms of policy – planning guidance notes, circulars and Ministerial statements – there will be difficulties in determining the current policy on any one issue.

4.10   One option for reform would be to adopt the Welsh model, which presents planning policy statements and guidance in one document. This option, which would result in an expanded Planning Policy Statement 1 and retraction of all the other documents, has a number of attractions:

- perhaps most importantly, it would allow a holistic approach to policy in a way the current range of subject-based guidance precludes. A planning system that is more responsive to prices, for example, has application across a range of subject areas, and would be more effective in a systemic document than in an individual statement;

- the range of topics on which there is a genuine national interest in spatial planning is, in practice, limited (see Box 4.2) and could be contained in one document of 50-60 pages;[3]

- it would reduce repetition in a more radical manner than is likely to be possible in a range of documents;

- it would increase certainty through its time frame – under the current system there will always be the pressure to update at least one of the long list of guidance notes, creating an uncertain policy framework for plan-making and development control;

- the alternative approach – asking Government to reduce the range of guidance on an incremental basis – does not appear to have delivered; at current rates it will take seven years to update policy with little reduction in complexity; and

- it would make it harder to add incrementally to the list of topics on which policy guidance was sought.

---

[2] Department for Transport, Local Government and the Regions, 'Planning: Delivering a Fundamental Change' (2002).

[3] On the potential to devolve many planning powers see, for example, M. Pennington, *Liberating the Land* (IEA, 2000), which explores these issues using a clear intellectual framework, drawing on the work of Hayek.

Box 4.2: Planning policy and spatial spillovers

England has a highly centralised system of land use regulation. There is extensive national policy on issues ranging from density levels to greenfield land targets. Plan-making processes and content are heavily regulated. The Secretary of State also has broad powers to make decisions on planning applications. However, it is notable that many of the spillover that planning seeks to address, including the protection of open space for recreation or the costs of increased noise of new development, occur at a local level, while others have regional or sub-regional impacts. This suggests that – national policy-focused on issues of genuinely national interest – could be concisely stated.

	National	Regional	Sub-regional	Local
Protection of open space for recreation				*
Provision of major infrastructure	*	*		
Quality of design of new buildings				*
Protection of historic built environment	*			*
Preventing merging of towns		*	*	
Disruption caused by new development				*
Vitality and viability of town centres			*	
Nature conservation and biodiversity	*			*
Pollution (air/noise) and congestion costs				*
Emissions and climate change	*			

While there may be a rationale for central government intervention independently of the level at which spillovers occur (as when there are benefits to be derived from a consistent approach to issues across the country to reduce transaction costs) there is a question about whether the current levels of centralisation are desirable. This is particularly the case given that increased decentralisation provides the opportunity for experimentation and innovation as well as allowing greater sensitivity to local economic and environmental conditions. It also is an effective means of minimising risk – if a nationally imposed policy is found to have hidden costs, these will be felt across the entire country. For this decentralisation to occur, however, appropriate incentives need to be in place so that all the relevant costs and benefits are considered – this issue is addressed in Chapter 7.

4.11   There are, however, disadvantages to having one planning policy statement. One issue is whether it would, in practice, be effective at reducing the tendency of central government to issue guidance. In Wales, for example, it is notable that the Planning Policy Document has attached to it an extensive range of technical notes, a companion guide, interim planning policy statements and a large volume of circulars and letters. A second issue is whether it would unduly restrain the flexibility of central government to issue policy changes to the planning policy statement in the light of changing circumstances or new information, conflicting with one of the aims of this Review – to increase responsiveness. A third consideration is that almost halfway through a period of revising statements and guidance is not necessarily the best time to consider this type of reform.

4.12   The most effective alternative is to recommit to the current streamlining programme. A desirable goal would be to reduce over 800 pages of policy to fewer than 200 pages. This would include completing the series of Planning Policy Statements, with a separation of policy from guidance, reducing repetition, shortening policy documents so that they are more strategic and obtaining a clear commitment from Government to cut the total volume of guidance. The challenge is to ensure that this requirement is made operational. This would involve:

- **establishing a framework for policy.** Current national policy has grown up piecemeal in recent decades, but in the absence of any logical framework. This makes avoiding duplication more difficult. Establishing a framework within which policy could be developed would both reduce the number of statements needed and provide greater clarity of objectives about what the planning system is in fact trying to achieve;

- **upfront timetabling for future publication of new policy statements,** in a manner similar to central government's demands for tighter project management by local government in terms of updating their own planning policies. This timetable should enable efficient production of updated policy – the length of time currently taken to update policy leaves planning in a constant state of flux;

- **rationalisation.** A cautious approach should be adopted to calls for further additions to planning policy documents and active consideration given to removing policy documents that are rarely used and whose content is covered by the new PPS1. The need for separate planning policy on simplified planning zones (PPG5), rural areas (PPS7), development on unstable land (PPG14), and planning for open space, sport and recreation (PPG17), for example, is unclear, while there is clear potential to merge PPG15 (historic environment) with PPG16 (archaeology); and

- **timing of supporting guidance.** Delaying the introduction of guidance notes aimed at interpreting policy statements causes unnecessary uncertainty. The Government should commit to policy guidance being published alongside the policy itself, or within a specified number of months and ensure that this is not an incentive for delaying the policy statement itself.

Recommendation 14

There should be a substantial streamlining of national policy, delivering previous commitments. The Government should publish proposals by summer 2007. This should include consideration of the potential to remove some of the current range of Planning Policy Guidance, and where necessary replace through an expanded PPS1. Any new policy should be consistent with the green paper principles of being strategic, concise and not mixing policy with guidance. Any new guidance should be published ideally alongside or otherwise within four months of publishing national policy. A desirable goal would be to reduce over 800 pages of policy to fewer than 200 pages.

PLAN-MAKING

4.13   The Planning and Compulsory Purchase Act 2004 reformed the plan-making system removing a tier of plans. In summary, the statutory development plan now comprises the Regional Spatial Strategy (or the Spatial Development Strategy in London) prepared by the regional planning body and the development plan documents in the Local Development Framework (LDF) prepared by the local planning authority (LPA).

4.14   The Regional Spatial Strategy (RSS) should provide a broad development strategy for the region over the next 15 to 20 years. It should identify the scale and distribution of new housing in the region, indicate areas for regeneration, expansion or sub-regional planning and specify priorities for the environment, transport, infrastructure, economic development, agriculture, minerals and waste treatment and disposal. Most former regional planning guidance is now considered part of the new RSS and forms part of the development plan.

4.15   At local level, the district or unitary authority prepares a Local Development Framework (see Figure 4.1) that sets out, in the form of a 'portfolio', the local development documents which collectively deliver the spatial planning strategy for the local planning authority's area. It includes Development Plan Documents (DPDs);[4] a project planning document called the Local Development Scheme (LDS); an annual monitoring report (AMR); a document outlining the consultation process called the Statement of Community Involvement (SCI); and supplementary planning policy documents (SPDs). Plan-making at the county level, other than for waste and minerals, has been removed.

4.16   As this new system has come into operation, a widespread view has developed – at the very least – that it is experiencing 'teething' problems that may be rectified over time. However, many contributing to the Review expressed concerns about the apparent complexity of the system and the processes required to produce the component parts of the LDF. Even though the new system is in its early stages and there is little appetite for a fundamental review, there is an emerging consensus that the system can be improved. This section looks at measures that could be taken to help streamline some processes and reduce some of the complexity. It will not be easy to introduce change at present, however. Care will need to be taken to ensure that the current process of plan development is accelerated, rather than being thrown off course.

---

[4] There are three required DPDs: the Core Strategy which sets out the spatial 'vision' for the local area; the Adopted Proposals Map showing the location of proposals in all current Development Plan Documents on an Ordnance Survey base map; and Site Specific Allocations.

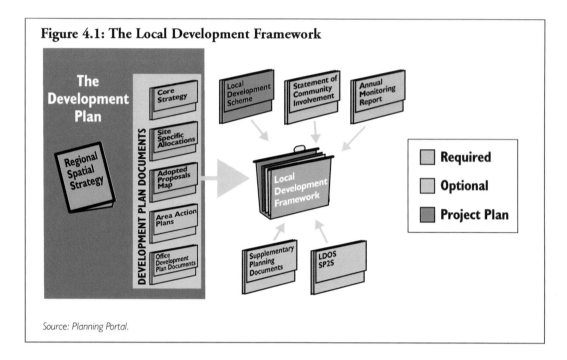

Figure 4.1: The Local Development Framework

Source: Planning Portal.

Streamlining the local plan-making processes

4.17   One of the major findings of the responses to the Review's Call for Evidence and the Review's own field research[5] was that the process for producing the content of an LDF is structurally too complicated, takes too long and is in need of adjustment. There is concern that authorities will focus on procedural requirements rather than planning content. As Birmingham City Council has noted:

> 'There is a real risk that authorities will find themselves concentrating on satisfying the procedures rather than the content of their plans – and if this happens the quality of the end product will almost certainly suffer.'[6]

4.18   Concerns with how the system is operating in practice centre on the extent to which it is over-engineered and takes too long for plans to be put in place. This is significant. If applications are determined primarily on the basis of the development plan then it and the RSS need to be as up to date as possible in order to inform decisions. The new development plan documents were designed to take three years to develop (refer to Figure 4.2) – which might be considered lengthy enough in the context of increasingly rapid economic and social change. But even this now appears over-optimistic. A recent report[7] suggests that there has already been some programme slippage during the production of Local Development Schemes, and early indications are that this has worsened (see Chart 4.1), with large numbers of development plan documents scheduled for examination four years after the new Act. (In addition the examination process could take a year to complete.) It may not be until around 2011 that many site-specific allocations emerge, seven years after the 2004 Act. If action is not taken, the adoption timescale for development plan documents could represent only a modest improvement on the previous system of Unitary Development Plans and district plans.

---

[5] The Barker Review conducted a series of regional workshops to investigate stakeholder views on the strengths and weaknesses of the current plan-making and development management processes. The details of the workshops can be found in Annex C of this report.

[6] Birmingham City Council, Response to the Interim Report of the Barker Review of Land Use Planning, p. 4.

[7] ODPM, *Starting Out With Local Development Schemes. Spatial Plans in Practice: Supporting the Reform of Local Planning* (April 2006).

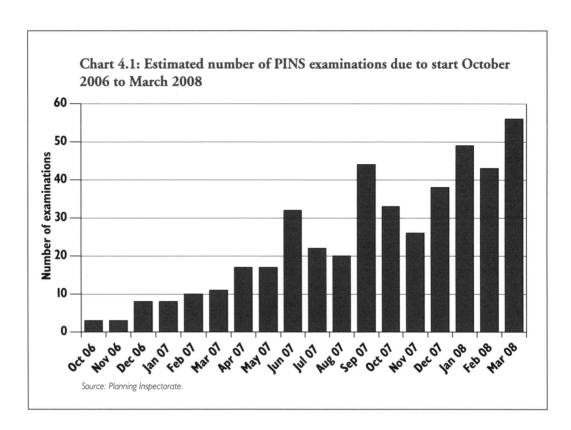

Chart 4.1: Estimated number of PINS examinations due to start October 2006 to March 2008

Source: Planning Inspectorate.

4.19   Many of the recent changes were adopted with the aim of encouraging community involvement. However, while effective engagement with the public and other bodies is essential to good plan-making, there is concern about 'consultation fatigue' caused by attempts to guard against public challenge through greater public involvement early on in the process. The key issue here is establishing which elements of the process should be conducted early on to add value. This is important because these processes are time consuming and costly. The practicalities involved in engaging individuals with high-level strategy should be carefully considered. Past research[8] suggests that the most successful consultation exercises in participation initially tended to involve smaller group discussions with the various interest groups. These allowed agendas to be established and mutual trust to emerge, before wider public meetings were held. Beyond this, there is also a question concerning how much time individuals have available to commit to engaging with strategies and how readily they can access the process, including travelling to meetings. In this context the jargon and complexity associated with acronyms (Local Development Frameworks, local development schemes, development plan documents, etc.) may impede effective community involvement.

---

[8] James Barlow, *Public Participation in Urban Development: The European Experience*, Policy Studies Institute (1995).

Figure 4.2: Preparation of a Development Plan Document

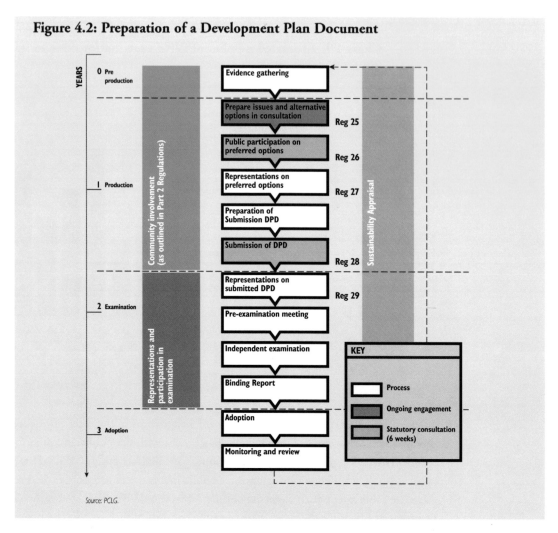

Source: PCLG.

4.20   Reforms to expedite processes would be valuable in terms of cost savings to the LPAs and, more importantly, in the broader benefit of having an efficient plan-making system to support development decisions. Once the initial round of core strategies is in place, the aim should be a process for Development Plan Documents that takes no longer than two years (see Figure 4.2). The priority here should be to:

- **deal with consultation fatigue.** An example is the City, which intends to produce six Development Plan Documents and twelve Supplementary Planning Documents. This will mean a minimum of 19 consultation exercises over five years – including the SCI consultation. While the City is in many respects unlike other local authorities, the example does illustrate the extent of consultation that authorities could face and in some cases are already receiving complaints about. Data collected by DCLG shows that 29 per cent of local authorities are planning to produce five or more Development Plan Documents. In some instances authorities have combined departmental consultation requirements to reduce this burden but the current system is 'consultation heavy'. This seems to be occurring despite Government guidance which suggests that the programme of document production should be realistic. The following three proposals would all help to relieve the consultation burden and associated costs;

Box 4.3: Potential two-year process for Development Plan Document preparation

Stage	Timeline (maximum time needed)
1. Development of preferred options	1-8 months
2. Consultation	9-10 months
3. Development of final proposals	11-16 months
4. Consultation	17-18 months
5. Preparation for Examination	19-20 months
6. Examination	21 months
7. Final report	24 months

- streamline the consultation process. The former development plan system permitted the LPA to develop a draft plan to 'consult' on without engagement with any other public bodies. Not only did this approach fail to engage the general public but it could also lead to the plan being undeliverable, as key delivery stakeholders had not been involved in it. There is therefore a need for genuine community and key stakeholder engagement in the development of preferred options. However, a formal separate issues and options phase can add six months to the timeline and additional cost of the issues and options stage for its Core Strategy alone may be around £100,000 for each authority or £36 million across all authorities.[9] Moreover, experience with the new system to date has questioned the added value. Some local planning authorities have said that they have to create additional options to consult on, all of which require a Sustainability Appraisal. An alternative would be for Development Plan Documents to undergo just two stages of statutory consultation – at preferred options stage and at submission stage, rather than three. This two-tier style of consultation is already standard across government. National policy, for example, undergoes both Green and White Papers. A third prior set of consultation on high level options adds costs and delay for little additional benefit. As the Planning Officers' Society has observed:

  'Experience suggests that the general public, at least, find it much more difficult and less rewarding to engage in consultation at the higher, strategic levels of planning';[10]

- streamlining sustainability appraisal requirements. Easing Sustainability Appraisal (SA) requirements would result in a significant reduction in direct costs (use of consultants, etc.) and administrative burden. Currently, SAs are needed for all Development Plan Documents (DPDs)[11] and Supplementary Planning Documents (SPDs) to assess the economic, environmental and social effects from the outset to ensure that they accord with sustainable development. It has been suggested that these often add no value or are merely a 'tick box' exercise. A revised

---

[9] The £100k saving per authority estimate is based on a breakdown of costs from the Core Strategy issues and options stage across three local planning authorities. The cost breakdown includes: internal staff costs; public consultation costs including document printing, distribution, consultation events; consultants costs to independently assess the Sustainability Appraisal reports. The figure is indicative only, as it is based on a small sample size.

[10] Planning Officers' Society, Response to the Barker Review of Land Use Planning Interim Report, p.2

[11] Refer to Figure 4.2 which shows how a Sustainability Appraisal should be conducted alongside the development of a Development Plan Document. This process is similar for the development of a Supplementary Planning Document.

preferred options stage would instantly reduce the number of SAs required. In addition, the case for removing the SA stage on Supplementary Planning Documents is particularly strong because these are underpinned by policies that have already been appraised. There are references in Government guidance to a reduced requirement for Sustainability Appraisal of SPDs where SA of the 'parent' DPD has addressed the relevant considerations. However, given that an SPD should not introduce new policy but should just expand on or supplement DPD policies, there is a case for SAs here being the exception rather than the rule. This activity will have to ensure the need to continue to meet the EU Strategic Environmental Assessment (SEA) requirements is met.

- Further, if a Supplementary Planning Document were to result in significant inputs, it is likely to be going beyond its role of expanding or supplementing existing policy, and should be a DPD in its own right. The argument can be taken a step further. Given that DPDs must be in conformity with the Core Strategy and must be in general conformity with the Regional Spatial Strategy, or Spatial Development Strategy in London, there should be a review of SA requirements of DPDs, particularly in the context of Articles 4 and 5 of the SEA Directive,[12] which relates to the avoidance of duplication of assessment where plans and programmes form part of a hierarchy; and

- **reform of the Statement of Community Involvement.** There is clear value to a local authority setting out its strategy for public involvement across its functions, but the requirement for a separate document setting out how this will operate in a planning context appears to add little value. There is also considerable opportunity for the public to exert influence through committees, local councillors and the proposed Community Calls for Action, especially as minimum standards for community involvement are set out in the Town and Country Planning (Local Development) (England) Regulations 2004. There is a good argument that SCIs should be integrated into the authorities' wider strategy and this has been taken up in the Local Government White Paper 2006[13] which proposes that local authorities should draw up 'comprehensive engagement strategies'. The Local Government White Paper also announced that the requirement for independent examination of the SCI by the Planning Inspectorate will be repealed at the earliest opportunity.

Examination in Public   4.21   In addition to this streamlining, it is important to ensure that the process for examining plans for soundness is not too protracted. Under current arrangements this whole final stage (through to presentation of the binding report) takes a year. This should be reduced. It is, however, critical to ensure that the examination in public itself is a robust process, particularly in the context of a plan-led system with binding Inspectors' reports. Policies emerging from regional or local plans should be based on sound evidence and properly scrutinised. While the examination in public should be efficiently operated, the risk of inadequate quality control presented by a structured discussion forum with no opportunities for questioning or cross-examination of evidence must be minimised.

---

[12] Directive 2001/42/EC on the assessment of the effects of certain plans and programmes on the environment.
[13] DCLG, *Strong and Prosperous Communities: The Local Government White Paper* (October 2006).

The challenge 4.22   A further important reform concerns the provision by which development plans can be
provision challenged. Under current provisions (based on section 113 of the PCPA 2004), if a court quashes all or part of the plan on a point of law or for substantial prejudice through a procedural failing, the plan process has to be recommenced from the beginning. With the alteration to the RSS for the East of England, East Midlands and South-East of England published by the Secretary of State in March 2005, the court found that the Secretary of State had made a mistake in his consideration of the report of the panel concerning required levels for housing provision. There was no provision for the matter to be resubmitted to the Secretary of State for reconsideration. The consequence was that the relevant part of the RSS was quashed and there has been a policy vacuum is the housing requirements for the sub-region which will remain until the review of the RSS is brought forward and published.[14]

4.23   Reform of this system to enable the Courts to quash the adoption or publication of the relevant plan by the determining authority, whether that is the LPA or the Secretary of State (for RSSs), should leave the authority or Secretary of State to decide whether the flaw is so fundamental that the process should recommence or whether (as in the RSS case referred to above) it could be simply reconsidered by the Secretary of State and the relevant part of the plan republished with the error corrected.

Reducing the length and complexity of plans

4.24   Not only are there widespread concerns about the complexity of the processes for plan-making under the new system, there are also concerns about the complexity of the content of the plans themselves. The new Local Development Frameworks were intended to be shorter than their predecessors and avoid the tendency to repeat national policy guidance or to add a plethora of new policies. The best of the new plans appear to be succeeding, with thorough core strategies that focus on issues of genuine strategic importance for the local area. However, the length of the documents and number of policies within them is still a cause of concern.

4.25   There is no reason for plans to be of great length. Issues such as the need for high-quality design or the appropriate form of green belt development are covered in national policy and do not need to be repeated in plans. Instead of lengthy documents, local plans should simply set out where they intend to deviate from national policy, and the reasons for doing so, alongside any specific issues of local interest, such as the boundaries of green belt or the relationship of policies to particular areas. Of course, the top line of national policy must be made clear for those communities that are unfamiliar with it. This would also speed up decision-making, as planners and, where appropriate, Inspectors could simply focus on policies of direct relevance to the issue at hand. Length also has implications for community involvement. Medway, for example, submitted over 1,500 pages to the Inspectorate to test for soundness. It is difficult for the public to understand and engage with this volume of material in a productive manner within the six-week consultation period.

---

[14] The above position was analysed and confirmed by the High Court in *Charles Church Developments Limited v. South Northamptonshire District Council* (2000), *Journal of Planning and Environmental Law*, Case Reports 46. The limitation on the Courts' powers has been the subject of considerable criticism in the courts – see for example per Buxton LJ in *First Corporate Shipping v. North Somerset DC* (2001) EWCA Civ 683; similar criticism was made in the challenge referred to above by Sullivan J (*Ensign v FSS 2005*).

Recommendation 15

Local planning authorities and regional planning bodies should continue to develop their development plans as expeditiously as possible to provide a clear planning framework for decisions.

DCLG should urgently review the regulations and guidance behind the new plan-making system to enable the next generation of development plan documents to be delivered in 18-24 months in place of the current 36-42 months, while ensuring appropriate levels of community involvement. Draft guidelines should be published by summer 2007, drawing on the views of other stakeholders including the Better Regulation Executive. This will involve:

- streamlining of Sustainability Assessment (SA) processes including removing or reducing requirements where a related higher tier policy has already been subject to SA and exploring how SA requirements can be streamlined for Supplementary Planning Documents;

- streamlining of Local Development Scheme processes to a short programme of intended development documentation by local planning authorities;

- refashioning the Statement of Community Involvement into a corporate 'comprehensive engagement strategy' along with removal of the need for independent examination, as proposed in the Local Government White Paper 2006;

- increasing the speed with which Supplementary Planning Documents can be delivered;

- regional and local planning authorities and Inspectors should ensure that regional and local plans deliver against the original objective of being short documents that do not duplicate national policy;

- the removal of a formal requirement for an issues and options phase of plan-making, leaving the Preferred Options and Submitted stage. Preferred Options should be generated via effective and focused engagement with stakeholders, especially those vital to the delivery of the plan;

- a reform of the challenge provision so that if a plan or part of a plan is quashed in the Courts the plan can be amended without the plan-making process having to begin from the start; and

- ensuring that the new examination in public process enables an effective scrutiny and a testing of the evidence base of policy.

Local authorities should explore the potential for efficiency gains (which could be in excess of £100 million over a three-year period) to be reinvested in enhancing the quality of their planning service provision.

DEVELOPMENT MANAGEMENT

4.26   Development management is the process whereby a local planning authority receives and considers the merits of a planning application and whether it should be given permission. There are also substantial complexities at this level. Outside support can help here. Dealing with planning issues can be particularly difficult for start-ups and Small and Medium-sized Enterprises (SMEs), which frequently lack knowledge and may find it difficult to afford professional services. The Royal Town and Planning Institute (RTPI) has operated its Planning Aid service as a charitable activity supported by DCLG and using over 600 volunteers to help local communities, groups and individuals who would not otherwise have access to professional planning advice. This is very successful, now helping 14,000 people and over 4,000 communities each year, with telephone casework approaching 5,000 calls. In guiding and advising its own clients, Planning Aid also reduces pressures on local planning authorities. The RTPI wants to extend this service through a social enterprise company so as to provide a comparable service for start-ups and SMEs. The RTPI is looking for business support for this, with a view to a pilot project in 2007. This could be a very helpful development.

4.27   In addition to finding mechanisms to help applicants cope with complexity, it is also important to try to streamline processes directly. A number of issues could potentially be addressed here, but two stand out: the complexities associated with the wide variety of consent regimes and the volume of paperwork associated with growing information requirements.

Variety of consent regimes

4.28   Although in the public mind 'planning permission' is a generic regulatory requirement for the use and development of land, in practice over the past few decades a large number of separate consent regimes have grown up. These include:

- core regimes of planning permission, principally under the Town and Country Planning Act 1990, and listed buildings and conservation area consents under the Planning (Listed Building and Conservation Areas) Act 1990;

- other regimes of advertisement regulations consent, building regulations approval, scheduled monument consent, highway works, felling licenses, hazardous substances consent, tree preservation order consents, trees in a conservation area consent, protected hedgerow and footpath order consents; and

- infrastructure regimes including for harbours development under the Harbours Act of 1964, heavy and light rail and inland waterways under the Transport and Works Act 1992, highways under the Highways Act 1980, electricity under the Electricity Act 1989, gas storage under the Gas Act 1965, pipeline construction under the Pipelines Act 1962, water infrastructure under the Water Industry Act 1991.[15]

4.29   The Halcrow Report, government-sponsored research conducted in 2002-04, investigated the merits of unifying twelve non-major infrastructure consents.[16] The starting point for the study was that the current system involved duplication and was confusing, complex and time consuming for all concerned. With the exception of building regulations (where the legal review highlighted a number of potential problems but suggested this could be reviewed at a later date) it concluded that, in general, there were a number of benefits to be gained from merging of consents. A legal review also found that on a procedural and legislative level unification would allow EU legislation and related Environmental Impact Assessment (EIA) regulations to be built into any new regime more easily than the current array of regimes. The review was unable to quantify the scale of the likely cost savings from unification, but concluded there was no reason why all the consent regimes

---

[15] Annex B of the Interim Report of the Barker Review of Land Use Planning, 2006, supplies further details of these infrastructure-related consent regimes.

[16] Halcrow Group, *Unification of Consent Regimes*, Report for the Office of the Deputy Prime Minister (June 2004).

explored, including planning, listed buildings, conservation areas, advertising regulations, tree protection, protected hedgerow and footpath order consents should not eventually be brought together into a single consent regime, given that:

> 'we are clear and convinced that the unification of some of the regimes is to be supported and will achieve real improvements – there is a case for change.'[17]

4.30   An essential insight of the Halcrow Report (endorsed by the relevant House of Commons committee) is that having a large number of different forms of permission related to land use and development is inefficient and cumbersome. This is important as part of wider streamlining reforms to the planning system. An applicant for a new office block might, for example, have to apply for general planning consent, listed building consent, conservation area consent and consent to carry out works to a tree protected by a tree preservation order, in addition to building regulation requirements. Additionally multiple applications require multiple appeals and multiple enforcement notices. (The various consent regimes for Major Infrastructure Projects produce similar levels of complexity and this was dealt with in Chapter 3.)

4.31   How should unification best be delivered? It is clear that change would require reform to primary and secondary legislation. It also would necessitate change at central government level, given that the ultimate decision-maker for some regimes is the Secretary of State at DCLG but for others, such as scheduled monuments, is elsewhere. More debatable is the issue of whether a 'big bang' approach is desirable, or whether a piecemeal set of reforms is preferable, starting with unifying the listed building and scheduled monument consent regimes as proposed in the DCMS Review of Heritage Protection. The merit of the holistic approach is that it would enable the issue to be addressed once and for all in a defined time period. However, a step-by-step process along a route to unification could be more readily achieved. That is the approach recommended in this report. One option would be to bring together the advertising, heritage and planning consents.

4.32   In some instances steps to unification need not be a complex process. Bringing the display of advertisements within the definition of 'development' would be relatively simple, with the categories currently obtaining deemed consent being another class of permitted development (as in Ireland). Similarly, including as development all works affecting the character of a listed building or scheduled monument could remove the need for these consents, with certain works relating to listed buildings included in permitted development. However, the issue of whether the natural world consents (tree preservation orders, felling licences, hedgerow consents) are best unified within broader planning permissions or kept as a separate (though rationalised) category, requires further consideration.

4.33   More immediately, the national standard application form, 1APP,[18] should make the process of applying for the various consents simpler. Due to be rolled out by DCLG and the Planning Portal in July 2007, the on-line form will bring together the various consent requirements and help the applicant to navigate through the process. 1APP also means that applicants will not have to produce different application forms for different local planning authorities.

---

[17] Halcrow Group, *Unification of Consent Regimes*, Report for the Office of the Deputy Prime Minister (June 2004).
[18] 1APP is a single standardised planning application form and is designed to end decades of inconsistency in the planning process. Existing planning application forms vary greatly between different local authorities, with different requirements on numbers of copies and additional information. This inconsistency is a major challenge to planning agents submitting applications in different localities, as they are unable to put one simple application process in place. The form would allow users to select the type of planning permission required and systematically complete and validate one seamless application form in a logical sequence.

Recommendation 16

The Government should formally commit to the gradual unification of the various consent regimes related to planning following the proposed unification of scheduled monuments and listed building consents, and should set out proposals in 2007. One option would be to bring together the heritage and planning consents.

Reducing the volume of paperwork

4.34   As the Interim Report made clear, information requirements to support planning applications have grown substantially in recent years. There are a number of reasons for this. Planners, committee members and third parties should be able to access high-quality information on the range of issues that are likely to affect a development, in order to come to a decision on whether or not the development should proceed. In addition, adhering to European legislation requires a large amount of paperwork. The use of professional planning consultants often results in comprehensive but lengthy reports. There is a theme of risk aversion within the system stemming from the threat of legal challenge that may lead to overproduction of documentation, and finally there are no current processes to ensure resource transfers before other government departments implement policies through the planning system. The incentives to reduce bureaucratic loads are lacking.

4.35   However, it is important that progress is made towards a risk-based and proportionate approach to the amount of information required to accompany planning applications; particularly given the cost involved and concerns that some of the detailed information does not add value. In this instance it is not efficient for local authorities to process excessive paper loads and businesses, facing costs in the form of application fees and consultants' fees, should not be put in the position where they are asked for unnecessary information. Information provided in support of a planning application should be of real benefit to the outcome of the application. It is not clear that any progress has been made in reducing the volume of paperwork associated with applications (indeed, requirements have been rising) although the 1APP national standard application form (which will be mandatory in the second half of 2007) is welcome here. Closer monitoring of progress using like-with-like cases would help here.

4.36   One particular issue is whether a separate, parallel environmental assessment regime is needed. The information submitted with a planning application should make it quite clear what the environmental impact of a proposal would be, and should not require separate environmental statements that can take a year and may cost upwards of £100,000 to complete, although they are only required for a relatively small number of overall applications (460 were required in 2005). Even if it is accepted that separate Environmental Statements should be produced, there is a real issue regarding the extent of information required. As one leading planning lawyer has observed:

> *'It is difficult to avoid the suspicion that the EA regime has grown out of all proportion, with the complex litigation that has taken place in recent years arising not because the challenger was unaware of what was proposed, but simply because the absence of an adequate statement provided a handy stick with which to beat the developer. In any event, the result has been the growth of a parallel system of environmental assessment, causing huge delay and costs to developers.'*[19]

---

[19] Charles Mynors, Planning Law and the Need for Reform, paper presented to the Planning Summer School (September 2006).

4.37   In terms of reducing the length or number of Environmental Statements, there are limitations to what is possible – the criteria for producing a statement and the items it must cover stem from EU Council Directive 85/337/EEC (as amended by 97/11/EC), and Departmental guidance (Circular 02/99 *Environmental Impact Assessment*) states that the Environmental Statements should concentrate on the 'main' and 'significant' effects and be prepared 'without unnecessary elaboration'. However, given the scale of costs that can be imposed, regulations setting out the thresholds which trigger the requirements to produce Environmental Statements should be re-examined.

Recommendation 17

The Government should, as a matter of priority, work with local planning authorities and other bodies such as the Better Regulation Executive to reduce substantially the information requirements required to support planning applications. The principle should be to move towards a risk-based and proportionate approach to information requests. Action should include:

- a review of the guidance on validating planning applications including the introduction of proportionality thresholds and the phasing of information required at different stages of the application process;

- the introduction of strict criteria to be fulfilled by Government, regional planning bodies and local planning authorities before any additional information requirements on applicants are introduced;

- an examination of the potential to raise the thresholds for EIA applications and limit the paperwork associated with Environmental Statements;

- a tighter enforcement of processes aimed at ensuring that resource transfers and training provision occur before other government departments implement policy via planning; and

- formal monitoring of progress based on representative samples of volumes of information, and associated costs, for like-with-like cases for both major and minor developments across a range of sectors. The first assessment should be published in 2009, benchmarking against 2006 volumes and costs.

5 Improving the performance of local planning authorities

INTRODUCTION

5.1   The planning service of a local authority is an important component of its customer-focused responsibilities. Over 650,000 planning applications are processed by local planning authorities each year, ranging from relatively small-scale applications for household extensions and advertising consents, to large-scale mixed-use developments that can impact positively or negatively on whole communities.

5.2   The best local authorities discharge this service to a high standard. In these authorities clear leadership and strong management deliver a high quality service with an efficient use of resources and effective customer care. The Review visited four local authorities that had made significant improvements to their planning services; these are detailed in Annex B. The wider ability of the system to cope with rapidly expanding volumes of applications in recent years has also been impressive, with additional funding in the form of the £600 million Planning Delivery Grant helping to ensure that progress is made towards better service provision in some areas.

5.3   However, as the Interim Report made clear, it appears that many planning departments could further improve the quality of service that businesses and other applicants expect in return for their taxes and planning fees. A recent survey of businesses[1] showed that 69 per cent were dissatisfied with the record of improvement in local authority planning departments. Cost, uncertainty, quality of service and extent of delays are all commonly cited problems. This affects not only the applicant firms and individuals, but also the quality of life of communities as a whole, with the benefits of regeneration, job creation, inward investment and lower prices lost or deferred. This chapter sets out recommendations to improve the performance of service delivery. It focuses on four main issues:

- reducing the volume of applications (the flow into the system) so that resources can be better targeted towards value-added activity;

- enhancing the efficiency and quality of process and service delivery, in part to minimise the resource required to process each application;

- addressing perceived deficiencies in resources and skills, so that planning departments are in a position to provide a high quality service; and

- the change in culture needed to raise the position of the planning department in local authorities and its status as a delivery tool more broadly.

Focusing resources on issues that matter

5.4   A central difficulty with which local planning authorities have had to grapple in recent years has been the marked increase in applications. In 1999-2000 there were 526,000 applications; by 2005-06 this had grown to 650,000 – a growth of 24 per cent. This has resulted in available resources being spread more thinly, putting pressure on desired delivery outcomes such as speedy

---

[1] CBI, *Public Services Survey* (London, 2006), referred to in K. Barker, *Barker Review of Land Use Planning: Interim Report* (2006), p. 46.

determination of cases. It is difficult to determine future trends for planning applications with any degree of certainty, but it is very likely that a combination of a rising population and stable economic growth will result in further growth in demand. If the trend growth rate for 1981-2005 were maintained over the next ten years, by 2016 there could be around 720,000 planning applications, while if the higher growth rate of 1995-2005 is maintained there could be 820,000 (see Box 5.1 below).

Box 5.1 Planning application forecasts

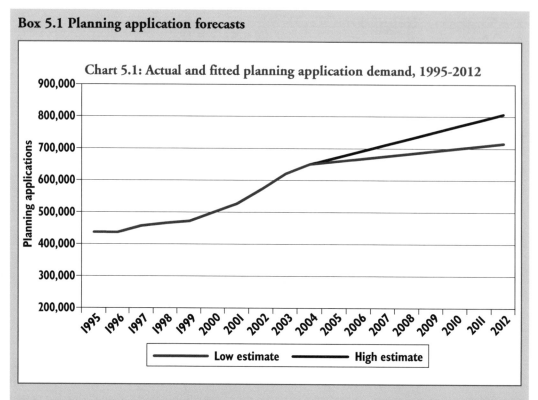

Chart 5.1: Actual and fitted planning application demand, 1995-2012

Source: Analysis based on DCLG development control data from 1981-2006.

The above graph is intended to provide an indication of the potential scale of future demand for planning services. Taking the growth between 1996 and 2004, the upper line projects this into the future, suggesting there will be over 820,000 planning applications in 2016. The lower line takes the average growth from 1986 to 2004 and projects forwards, giving a prediction of over 720,000 applications in 2016. (These examples are intended solely as illustrations of potential future demands on the planning system, and should not be taken as precisely modelling future planning demand.)

5.5   In this context, it is critical to ensure that the rules for whether a development requires planning permission are appropriate. While the public interest needs to be protected, planning applications should only be requested where they are needed. Local authority resource should not be taken up disproportionately on small-scale planning permissions that have little potential impact on the public interest, rather than on engaging positively with larger scale residential and commercial developments.

5.6   The Government has already begun to address this issue. Town and Country (General Permitted Development Order) 1995 is already in place as a deregulatory measure aimed at ensuring that minor developments such as small extensions do not need planning permission from the local authority to proceed. The Householder Development Consents Review[2] put forward proposals to reduce householder consent requirements. This could potentially remove tens of

---

[2] DCLG, 'Householder Development Consents Review: Steering Group Report' (July 2006).

thousands of cases from the system, following a 115 per cent rise to 340,000 over the ten years to 2005. It will do so on the basis of the 'impact' principle, i.e. that planning permission should only be required for developments that have non-negligible third-party effects. This should also address issues of perverse impacts caused by current volume-based measures such as demolishing outbuildings to comply with the requirement that the volume of the original terraced house must not be increased by more than 10 per cent (or 50 cubic metres whichever is the greater) to avoid the neccesity for making a planning application.

5.7   However, it is possible to overestimate the benefits of this reform from the local planning authority perspective. Although householder consents form a large proportion of application numbers (see Box 5.2 below) they form a small proportion of total resource due to their relative simplicity. Even a 30 per cent reduction in volume may only result in overall saving of around £15 million for local authorities out of a total cost of between £199 million and £242 million.[3] Where householder application fees cross-subsidise the processing of other applications it could actually reduce available resources within local authority planning departments. Nor can it be assumed that staff freed from working on householder consents will be suitable for transfer to more complex projects. However, it is clearly sensible and welcome that effort and energy is diverted to where it most matters and householders freed from unnecessary burdens.

5.8   It is also possible to go further. Householder consents are only Parts 1 and 2 of a 38-part General Permitted Development Order. There is the potential to extend the principle behind the reform to minor development. While householder consents have seen by far the largest growth in recent years, making it right that they were the priority for review, other consents have also risen somewhat, up 10 per cent since 1999-2000. There are now around 122,720 minor consents each year[4] (refer to chart 5.2). Removing some of these cases from the system would further benefit local planning authorities, as well as providing welcome extra flexibility (and cost-reduction) for potential applicants. Of course, simply because a development is minor does not mean it is uncontentious. There are often both indirect impacts (such as car parking) and aggregate impacts (such as the appearance of a street) to consider. But the central principle is clear: consent should not be required for development unless it has non-marginal third-party impacts.

5.9   The impact principle could also be brought to bear on the use classes order. This currently acts as a proxy for impact through, for example, prohibiting any change of use from a hotel without applying for planning permission. But in reality there may be numerous instances where a change of use has no impact. Requiring planning approval in these circumstances loads extra burdens onto the system for no public interest benefit. However, the use class order has only recently been revised, and this may not be the best time to revisit this issue in the short term.

---

[3] Estimates of the cost of existing fee-paying development control activities outlined in ODPM, *The Planning Service: Costs and Fees*. Arup Economics and Planning with The Bailey Consultancy, Addison & Associates and Professor Malcolm Grant, November 2003.
[4] DCLG, Development Control Statistics 2005-06, http://www.communities.gov.uk/pub/642/DevelopmentcontrolstatisticsEngland200506_id1503642.pdf.

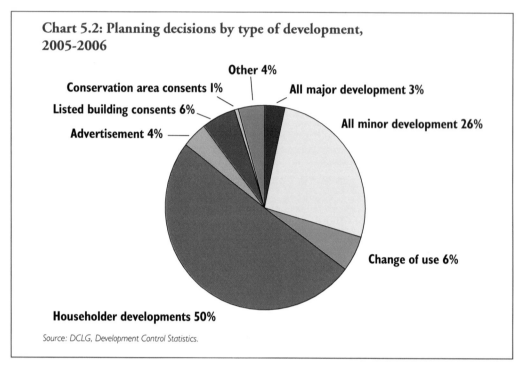

Chart 5.2: Planning decisions by type of development, 2005-2006

Other 4%

Conservation area consents 1%

Listed building consents 6%

Advertisement 4%

All major development 3%

All minor development 26%

Change of use 6%

Householder developments 50%

Source: DCLG, Development Control Statistics.

Microgeneration 5.10 A particular area that would benefit from reform is the microgeneration of electricity. Currently, the planning process can present a barrier to installing microgeneration equipment in both domestic and commercial buildings. This particularly applies in the case of wind turbines, which are subject to acoustic testing at a cost to the applicant of up to £450. In addition to extending permitted development rights for small-scale microgeneration equipment on domestic buildings, including small wind turbines and solar panels, the Government should also extend these rights to small businesses.

5.11 For this to provide a genuine benefit to the environment there is a need to ensure that the environmental cost of manufacturing microgeneration equipment does not outweigh the benefits of its use, and clarify which technologies this applies to. This could be addressed by the introduction of an approved system of industry standards. This should help to give consumers (whether businesses or householders) confidence that the equipment they are buying is manufactured in an environmentally sustainable way.

New system of side-agreements 5.12 Extending the 'impact' test beyond householder consents to minor consents such as commercial development would be a significant move towards reform. But while the impact test is an important determinant of whether planning permission should be required, there is also a strong case for further refining the types of cases that require permission. In particular, where the potential impact can be mitigated through negotiated agreement between affected parties, there seems no need for government intervention. For example, an extension to a small business property as a result of an increase in trade might result in the view from the living room of an adjoining residential property being impaired. Under the 'impact' test, this would result in the development requiring planning permission. It would therefore rest with the local authority to determine whether the development should proceed. An alternative arrangement would be for the potential applicant to talk to the neighbour and discuss the available options. It may be, for example, that the neighbour would consent to the development if the firm agreed to build a wall to block the overview. Where this agreement can take place independent of the planning authority, there would therefore be no need for full planning permission as there would be no outstanding negative impact that the authority needs to take into account. A similar system is currently operated in New Zealand (see Box 5.3 below). This has merits that extend beyond the narrow issue of planning through actively promoting neighbourly interaction along the lines desired in the Government's neighbourhood renewal policy.[6] It is likely that this system would only work in practice where the impact was felt by only a small number of parties.

Box 5.3: New Zealand system of side-payments

New Zealand had a similar system of planning law to England, alongside a very similar structure of governance, complete with parish councils and unitary authorities. A feature of its recent Resource Management Act is the use of side-agreements/payments to allow for a proportion of planning issues to be determined outside of local authorities. This sorts out disagreements or potential disputes without involving the council or the courts, where a development is likely to have an impact on a third party. They are most commonly applied for minor developments. For example:

- a neighbour wants to build an additional storey on their house. Your agreement may be that they pay for opaque glass to be installed in your bathroom window to protect your privacy; or

- a neighbour wants to double the size of a garage on your property boundary. Your agreement may be that they will seal the driveway that you both share.

There are no limits to what can be asked for in a side-agreement, but affected parties are encouraged to think about how they might be affected and limit what they might request to things that might reduce or remove that effect.

Wider use of development agreements

5.13 More generalised permissions may also contribute to a reduction in workload. Local Development Orders (LDO), for example, have been designed to allow local authorities to extend permitted development rights locally in response to local circumstances, negating the need for planning applications. They can apply to the whole area or a designated part. In principle, they have much to commend them. But critics note that Simplified Planning Zones (SPZs),[7] which came into force in 1987, were not successful in achieving a similar aim. By 1993 only six SPZs had been approved, in Corby, Derby, Birmingham, Knowsley and Gedling, and these were restrictive, lacking the intended flexibility. Part of the problem was the lack of incentive for the local authorities to develop such zones, particularly as they took over a year to draw up due to elaborate procedural hoops. LDOs risk facing similar issues unless incentives are addressed. Nevertheless the concept is a good one, and the extension of it in other areas should be encouraged. In terms of heritage issues, for example, management agreements that provide pre-agreement for routine development have the potential to reduce the volume of individual heritage applications, as with the London Underground where agreements have been reached that minor upkeep work can proceed without individual applications.

---

[6] The Social Exclusion Unit, 'A New Commitment to Neighbourhood Renewal: National Strategy Action Plan' (January 2001), http://www.socialexclusionunit.gov.uk/downloaddoc.asp?id=33
[7] Simplified Planning Zone (SPZ) is an area in which a local planning authority wishes to stimulate development and encourage investment. It operates by granting a specified planning permission in the zone without the need for an application for planning permission and the payment of planning fees.

Recommendation 18

There should be a rebalancing of the focus of planning on the cases that matter most, in line with the principles of risk-based regulation by:

- a widening of permitted development rights for minor consents by extending the 'impact' principle of the Householder Development Consent Review, so that in future only those cases where there will be non-marginal third-party impact will require planning permission, with the objective of an appreciable reduction in volumes of applications. This should be completed within the next two years; and

- the development of a voluntary new system of negotiated side-agreements between affected parties, so that where agreement can be reached a full planning application will not be required. This is likely to be most practical with smaller scale applications.

The permitted development rights should also be widened to help combat climate change. In particular, proposals to extend rights to domestic microgeneration should be extended to commercial settings.

MORE EFFICIENT PROCESSES

5.14   Reducing the number of minor planning applications will release additional capacity to improve the speed with which the remainder of applications are dealt. However, the impact of these reforms will only be felt after a number of years, and though they may remove tens of thousands of applications from the system each year, they will not release a proportionate volume of resources, given that they are the simplest and cheapest applications to process. Reforms to enhance the efficiency with which remaining applications are dealt are also needed. This will release resources that can be used either to lower the cost burden on the taxpayer and business, or to enable a faster and higher quality of service to be delivered.

5.15   There is no one solution. Case studies conducted by the Planning Advisory Service[8] and for this Review clearly demonstrate that effective leadership at the local level is often as important as the systems and processes that can be influenced in a national policy review such as this. The simplification reforms set out in Chapter 4, however, should have an impact on the resource burden per application. Reducing the volume of paperwork that needs to be processed with each application will free up officer time and reduce the need for planning departments to pay for expensive consultants to write lengthy technical documentation. In addition to these efforts to streamline the planning system, the following reforms are proposed.

Increased use of pre-application discussions

5.16   Pre-application discussions are widely recognised as enhancing the speed and quality of the planning system.[9] By enabling early identification of relevant issues, applicants are provided with greater certainty of process and outcome. It also allows complex negotiations, such as the heads of terms for Section 106 agreements, to be raised in advance, permitting drafts of these agreements to be submitted along with the application rather than being introduced later in the application process without any opportunity for discussion. However, not all local authorities offer pre-application discussions, and in some instances there is a perception that these discussions have a relatively low status, so an applicant may have a discussion with a junior officer and subsequently receive different advice about the issues on submission of an application. Research[10] also suggests

[8] Planning and Advisory Service, 'Success Stories' at http://www.pas.gov.uk/pas/core/page.do?pageId=10389
[9] The Audit Commission, *The Planning System: Matching expectations and capacity* (February 2006).
[10] Ibid. The Audit Commission, *The Planning System: Matching expectations and capacity* (February 2006) pp. 53-56.

that it is beneficial to involve council members at this early stage.[11] Although care needs to be taken that this involvement is not prejudicial to the independence of the decision-making, it is appropriate that issues which may arise in committee are aired and discussed at an early stage so that mitigating action can be taken before an application has progressed to its last stage. Addressing such issues at a later stage adds to delays in the system. The Audit Commission identified this as one way in which pre-application discussions could be enhanced.[12]

5.17 Local planning authorities need further encouragement to offer pre-application discussions. At present planning fees do not fund the work involved in preparing and carrying out these discussions because they are a voluntary, not statutory, activity. Although a local planning authority can charge a fee (as per section 93 of the Local Government Act 2003), in practice local planning authorities tend to charge only the larger, commercial developer, so as not to dissuade householders and other small developers from seeking early advice. Government policy has been that planning application fees should be set at a level to allow 100 per cent cost-recovery but there continues to be some shortfall. The effect of this is exacerbated as local authorities are not compensated for the time and resource they devote to non-fee work, such as pre-application discussions, applications for listed building consent and so forth. There is, of course, a risk that many smaller applicants would resist paying extra for a pre-application discussion: the universal imposition of a new separate charge for the service could have the perverse effect of reducing demand for these useful discussions. Accordingly it may not be appropriate to create a fresh, compulsory charge under the planning fee regulations when these are reviewed in 2007, although a standard fee could be levied above a set threshold. Businesses must take a role in supporting the use of pre-application discussions by showing a willingness to participate early in the process and by submitting complete applications as a result.

Roll-out of Planning Delivery Agreements

5.18 The Government has set local planning authorities targets to determine 60 per cent of major applications within 13 weeks; and both 65 per cent of minor applications and 80 per cent of other applications within 8 weeks. These targets have focused attention on the need to deliver a more efficient service, and have, in combination with the Planning Delivery Grant,[13] encouraged local authorities to reform their processes to drive delivery. However, there is much concern about perverse impacts, such as applications being turned down to meet deadlines, fewer pre-application discussions and longer delays in considering conditions. Given these concerns, alternatives to the current system should now be considered to see if it is possible to enhance the speed with which planning applications are processed without compromising the quality of decisions and outcomes.

5.19 One such system is currently in pilot phase: the use of Planning Delivery Agreements. This is a process whereby the local authority and applicant discuss up front the timetable for delivery and work towards it. It has a number of potential advantages.[14] It is flexible, enabling timetables to be set which are tailored to specific circumstances. It enables all major applications to be processed in a timely manner, whereas the current system tends to focus disproportionate effort on those

---

[11] There is guidance available on the involvement of councillors in pre-application discussions, see Planning Advisory Service, 'Positive engagement – a guide for planning councillors' at
http://www.pas.gov.uk/pas/core/page.do?pageId=11660

[12] The Audit Commission, op. cit.

[13] Planning Delivery Grant (PDG) is an incentive grant that rewards planning authorities for progress in development plans, performance on development control, delivery of housing numbers in areas of high demand, and enterprise areas. For 2005-06 its scope was widened to recognise achievements in e-planning and to tackle housing issues in areas of low demand.

[14] For a discussion of the issues and best practice see Advisory Team for Large Applications (ATLAS), *Planning Delivery Agreements Report* (January 2006). Located at:
http://www.englishpartnerships.co.uk/publications.htm#programmesandprojects

medium-sized cases which can reasonably be completed within the 13-week time frame, and it enables, through a formal inception day at the start of the process, the early consideration of issues that may otherwise only emerge later in the process. For this system to be effective it is necessary that:

- delivery agreements become a requirement for local authorities if the developer wishes to have them. Without this there will be no incentive for the local authority to agree to setting out these time frames. Clearly it is preferable for these agreements to remain voluntary, not least because if the authority feels the agreement is imposed it may be less cooperative in delivering the time frame. But developers pay large application fees for big applications and it is reasonable that they are provided with some certainty of time frame as part of standard service delivery;

- there is some form of penalty for failure of either party to meet milestones along the established time frame. If the local authority fails to deliver to target, for example, there should be a reduction in fee charged. Conversely, if the applicant misses a target there could be an increase in the fee;

- the definition of major and minor developments is re-examined. Currently, both a ten-unit housing development and a 100,000 square metre mixed use development both classify as 'major'. There should be a threefold classification of development: minor, medium and major, with only this new major category being covered by the delivery agreements;

- minor and medium-sized applications would continue to be monitored along the current 8- and 13-week timetable (or 16 weeks where an Environmental Impact Assessment is required), to ensure that there is the incentive to continue to deliver an efficient service for these types of development;

- where an agreement is not reached within the timeline for processing the application, the default of the 13-week timeframe would be reverted to; and

- the Government publishes data for the average length of time taken to process applications under Planning Delivery Agreements so that, in addition to knowing the proportion of cases determined within 8 and 13 weeks, it is possible to monitor the time taken to process the largest and most complex planning applications. In the current system these cases are hidden by the statistics; this is true both of local authority decisions (where there is no published data on the time taken to process those that fall outside the 13-week period) and also of the Planning Inspectorate and Secretary of State call-in data.

Greater delegation to officers

5.20   Delegated powers are conferred to designated planning officers by locally elected councillors, so that the officers may take decisions on specified planning matters on behalf of the council. A substantial proportion of cases (89 per cent nationally) are devolved to officers to make decisions but this varies significantly across local authorities. Where a decision is not delegated there can be additional delays to the system, largely because the case will need to coincide with committee cycles and related lead-in times for circulation of papers. Greater delegation will not undermine the important democratic legitimacy of decision-making within local authorities; it will simply ensure that members' time is appropriately targeted.

5.21   Where members' views are genuinely required it is important to ensure that they are engaged as early in the process as possible. Mid Devon Council, for example, have devised a system of giving councillors sight of major applications before committee meetings so site visits can be conducted and discussed at the earliest possible time.

Better engagement with statutory consultees

5.22   A key part of the planning application process is to ensure adequate opportunity for engagement with members of the public and other interested parties, so that their views and expertise may be brought to bear on the desirability of the application. While many aspects of the current system appear to work well, there are a number of issues relating to the effectiveness and timeliness of advice provided by statutory consultees (those with whom local authorites are required by law to consult, such as Natural England, the Environment Agency and English Heritage). These consultees often provide specialist advice on important issues and e-planning tools are helping to streamline engagement processes, but there are still questions about the threshold at which these bodies become involved. Housing developments of only ten units, for example, can trigger the requirement to consult a range of statutory bodies. There might also be potential to narrow the non-statutory consultation lists or reduce the number of statutory consultees. While statutory consultees have been set targets for responding to local authority representations – which has resulted in an improvement in performance – there is no system of incentives attached to this system. Better incentives could mean that their advisory functions were resourced effectively in order to provide timely advice.

Highway delays   5.23   In particular, there is widespread concern about how the Highways Agency uses its Article 14 directions to hold back development, both in terms of the number of directions used (570 between 2004 and 2006) and the time they take to resolve.[15] The case was made to a recent Transport Select Committee inquiry that 'the Agency causes endemic delay in major road building and regeneration projects across the country, particularly in poorer areas of the North East', though the report noted that the Agency and the Department for Transport argued that the directions were used proportionately to ensure planning and development is carried out in a coordinated way.[16] The use of a 'holding direction' to direct a planning authority not to approve an application for up to six months (renewable) is of particular concern among regional bodies and local authorities. Further progress is needed to ensure the Agency is more proactive in solving issues of dispute and works to engage earlier in the development process. It should not employ holding directions at a late stage.

Speeding up the final stages

5.24   There is also scope to improve the speed with which development is able to proceed after the granting of planning permission. Part of the issue here relates to appeals and call-ins, and these issues are considered in Chapters 3 and 6 of this report. This chapter looks at how to enhance timeliness for those cases that are not appealed or called-in, by addressing three areas:

- enabling the delivery of planning conditions – planning conditions are conditions attached to an application which result in it being accepted. The conditions can include, for example, the design of buildings, noise control, access requirements, road junctions, car parking, inclusion of play areas and landscape issues. While these conditions are important, fulfilling them can add to delays. The widespread

---

[15] According to Land Securities, for example, 'in our experience large and small planning applications across the country are frequently held up for months by the extended time it takes to resolve highway disputes'. Response to the Barker Review Call for Evidence, 2006, p. 2.

[16] House of Commons, Select Committee on Transport, Ninth Report, Session 2005-06 (July 2006), paragraph 136.

use of standard conditions helps create certainty but there also needs to be processes for ensuring that public bodies with responsibility to allow discharge of those conditions act in a timely manner;

• **planning obligations** (sometimes referred to as Section 106 agreements) are legal agreements between a planning authority and a developer, or undertakings offered unilaterally by a developer, which ensure that certain extra works related to a development are undertaken – for example, the provision of highways. There is the potential for Section 106 agreements to add substantially to delays to planning permission. In around 45 per cent of cases (around 11,500 developments) these take more than six months to complete and 11 per cent (around 3,700 developments) take over a year[17] (refer to Chart 5.3 below). Protracted discussions to negotiate Section 106 agreements, arising partly from indeterminacy of process, can cause delay and frustration.[18] The introduction of the Planning Gain Supplement, which was proposed to capture the value uplift accruing to land going through the planning process, combined with a pared back Section 106 should help to reduce the need for negotiation. In addition, discussions about Section 106 payments should occur during the early phases of the application process, preferably pre-application and as part of the Planning Delivery Agreement, to minimise subsequent delay and surprise. Use of the Law Society's new model Section 106 should be encouraged in the context of some remaining concerns that Section 106s are often badly drafted, producing extra legal uncertainties.

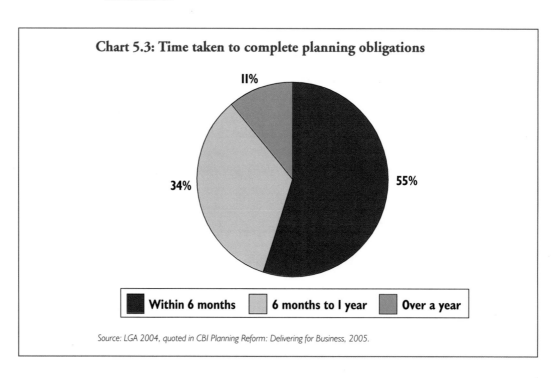

Chart 5.3: Time taken to complete planning obligations

11%

34%

55%

■ **Within 6 months**   ▨ **6 months to 1 year**   ▨ **Over a year**

Source: LGA 2004, quoted in CBI Planning Reform: Delivering for Business, 2005.

---

[17] Figures derived from DCLG, *Development Control Statistics 2005-06* provide the data on number of cases processed and proportion accepted; University of Sheffield and Halcrow Group, *Valuing Planning Obligations in England: Final Report* (2006) provide the figure of 6.9 per cent of cases accepted having Section 106 agreements in 2003-04; and LGA figure on negotiation times is given in CBI, *Planning Reform: Delivering for Business* (2005). It should be noted that not all planning permissions result in a development going forward and so the figures will be slightly lower.

[18] Advisory Team for Large Applications (ATLAS), *Planning Delivery Agreements Report* (January 2006) p. 12.

- judicial review procedures. Although there are few judicial reviews compared to the total number of planning applications, the cost, added uncertainty and increase in delay that can be caused by a judicial review (or even the threat of such a review) can be substantial. It is therefore desirable that the Goverment reduce this uncertainty by streamlining the processes.

Recommendation 19

The planning application system should be made more efficient so that high quality outcomes are delivered through a value-for-money process. This should include:

- more widespread use of pre-application discussions, which are often of great value to both planning departments and applicants. Where appropriate these should be used as an opportunity for early community involvement. Local authorities should charge for these only when this is unlikely to significantly reduce demand for the service;

- the roll-out of Planning Delivery Agreements (PDA) to ensure all applications are dealt with in a reasonable time frame. There should be a requirement for local authorities to offer these for large applications – revising the current thresholds for 'majors' by separating them from medium-sized applications would help here. Where a PDA has been agreed the application would be removed from the current national targets;

- a review of the statutory consultee arrangements to improve efficiency, to include consideration of the thresholds at which these bodies become involved with applications and better incentives to ensure a quicker response to enquiries;

- early engagement from statutory consultees such as Natural England, the Environment Agency and English Heritage. In particular, the Highways Agency should ensure it adopts this approach rather than relying on late use of Article 14 holding powers; and

- speeding up the final stages of the application process, in particular by earlier negotiation of Section 106 agreements or use of tariffs, and discharging planning conditions.

Businesses should engage with pre-application discussions to enable issues to be identified at an early stage and ensure that they submit complete applications.

ENHANCING RESOURCES

5.25   Reducing the number of minor planning applications, streamlining the system and introducing further efficiencies will help the planning system to deliver a more timely and better quality service. These should be the focus of reform activity in the coming years, and should mean that the cost per application for the public and private sector should fall in the long term. While the benefits of long-term reform measures accrue there may be a case for additional resources in the short-term where this can be linked to improved services and supporting best practice. The Interim Report outlined the background to increased resources pressures.[19] This section considers how additional resources could be found. The planning system has already had £600 million additional Government funding provided through the Planning Delivery Grant as a performance-raising measure[20] and the recent increases in fees have resulted in over £200 million being raised annually through fee payments. There are two principal sources of further funding – private applicants and taxpayers.

---

[19] Kate Barker, *Barker Review of Land Use Planning. Interim Report – Analysis* (July 2002) pp. 75-76.
[20] The Planning Delivery Grant (PDG) is providing about £605 million over six years (2003-08), to resource and incentivise regional planning bodies and local authorities to improve the planning system and deliver sustainable communities. Allocations are based on assessment of performance across a range of planning functions.

Private sector options   5.26   In terms of additional private sector contributions, there are seven main options, although there is also a need for caution about adding further private sector costs to the planning system:

- **raising the cap on fees.** The current national fee structures cap the fee per application at £50,000,[21] but the cost of processing the largest planning applications can be very much higher. For instance, rough estimates from the City of London suggest that it costs around £100,000 to process a large office development. The cap therefore essentially represents a subsidy of large developers by the taxpayer or other commercial and residential planning applicants;

- **an across-the-board increase in fees.** Planning fees have already risen substantially in recent years – around £68 million extra a year as a result of the most recent rises, which saw fees rise by 39 per cent on average (but in some cases by up to 350 per cent). Certain business groups argue there is a little to show for the recent rises. But calls for more resources to manage increasing demand on the planning system, raises the possibility of a further rise to more accurately reflect average costs;

- **a variable fee structure.** At present fees are set nationally – they do not necessarily cover the cost of individual authorities, which can vary substantially, partly due to different costs of living. A flexible fee structure (or at a minimum a London premium) could address this. However, moving to a local system effectively risks requiring applicants to subsidise inefficiencies (there would be no incentive to operate an efficient service if charges could be raised to cover costs) and introducing increased complexity caused by local variation. It would also need to be subject to a cap, as the local authority is in effect a monopoly service provider;

- **ring-fencing of fee income.** One option would be to ensure that fees which are paid for planning applications (which net £200 million a year) go to improve the planning service rather than being used in the local authority more widely. There is a strong case for this – the fee is for a service and is not an additional form of taxation. But hypothecation goes against the grain of wider reforms to local government. As money is fungible, there is also no way to stop local authority finance departments reducing the funding they provide to planning even if fee income is ring-fenced;

- **allowing charges for a premium service.** Many public services now have differential tariffs according to the quality of service that is desired. The Passport Agency, for example, charges £91 for a premium one-day service and £66 for a standard three-week service on adult passports. In planning, however, there is a still a 'one size fits all' approach. This means that those who value a higher quality or faster service are not able to procure for it;

- **allowing applicants to buy in extra resources.** A more flexible approach to the above would be to allow applicants to pay for extra resources when needed. There are some instances where this has already happened, but they are not widespread. There are particular grounds for this where, for example, a small authority receives a large one-off application that it simply does not have the resource to finance. It could, however, give the impression of 'buying' planning permission and care would need to be taken to ensure this did not occur by ensuring that the payment went to the local planning authority or some accredited agency rather than directly to the consultants. Planning Advisory Service (PAS) or Advisory Team for Large Applications (ATLAS) could be used as an intermediary, or 'blind trusts' could be used, where the developer pays money into a trust that the local authority controls. Whichever approach was adopted, care would need to be taken to ensure this process did not become anti-competitive through favouring large, incumbent firms; and

---

[21] £13,250 plus £80 for each additional 75 square metres to a maximum of £50,000 for commercial and £13,250 maximum (50 dwellings or more) plus £80 for each dwelling-house in excess of 50 to a maximum of £50,000.

- allowing charges for services which are currently free. Although planning generally operates on a principle of 100 per cent cost recovery for applications, not all aspects of planning are covered by this principle. For instance, conservation area and listed building consents are free but cost around £20 million per annum[22] to administer, while pre-application discussions cast around £40 million. There are issues of propriety linked to charging for appeals or for penalising those who live in areas protected due to the public interest so this should be limited to charging for pre-application discussions.

Public sector funding

5.27   Options for incoming public sector contributions to the planning system involve greater local authority resources being committed to the planning department, maintenance and extension of the central government Planning Delivery Grant and the introduction of a new form of grant linked to planning performance. While the first of these options may be desirable, it is arguably not the place of central government to dictate local spending priorities, so decisions here need to be made at the local level. In terms of the Planning Delivery Grant, analysis has suggested[23] that it has had a number of benefits for local authorities, from raising the status of planning to increasing resources for both development control and plan-making, although there are concerns about perverse outcomes related to the target regime. It is also clear that around 97 per cent of the funds appear to have stayed within the planning department. However, 'additionality' of specific grant funds tends to reduce over time as finance officers factor in the size of the grant when distributing annual budgets between departments, leading to diminishing returns.

5.28   All of these options, both private and public, have drawbacks. Raising business fees across the board is not necessarily desirable in the context of recent average fee rises of 39 per cent, particularly when many businesses believe they have yet to see any proportionate improvements to the service from this increase. However, there is no reason why larger developers should pay proportionately less of their planning application costs than others, and there is therefore a reason to raise the threshold for fees beyond £50,000. The rates per square metre or hectare could be applied on a tapered sliding scale on the basis that costs should fall at the margin. There is also a good case for allowing applicants who are willing to pay for extra staff and resources to be brought in so that their application can be processed expeditiously. This could be achieved through direct additional payments to local authorities or a large-scale expansion of the Advisory Team for Large Applications (ATLAS) team. ATLAS was set up in 2004 as a pilot scheme to provide an independent advisory service to local authorities in London and the wider South-East where the pressures of increased development activity were being felt most acutely. It offers direct support to individual local authorities in delivering key Government objectives such as large-scale housing developments or regeneration projects. This would effectively tackle bottlenecks while ensuring that additional resource was procured on a voluntary and discretionary basis.

5.29   Government has already contributed public funding of over £600 million in the form of the Planning Delivery Grant, but in the context of short-term resource pressures there should be a commitment to maintain some form of Planning Delivery Grant into the future. Care will need to be taken to ensure that it is not diverted away from front-line service delivery to process issues. Reforms to reduce the complexity of the new Local Development Framework (LDF) process as set out in Chapter 4 should help to limit extra demand for resources.

---

[22] DCLG, 'The Planning Service Costs and Fees' (2003).

[23] DCLG, 'Evaluation of Planning Delivery Grant,' Addison and Associates with Arup (2006).

> **Recommendation 20**
>
> The Government should review current resource arrangements for local planning authorities, related authority services (such as conservation) and key agencies. This should take account of the efficiency gains to be derived from other recommendations. In particular it should explore:
>
> - raising the £50,000 threshold for fee payments on a tapered basis;
>
> - making it easier for applicants to pay for a premium service or to pay for additional resource/consultants to help process their application expeditiously, if this can be done in a manner that avoids anti-competitive effects; and
>
> - maintaining a form of Planning Delivery Grant beyond 2007-08, ensuring some form of benefit for commercial speed and delivery outcomes alongside other goals.
>
> Any fee increase should only be allowed on the basis of a clear mechanism for indicating the higher quality of service that will be delivered as a result.

Supporting skills

5.30   There are many highly skilled and competent professional staff within the planning profession. However, there are a number of concerns about maintaining the skills base.[23] These include: recruitment and retention challenges, measured in part by high vacancy rates; concerns about the training of planners (13 per cent of departments lack a training budget) and council members; the demands for specialist skills (negotiating complex Section 106 agreements, for example, requires some knowledge of development finance that planners have previously never needed); poaching by private sector consultancies; and worries about the high proportion of agency staff and the turnover of these groups.

5.31   Part of the solution here is addressing supply constraints. Until current training and bursary initiatives take effect, the community of planners will remain limited and the public sector will often find it difficult to compete with the private sector because of the nature of the work and the private sectors greater ability to pay. The Government has started to act in this area by supporting the Planning Advisory Service, which works alongside local authorities to help them improve performance. The Academy for Sustainable Communities[24] should also help capacity building and the 180 credit point Postgraduate Diploma in planning, which can be completed within one calendar year, should facilitate entry possibilities for those unwilling to commit to a four-year course.

5.32   In addition, DCLG bursary payments are a positive step (£3.9 million has been spent on some 412 postgraduate bursaries), but with the top 30 planning consultancies growing at the rate of 150 planners a year, this has limited effect for the public sector. Indeed, in the academic year 2004/05, DCLG distributed 136 postgraduate degree bursaries for students who wished to pursue planning careers in Local Planning Authorities (LPA), but out of the students who completed their courses 45 per cent now work in planning consultancies.

---

[23] See, for example, Local Government Association and Office of the Deputy Prime Minister, *Skills Base in the Planning System* (November 2004) and Tim Edmundson, Planning Research, *An investigation of potential measures to address London Local Planning Authorities' recruitment and retention problems* (April 2004).

[24] The Academy for Sustainable Communities (ASC) is a new national and international centre of excellence for the skills and knowledge needed to create communities fit for the 21st century. The ASC's focus is on increasing skills and learning, targeting skills shortages and sharing knowledge and expertise. http://www.ascskills.org.uk/pages/about-ASC

5.33   These actions may therefore not prove sufficient. Some potential solutions raise wider sets of issues. Skills may be closely bound to broader issues of local authority empowerment. Allowing planning services more autonomy could increase the status of the work, thus making it easier to attract and retain high skilled employees. Empowerment is being addressed in other areas of government, most notably the Lyons Inquiry into Local Government.[25] Within the remit of this Review the main areas for further action are:

- incentivising local authorities. There are currently few financial incentives for local authorities to adopt growth strategies. If incentives could be aligned so that authorities received better returns from growing their tax base, this would raise the status of planning within the authorities, and potentially the attractiveness of planning as a career. Incentives are explored more fully in Chapter 7;

- improving perception of planning as a career. For at least the past two decades, the perception of planning as a profession has been relatively low and has slipped down the list of desirable places to work within local authorities. Some progress is being made, good planning schools can now require a minimum of a 2.1 degree for postgraduate courses. Further progress could involve partnership work at a national level between the Local Government Association (LGA), the Royal Town Planning Institute (RTPI), and the Town and Country Planning Association to ensure a continued focus on recruiting new entrants into the profession. At the local level, planning departments need to improve job design and offer more opportunity for progression. Where this is currently happening it is showing positive outcomes in terms of retention and service quality.[26] One option here would involve making the chief planner a more central post within the local authority. This is something that the Local Government White Paper (LGWP) supports: 'we encourage local authorities to make planning a prime responsibility of one of the corporate directors who should be professionally qualified';[27]

- encourage or require more business process reviews. It is also key to ensure that the current available skills are utilised effectively. A number of studies have concluded that non-planners can do more of the basic work. Simple householder applications, for example, could be dealt with by relatively unqualified staff, freeing up resource for use elsewhere. The best authorities are already doing this. However, the investigations for this review[28] suggest that for some poorly performing authorities there could be scope for reorganisation of work. In addition, the processes by which the planning department is integrated within the local authority should be reviewed to ensure that all strategic areas are working closely on spatial outcomes. While the Planning Advisory Service and Audit Commission are already doing some good work on leadership, more can be done. Best Value Reviews, Comprehensive Performance Assessment, user-friendly guides, an efficiency award or a team of consultants could be further useful approaches;

- enhance scale economies. Many local authorities are too small to exploit fully economies of scale. However, this can be addressed by pooling resources between authorities, which is currently not a widespread practice among local planning

---

[25] More information about the Lyons Inquiry can be found at http://www.lyonsinquiry.org/

[26] Refer to the case studies conducted by the Barker Review in Annex B of this report.

[27] DCLG, *Strong and Prosperous Communities: The Local Government White Paper, Volume II, E36 p. 45* (October 2006).

[28] Refer to the case studies conducted by the Barker Review in Annex B of this report.

[29] Audit Commission, *The Planning System: matching expectations and capacity* (February 2006).

authorities.[29] A pilot scheme in Hampshire, supported by £50,000 from the Planning Advisory Service, shows how this could work. New arrangements such as City/Regions or LPA mergers could help exploit these more fully, although on a more modest basis the development of specialist expertise within larger authorities could be of benefit. An alternative would be to try to incentivise wider-scale sharing service arrangements or a sub-regional Major Projects Team. This Review supports the Local Government White Paper, which states: 'we encourage authorities, wherever possible to combine expertise at sub-regional level and draw on the expertise of partners'.[30] Potentially, high performing local authorities could take over the services of others or franchise their management functions/loan their staff out on a fee-paying basis;

- **improved officer training and compulsory member training.** Tackling skills issues among planners involves not just ensuring an adequate flow of highly skilled new entrants, it also requires effective Continuing Professional Development for those who may have received their professional training many decades ago. Progress here would, as with all training, ideally need to move beyond crude input measures such as the number of recommended days spent training in the course of a year to keep RTPI accreditation. The University of West England at Bristol has recently created a distance learning course in spatial planning with £250,000 of government funding. This is welcome. There is also the need to improve council member skills. More extensive member training would help, targeting new members in the first instance.

- **increased use of alternative service providers** for whole service (i.e. partnership working, competitive tendering and contracting out). Some local authorities are now contracting out decision-making in certain areas, e.g. highways, education and housing benefit. This is increasingly occurring in planning departments, but from a very low base. It offers a useful mechanism to enhance customer service and improve value for money, by drawing private sector expertise and processes into the public sector. The Planning Officers Society (POS) argues that legislative arrangements, probity and transparency requirements mean decision-making must lie with the planning authority. However, they also state that 'many examples exist where external consultants have been used to help deliver the service', and experience shows that there are no legal impediments to contracting out.[31] Closer working with the private sector via these means has considerable potential and should be encouraged; and

- **use of intermediary accredited agents for particular services.** A less radical version of the above would be to use accredited agents for technical services. These could be used, for example, to bypass the validation stage, as currently being adopted by Waverley Council and Planning and Regulatory Services Online (PARSOL). They could also be used for Certificates of Lawful Development, used to establish whether an existing use or proposed use is lawful for planning purposes. Home improvement companies or local planning agents would be happy to compete for this service. Regulation of accredited agents could, however, be complex.

---

[30] DCLG, *Local Government White Paper, Volume II:* E39 (October 2006).
[31] http://www.mvm.co.uk/planningofficers/planningguide/planning.asp?id=467&p=462&h=

5.34 Many of these reforms can be undertaken unilaterally by local authorities seeking to improve their own performance. However, in the context of some of the challenges raised in Chapter 1 in terms of the need for culture change within the profession to develop a planning system that adopts positive planning and is responsive to change there is also a case for a more coordinated programme of reform. The Local Government Association and the Planning Officers Society are both well placed to draw up a change management strategy/programme to help deliver culture change in local authorities, and this would help to ensure that the benefits that positive planning can bring are embedded in authorities throughout the country.

Recommendation 21

The skills of decision-makers and others involved with the planning system should be enhanced and more effectively utilised. To achieve this:

- the Government should ensure continued funding for the Planning Advisory Service to promote continuous improvement, raise underperformance and facilitate joint working;

- the Government should work with the RTPI, TCPA and other bodies to ensure a continued focus on getting new entrants into the profession. Postgraduate bursaries funded by DCLG should be tied to a number of years of public sector service, so that a return is provided for the public purse;

- the Government should raise the status of the Chief Planner within local authorities, potentially on a statutory basis, to reinforce the status of the profession for all parties, including members;

- wider use of business process reviews and best practice guidance to ensure that the time of more qualified planners is freed up to focus on the most complex cases;

- compulsory training should be provided for planning committee members, focusing resources in the first instance on new members, with increased training for officers; and

- the LGA and POS should establish a change management strategy/programme to help deliver culture change in local authorities.

Recommendation 22

Local planning authorities should enhance the quality of service provided by their planning department through more effective interaction with external organisations, via:

- the introduction of more 'shared services' by local authority planning departments (or contracting to more efficient LPAs) to enable economies of scale and scope;

- increased use of outsourcing and tendering for development control services, so that private sector expertise is more effectively leveraged; and

- exploring the potential for greater use of accredited consultants to carry out technical assessments for selected tasks should be considered.

The Government should also expand the role of ATLAS both in scope, to remove bottlenecks in the delivery of large commercial development as well as housing developments, and in geographic range, so that the benefits of this model can be felt beyond southern regions.

Addressing continuing poor performance

5.35   A robust response to local authority performance that is poor is also likely to be an important factor in improving standards. A good quality of life in local communities is supported by excellent planning services. Heavy-handed forms of central government intervention should always be used with caution but the necessary corollary of increased local authority autonomy is that there will be variability in performance and persistent poor quality performance within local authority planning departments must be addressed.

5.36   The recent Local Government White Paper sets out a general approach whereby the response to poor performance is tailored to the severity of the problem, suggesting seven processes for tackling poor performance:

1.   **sectoral improvement support:** support and advice from within the local government sector and other sectors involved with local service delivery;

2.   **Government Office coordination:** where underperformance is not being appropriately addressed Government Offices may intervene, coordinating and monitoring the action taken;

3.   **inspection:** the need for targeted inspection will be determined by inspectorates, usually as part of the annual risk assessment;

4.   **referral to the Secretary of State:** if problems are severe the Secretary of State may decide to intervene formally;

5.   **improvement notices:** these will be introduced to address significant or enduring underperformance in a single body or across partnerships;

6.   **directive action:** in cases where more directive action is required the appropriate Secretary of State, taking advice from Government Offices, other relevant bodies and Inspectorates may direct the organisation to take some specific action; and

7.   **removal of functions:** this option is the most extreme step on the ladder of improvement support and intervention, and is only proposed to help tackle the most serious circumstances.

5.37   In many respects this builds on the approach that has been taken to planning in recent years, with those local planning authorities failing to improve being identified as 'Standards Authorities' subject to investigation and close monitoring by Government Offices. Support in identifying and tackling problems and in building capacity has been provided by the Planning Advisory Service. This 'carrot and stick' model has much to commend it.

5.38   The priority for the future will be to develop this approach, using increasingly effective options for intervention. In line with the White Paper, this means (in particular) developing better sector-led approaches to providing support and tackling underperformance at the earliest possible stage. The experience of the Planning Advisory Service provides a firm basis on which to build. Where performance remains poor in spite of sector-led support, a strong case for Government to act exists. In 2004-05, for example, the Chief Executives of persistently poorly performing local authorities were invited to discuss their improvement programmes with senior government officials and, in some cases, subsequently with Ministers. This approach appears to have produced results, providing a good case for adopting it again in 2007-08 – when the proposed new performance framework for local government will not yet be in place.

5.39   Equally, in terms of removal of functions, the Government should not avoid making these tough decisions when, in exceptional circumstance, they are needed. The 'take-over' model of removing functions, whereby a new team of planners is parachuted into a failing authority to improve performance, does, however, have a number of drawbacks. In particular, it is a short-term intervention that fails to build long-term capacity. However, a model whereby consistently failing authorities are directed to enter into a joint-venture company may provide a sustainable and effective solution in the right circumstances. This approach has been adopted on a voluntary basis by Salford City Council to improve the performance of their in-house development services directorate (see Box 5.5 below). While it is clearly preferable that such models are entered into on a voluntary basis, where performance is routinely poor the Secretary of State could, based on the final two elements of the Local Government White Paper intervention framework, direct that this or similar steps must be taken.

Box 5.5: Joint-venture case study

In 2005 Salford City Council set up a joint venture with Capita Symonds and Morrison to create a multidisciplinary company called Urban Vision providing high quality professional services covering planning, highways and property management. With the exception of Berkshire, this was the first time a council had sought to provide a comprehensive development control function through the private sector. After a comprehensive selection process (which involved the staff and unions) five consortia of firms were short-listed, with the winning bid resulting in the formation of Urban Vision on 1 February 2005. Each party has a share in the company and shares any resulting profits. A total of 392 council staff were seconded from the Council to the new company. According to a recent Audit Commission report, the company's early performance is encouraging.

5.40   For the joint venture approach to be successful, it will clearly be important to ensure that robust measures are adopted in order to monitor performance. Although speed is an important element of quality of service, caution should be exercised concerning over-reliance on national targets given the extent of concerns relating to perverse outcomes. Among the indicators on which greater reliance should be placed relating to are customer satisfaction surveys (already used by the best local authorities and by the Planning Inspectorate) in order to determine whether the fee-paying customers are satisfied with the quality of service being provided. These surveys would also provide useful data from which local authorities can identify how to improve their planning function.

> **Recommendation 23**
>
> A robust system of performance management should be put in place to address continued poor performance, in line with proposals in the Local Government White Paper. DCLG should:
>
> - conduct a review of measures to judge effectiveness of planning departments in the context of local government reform. A review should consider how best to measure the quality of service provided by the planning system, including consideration of development outcome measures and labour productivity figures, alongside a greater emphasis on customer satisfaction survey evidence. In addition, the end-to-end time taken to process the larger applications that fall outside current targets should be included in the DCLG annual publication of development management statistics;
>
> - encourage the development of stronger sector-led support and intervention models;
>
> - use the new performance framework to set improvement targets in the worst performing authorities; and
>
> - encourage and, where necessary, direct local authorities that continue to underperform to tender their planning function, along the lines of the successful Urban Vision model or to contract with other more successful authorities to provide or share services.
>
> For 2007-08, DCLG should require the chief executives of persistent poor performers to discuss improvement programmes with senior officials and, where appropriate, Ministers.

Improving the quality of design of new development

5.41   While the focus of this chapter has been on local authority processes, it is important to recognise the importance of local authority performance in other key areas. One such area is design. It is critical that the substantial new development anticipated over the next twenty years is well-designed. Planning plays a crucial role in the design, performance and appearance of cities, towns and villages. Good design in planning attracts people, investment and activity to places. Many spillovers associated with new development, such as local traffic disruption, may prove relatively short-lived, but the costs of poor design are felt for the lifetime of the building: poorly designed housing estates or office blocks impose costs on very large numbers of people.[32] Good design can also bring economic benefit, increasing labour productivity: one survey suggested that 94 per cent of employees regarded their place of work as a symbol of whether or not they were valued by their employer, and staff turnover has been reduced by 11 per cent after moving to new premises.[33] There are also social and health benefits to living in pleasing surroundings which function well.[34] Well-designed neighbourhoods and towns can give rise to a durable and sustainable virtuous circle.

5.42   What constitutes good design is well-documented, not least by Government and its agencies including Commission for Architecture and the Built Environment (CABE), its design adviser. However, creating a policy environment that fosters that good design has proved more challenging.[35] Nevertheless, a number of initiatives have recently been introduced to raise the quality of design. These include:

- national policy which provides for good design as a central objective of many key government policies on regeneration, sustainable communities in the key growth

---

[32] CABE, *The Cost of Bad Design* (2006).

[33] CABE, *The Impact of Office Design on Business Performances* (2005).

[34] DETR, CABE and UCL Bartlett School of Planning, *The Value of Urban Design* (2001). The report found that good urban design adds value though producing high returns on investment and reducing management, maintenance, energy and security costs.

[35] CABE, *The Cost of Bad Design* (2006).

areas and the delivery of affordable housing. The Government's policies on urban design are set out in *Planning Policy Statement 1: Delivering Sustainable Development* which states that good design is indivisible from good planning, and that planning authorities should plan positively for the achievement of high-quality and inclusive design for all development, including individual buildings, public and private spaces and wider area development;

- Local Development Frameworks and non-statutory planning documents (such as masterplans and site briefs) provide opportunities for local planning authorities to embed local design policies that reflect the distinctiveness of particular areas and sites;

- Design and Access Statements which explain the design rationale behind a planning application have been introduced in an effort to raise the quality of the design proposal being placed before the local authority.[36] They are required on both outline and full applications for all development proposals and should show that the applicant has thought about how their proposal will help to create well-designed accessible and safer places;[37]

- Design Codes are one way to secure high-quality design across a spatial form. Encouraged by DCLG, urban coding has been applied at Upton in Northamptonshire to provide a consistency of design across new developments without imposing uniformity. Pilot schemes suggest that these can have a positive impact on the quality of outcomes.[38] However, they are not uncontentious and should not be applied in ways which result in formulaic design responses or stifle design creativity. Government evaluation has noted that design codes are delivery tools and not 'vision-making'.[39] In the circumstances where they are useful – such as masterplanning – it is important that they are flexible and able to develop over time. Local planning authorities should work with architects alongside urban designers and other built environment professionals in the development of individual codes;

- the Design Review Panel run by CABE has been acknowledged as a success improving the quality of the schemes presented to it.[40] The Panel offers expert advice and assessments of schemes that will have a significant impact on their environment. This includes schemes of national importance, which have a significant impact on the local environment, or which set standards for future development. The schemes vary greatly in type and size, ranging from tall buildings in city centres and major masterplans to smaller proposals for public buildings such as arts venues and schools; and

- design commissions such as the commission into affordable housing design in the Thames Gateway. This will draw together stakeholders from across the Gateway to deliver a document that will specify design standards to apply to all Housing Corporation-funded properties developed in the Gateway. The aim is to set a high standard that all providers of affordable housing must meet.

---

[36] Section 42 of the PCPA 2004 substitutes a new section 62 of the 1990 Act and amends section 10 of the Listed Buildings Act in order to provide that a statement covering design concepts and principles and access issues is submitted with an application for planning permission and listed building consent. Section 42 also inserts a new section 327A into the 1990 Act, which prohibits, among other things, a local planning authority from entertaining an application unless it is accompanied by a design statement and an access statement, where required.

[37] DCLG (2006), Circular 01/06: Guidance on Changes to the Development Control System; CABE, *Design and Access Statements: How to Write, Read and Use Them* (2006).

[38] CABE, ODPM and English Partnerships, *Design Coding: Testing its Use in England* (2005).

[39] DCLG, *Design Coding in Practice: An Evaluation* (2006).

[40] ODPM: Housing, Planning, Local Government and the Regions Select Committee, *The Role and Effectiveness of CABE. Fifth Report of Session 2004-05* (2005).

5.43   However, the planning system could do more to deliver high-quality design. The Urban Task Force Report of 1999 found that the majority of new developments were poorly designed, and a more recent study by CABE found that only 13 per cent of new housing developments were well-designed.[41] Planners themselves articulate the need for further development of their knowledge on design awareness and appreciation and urban design.[42] There is a growing number of prestige projects at the cutting edge of contemporary design, but beyond these developments the quality of design is too often lacking. There are several factors that are likely to underlie the poor quality of design in England, including the inadequate supply of new-build, which means that developers can sell without having to produce well-designed buildings. There can also be market failure in the provision of high-quality design and design diversity where developers have market power – market failure that requires public intervention.[43] The Urban Task Force recently warned that 'new measures are needed to ensure that private housebuilders – despite their best intentions – do not build a new generation of mono-functional enclaves based on lowest common denominator design'.[44]

5.44   Maintaining focus on the need for good design should include: the active use of design champions who are well-trained and active in the decision-making process; increasing design expertise within local planning authorities; and, critically, encouraging local planning authorities to turn down applications with poor quality design and the appointment of Inspectors to support this position. Planning authorities should also seek advice on design issues from professionally qualified advisors such as architects sitting on local design panels.

Recommendation 24

Decision-makers should give higher priority to ensuring that new development has high design standards – both for function and appearance:

- design coding may be used strategically and carefully in the context of master-planning to assist good design. Care is needed to ensure that design codes do not become formulaic or exclude contemporary architecture so that innovation and originality are restricted;

- pre-application discussions should be acknowledged as one tool in ensuring good design;

- design champions with high-level skills and expertise should be encouraged at all levels;

- design review panels should be facilitated at the local level and integrated within the pre-application discussion process; and

- local planning authorities and Inspectors should be encouraged to turn down poorly-designed proposals, particularly where the costs of bad design will be high.

---

[41] Lord Rodgers and the Urban Task Force, *Towards an Urban Renaissance* (London, 1999): 'the poor quality of the urban environment has contributed to the exodus from English towns and cities ... we have tolerated [too long] a lazy over-use of off-the-peg designs and layouts' (pp. 39, 51); CABE, *Housing Audit: Assessing the Design Quality of New Homes in the North East, North West and Yorkshire and Humber* (London, 2005).

[42] According to RTPI, *A Survey of Discipline Knowledge and Generic Skills of RTPI Corporate Members* (2005), 62 per cent of members desired further development of their knowledge on design awareness and appreciation and urban design.

[43] See J. Tirole, *The Theory of Industrial Organisation*, (1989) for an exposition of how, when there is market power, the unregulated monopolist may supply too little (or too much) quality depending on whether the marginal willingness to pay for quality by the marginal consumer is lower (or higher) than the average willingness to pay of the group of consumers.

[44] Urban Task Force, *Towards a Strong Urban Renaissance* (London, 2005), p. 6.

6

Enhancing the appeals process

INTRODUCTION

6.1   A well-functioning appeals process is a vital component of the planning system. If a planning application has been turned down, that decision can be appealed by taking the case to the national body charged with handling these matters, the Planning Inspectorate (PINS). There are currently over 22,000 planning appeals processed by PINS each year, ranging from small-scale household applications (the bulk in volume terms) to major commercial developments.[1] Only around 4 per cent of all planning applications are appealed, but the overall number is growing and among them are a number of the most controversial cases determined each year.

6.2   This chapter explores how to improve the workings of this appeal system, focusing on the need to speed up decision-making. It sets out the nature and scale of the challenge to be addressed and the reforms needed to:

- reduce the demand for the appeals system through a new Planning Mediation Service;

- increase the efficiency of the appeals process by allowing PINS to determine appeal routes; and

- improve the resourcing of the appeals system, including charging for withdrawn appeals.

6.3   The focus of this chapter is on the nature of the changes that the Government and PINS need to make in order to improve the efficiency of the appeals system, though appellants also have a role to play in ensuring readiness and timely case preparation.

NATURE AND SCALE OF CHALLENGE

6.4   The planning appeals system in England aims to deliver high-quality and timely decisions in a transparent and efficient manner. In terms of quality, the current system already appears to be operating well. Surveys consistently show that the majority of appellants are satisfied with the way their appeal is handled, and the low volume of High Court challenges that successfully overturn Inspectors' decisions provides further evidence of the professionalism of the service – in 2004-05 only 68 cases were challenged in the courts and, of these, PINS successfully defended 39.[2]

6.5   There are still important issues to be addressed in terms of timeliness, however. As the Interim Report set out:

- in 2001-02 only 1.8 per cent of appeals determined by written representations took over 24 weeks. By 2005-06 this had risen to 21.6 per cent;

---

[1] Most appeals are due to rejected applications, but appeals can also be lodged on wider grounds, such as non-determination, when the local authority has not proceeded the application within required time frames.
[2] In total, 14 were withdrawn, 25 were successfully defended, PINS submitted to judgment in 21 cases, and 8 were pending.

- in 2001-02 only 6.1 per cent of appeals determined by hearings took over 24 weeks. By 2005-06 this had risen to 89.8 per cent, with 49.3 per cent taking over a year;

- in 2001-02 42.2 per cent of appeals determined by inquiry took over 24 weeks. By 2005-06 this had risen to 81.2 per cent, with 34 per cent taking over a year; and

- customer surveys also clearly indicate that issues of speed are the primary concerns for users of the system, whether that is the time required to obtain a hearing/inquiry date, the time for the hearing/inquiry to be held or the time for the Inspector's report to be written and the decision finally made.[3]

6.6   This issue is of particular significance given the likelihood of rising pressures on PINS. Under the 'high scenario' of DCLG's projections model, appeal volumes could rise to 26,000 by 2009-10, up from 23,100 in 2004-05.[4] In addition, the Inspectorate is likely to face greatly increased demands from other sources over the next few years, in particular the requirement for PINS Inspectors to examine local authorities' development plan documents. The proportion of PINS resource expended on development plans has already grown from 7 per cent of total resource in 1999-2000 to 15 per cent in 2005-06, and further increases will put pressure on the amount of resources available for planning appeals and other areas of work such as compulsory purchase orders, Transport and Works Act casework and Highways Act cases.

REDUCING DEMAND

6.7   A principal cause of the increase in delays in deciding appeals is the rise in the volume of cases. There has been a 64 per cent rise in appeals from 1997-98 to 2004-05, from 14,182 to 23,160 (see Chart 6.1 for 2000-06 data). This mainly reflects a rise in the total number of applications to over 670,000. However, a rise in the proportion of cases that are likely to be appealed from 3.78 per cent of Section 70 applications in 1997-98 to 4.17 per cent in 2004-05 has also contributed. A central issue here is whether there are grounds for believing that the appeal system is 'over the hump' in terms of volumes. There is no clear evidence that this is the case, although one-off factors such as the change in the time period for submitting appeals certainly contributed to some of the rise in numbers. While the volume of appeals did fall from 23,160 in 2004-05 to 22,011 in 2005-06, figures from 1 April to 31 August 2006 indicate that the full year figure for 2006-07 is likely to show a further rise to around 22,700-23,000. Continued economic growth is likely to bring further increase in volumes over the coming few years, given the correlation between the health of the economy and the demand for planning applications. Attempting to reduce demand for the appeal system should therefore be a priority.

6.8   It is unlikely that the reforms set out in Chapter 5 to reduce planning applications will noticeably reduce appeal volumes. Extending permitted development rights to certain householder and commercial developments is likely to remove only a small proportion of appeals, given that it should result in only uncontentious proposals being removed from the planning system. If anything is to be done about demand, the focus needs to be on reducing the volume of cases appealed.[5]

---

[3] Planning Inspectorate Customer Survey 2005, p. 7.

[4] DCLG unpublished data.

[5] There are five grounds for appeal. In 2005-06 the figures were refusal (20,298), failure to determine (963), refusal of consent required for conditional appeal (302), appeal against conditions (295), approval of details: refusal or imposition of conditions (99), approval of details: failure (54).

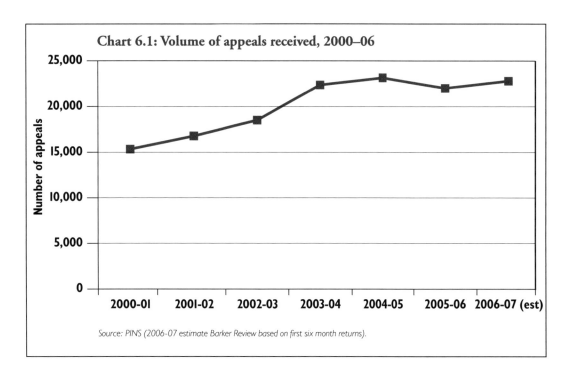

Chart 6.1: Volume of appeals received, 2000–06

Source: PINS (2006-07 estimate Barker Review based on first six month returns).

6.9   The Government therefore needs to consider ways to reduce the proportion of planning applications unnecessarily refused. There will be limits to what can be achieved here. The recent increase may, for example, in part be due to a buoyant property market, which increases the incentive for speculative applications. However, some other proposals outlined in Chapter 5 will help here. In particular:

- a more stable policy environment established by streamlining national policy should reduce turbulence in the system. Fewer policy documents would limit the extent to which policy will vary each year;

- getting the new local development frameworks into place more quickly may also reduce appeals. It should be noted, on the other hand, that there is no clear evidence that local authorities with more up-to-date plans have lower appeal rates (indeed York, which has not adopted a plan since 1956, determined 2,600 cases in 2004-05 but only had 33 appeals in that time – an appeal rate of under 1.3 per cent against the national average of around 4 per cent);

- promoting pre-application discussions by encouraging developers and planners to engage earlier should reduce refusal rates. Where appropriate, earlier member engagement could also help by limiting the potential for new issues to arise at committee meetings; and

- the roll-out of Planning Delivery Agreements for large applications should also tackle any perverse incentives in the current target framework. Responses to this Review's Call for Evidence suggested that an increase in refusals due to the current target framework could be widespread. This would be consistent with the timing of the rise in rejection rates (although the fact that appeal success rates are stable at around 33 per cent suggests, on the other hand, that the reasons for rejecting applications have not become more arbitrary).

6.10   These reforms may not, by themselves, be sufficient to reduce demand substantially. Reforms to the new plan-making system to deliver up-to-date plans, for example, will take time. Other approaches need to be considered. One option would be to take action to improve the performance levels of local authorities that have a high rate of appeals relative to the national average. While there is a national average of around 4 per cent of cases appealed, this varies substantially by local authority. There is also substantial variation in the proportion of cases that are allowed. In 2004-05 29 local authorities had 50 per cent or more cases allowed against them, while 39 authorities had 20 per cent or under allowed. The abatement of planning delivery grant where Local Planning Authority (LPA) performance on the proportion of appeals allowed is poor, as currently occurs, is a useful step.

Appeal fees 6.11   Another approach would be to introduce a form of fee structure for appeals. Demand for appeals could be reduced by more effective pricing. One example could be a 'loser pays' system that would increase the incentive for local planning authorities to make good-quality decisions and lower the incentive for developers to appeal on a weak case, particularly if the appeal was likely to prove costly. Arguably, this incentive already exists in some form: appeals are already expensive and not entered into lightly, by either developers or local authorities. Costs can also be awarded against parties that have acted unreasonably. This proposal could also lead to local authorities being over-inclined to grant permission to avoid having to face the prospect of a potential appeal, or defend their decision when appealed because of the costs they might have to bear. However, it is an option to consider and could help to ensure that the volume of unnecessarily rejected applications is reduced.

6.12   Another potential model would be to introduce a general fee for appeals, in the same manner that there is a fee for the original planning application, with different rates charged according to whether the appeal was determined by written representation, hearing or inquiry. However, this would introduce additional costs for those appellants who are ultimately successful at appeal, and already having to bear their own costs and suffering the costs of increased delay. It is not clear why these applicants should be further penalised, and for this reason it is not proposed that a general charging model be introduced to the appeals process. There is, however, the potential to ensure that all use is made of power to charge for unreasonable behaviour leading to unnecessary costs.

Introduction of a Planning Mediation Service

6.13   A more attractive option may be greater use of mediation of disputes between applicants and local authorities, so that potential issues are ironed out at an early stage without having to resort to a lengthy and expensive appeal process. Mediation is the intervention into a dispute by an impartial third party whose role it is to assist the parties in reaching their own mutually acceptable settlement. It has been found to be an effective form of alternative dispute resolution in a number of contexts, with an increased tendency for mediation to be used as an alternative to court proceedings. The changes to the civil justice system brought about by Lord Justice Woolf enacted in the Access to Justice Act 1998 firmly embedded mediation in court procedures. Allowing parties to agree a settlement rather than having one imposed on them also gives greater ownership of the end result. The benefits are therefore that it is:

- quick;
- cheap;
- flexible;
- voluntary;
- non-confrontational; and
- importantly, may deliver a 'win–win' situation rather than the 'win–lose' of imposed decisions.

6.14   There has long been interest in the application of mediation in the planning field. In the USA since the 1960s there has been widespread use of mediation in a variety of environmental disputes. It is a generally accepted means of resolving conflicts between local communities, local, state and federal agencies, and other interest groups. It is used in planning in New Zealand and Australia to some effect. Around 5 per cent of appeals in Australia are settled by mediation with 44 per cent of LPAs in New South Wales having in-house mediation services.[6] In England, action to date has taken the form of studies. In 1998 the Department for Environment, Transport and the Regions (DETR) included increased use of mediation as one of its policy proposals in its statement 'Modernising Planning' and the issue was explored in depth in a subsequent Government-sponsored study in 2000.[7] This report, which included a pilot study (see Box 6.1) concluded that:

- the use of mediation on a voluntary basis, but under formal arrangements, should be encouraged;

- it would be useful to establish a permanent mediation service for planning disputes, in the first instance based on trained volunteer mediators;

- a best practice guide on the uses of mediation in planning should be made available; and

- a study should be conducted on the use of mediation in planning beyond the appeals system.

6.15   These recommendations were not acted upon, despite continued interest in the issues raised, most recently in the form of the Householder Development Consents Review which highlighted the benefits mediation could bring to the planning system. However, there is a good case for the development of a planning mediation service that could be called on in cases where both parties were willing to try to resolve their dispute. There will always be certain types of case that are more amenable to mediation, such as those relating to design, than others. Adopting a policy of mediation would, however, involve a substantial culture change within the planning system, in that it breaks with the quasi-judicial role of the Secretary of State, or one of her Inspectors, in upholding or dismissing the appeal deflecting responsibility for decision-making from the Inspectorate to the appellant and the LPA.[8]

6.16   Introducing such a service would require a number of critical issues to be tackled. The first is when the mediation should be brought into effect. One model would be for the service only to be used following a rejected appeal, but this, in many instances, may be too late. In principle, mediation should be used as early in the process as is appropriate for the case. In any event there should be no artificial restriction imposed on the stage at which this service could be utilised, in some instances this may be before a decision has even been made, some after a refusal but before lodging an appeal, and some after lodging an appeal. The second issue involves ensuring a high-quality service. The skills of the mediator are often central to the success of mediation – the expertise could be drawn from a range of sources, which could range from private sector mediation specialists to a dedicated resource unit. Third, how should the service be financed? Given the cost savings to the public purse of mediation instead of appeals there is a case for this service to be provided free at the point of need, to reduce the perverse effect of having a free appeals service but a fee-based mediation service. Finally, there is the question of whether mediation should be voluntary or compulsory: one model here would be to require mediation before lodging an appeal, although as mediation is most effective when both parties want a solution, this might not prove to be the best approach. A voluntary approach is therefore more desirable.

---

[6] M. Stubbs, 'A New Panacea? An evaluation of mediation as an effective method of dispute resolution in planning appeals', *International Planning Studies*, 2/3 (1997), pp. 347-365.
[7] M. Welbank, N. Davies and I. Haywood, *Mediation in the Planning System*. A Report for DETR (2000).
[8] Stubbs, 'A New Panacea?', (1997).

> **Box 6.1: Mediation in practice**
>
> A pilot project on mediation in the planning system was run by the Planning Inspectorate as part of a wider study in 2000. This resulted in 48 mediations. Of these:
>
> - in 31 cases (65 per cent) the pilot projects were regarded as successful in delivering an outcome;
>
> - in 42 cases the local planning authority was satisfied with the outcome and in 43 cases were satisfied with process;
>
> - in 34 cases the applicant was satisfied with the outcome and in 43 cases they were satisfied with process; and
>
> - in all cases the applicant selected mediation to save time, expense and aggravation – in 36 cases they felt this expectation had been realised.
>
> There were also substantial time savings to proceedings, with 30 cases taking under three hours, and only two cases taking over six hours.
>
> *Source: Mediation in the Planning System, ODPM 2000.*

6.17   It is difficult to estimate the scale of the impact this could have on the volume of appeals, but in certain types of case there is good reason to believe, on the basis of international experience, that this form of alternative dispute resolution mechanism can add value. On the basis of the 2000 pilot study, of the 48 pilot cases all were assumed to be prospective appellants, borne out by the fact that all had applied for and received appeal application forms. However, subsequent to the mediation, only 13 appealed, i.e. 73 per cent of appeals were avoided. Obviously these figures would not be replicated on a national scale as this only applies to those interested in participating in mediation, but they give grounds for believing that an appropriately developed mediation system would result in a decline in the volume of appeals. Even if the percentage figure is relatively modest the potential cost savings could be significant: the annual cost of running appeals is now in the region of £30 million.

> **Recommendation 25**
>
> DCLG should establish a planning mediation service to act as an alternative dispute resolution mechanism within the planning system.
>
> PINS should also explore further means of reducing the demand for the appeals system. This should include greater use of powers to charge for unreasonable behaviour leading to unnecessary expenses.

Reducing wider demands

6.18   In addition to reducing demand for appeals, it is also important to consider the other demands on the Inspectorate's resources beyond planning appeals. The annual proportion of PINS resource spent outside planning appeals has been over 50 per cent in recent years (see Table 6.1). If demand on resource elsewhere in the system can be reduced, this will help divert resources to processing appeals. An issue here to which DCLG might wish to return is the degree to which PINS Inspectors need to approve all local authority development plans for 'soundness' – a task that has major resource implications and which represents a greater inspection burden than may be necessary. However, this independent examination may be required to ensure compliance of the planning process with the Human Rights Act 1998. This is not a reform to pursue in the short term, to avoid uncertainty during the current round of local plans. In the short term it is more critical to reduce the number and volume of development plan documents. As set out in Chapter 4, it appears that local authorities have been too ambitious in their commitment to producing more, and more complex, development plan documents than the system requires of them. This results in more resource being taken up in judging whether or not they are sound.

Table 6.1: Percentage of Inspectorate resource spent on appeals, plans and other activity 2001-06

	2001-02	2002-03	2003-04	2004-05	2005-06
Planning Appeals	48	46	46	42	49
Development Plans	8	10	10	11	15
All other activities	44	44	44	44	36

Source: Planning Inspectorate.

6.19   Part of the solution here is the removal of the requirement for the Statement of Community Involvement (SCI) to be independently examined by the Planning Inspectorate. Public participation in the planning system is essential, but it is not clear that this system has resulted in improved participation. While the resource pressures from this original requirement will reduce next year as local authorities put their first Statements in place, any subsequent revisions will, under the current system, need to go to the Inspectorate for approval. The resource savings here would only be relatively modest. However, in the context of wider pressures this is not a good use of the Inspectorate's limited resources, a position that is endorsed by nearly all stakeholder groups, including the Planning Officers Society and the Royal Town Planning Institute. Integrating the SCI into a broader corporate approach to community involvement should prove to be a more effective means of delivering community involvement. The announcement in the Local Government White Paper 2006 regarding repealing the inspection requirement for SCIs and calling for local authorities to draw up corporate engagement strategies is therefore welcome.

Recommendation 26

The Department of Communities and Local Government should reduce the non-appeal demands made on the Planning Inspectorate. This should include working with local planning authorities to reduce both the number and the length and complexity of their development plan documents, so that there is a reduction in the proportion of resources devoted to testing their soundness.

IMPROVING EFFICIENCY

Continuing to drive productivity gains

6.20   The Planning Inspectorate has already made considerable productivity gains, including the realignment of programmes of work which the Inspectors undertake each week to provide more intensive programmes of hearings in the same local authority. An initiative to bring together shorter sessional hearings to allow an Inspector to work in a single local planning authority area for a week is being rolled out following successful piloting. The Inspectorate is also introducing a range of improvements to the administrative processing of case work and to the full range of critical support services, while a number of further options for reform are also being considered, including rewards for continuing productivity improvements. These are all welcome initiatives.

6.21   However, it is questionable whether these will prove to be sufficient. Over recent years efficiency gains of 9 per cent a year have been delivered. Given rising workloads, the likelihood is that these improvements will only manage to maintain the current levels of service provided by the Inspectorate, rather than result in the required step-change in performance.

Determining the most efficient appeal route

6.22   In this context, the ability of the Inspectorate to determine the route of appeal is significant. There are three means whereby an appeal can proceed: written evidence, oral hearing and public inquiry, and there are substantially different resource implications with regard to the option chosen. Hearings are 3.2 times more expensive to conduct than written cases measured by days of effort, while local inquiries are 8.3 times as expensive (see Table 6.2). The proportion of the annual workload that is attributed to each route therefore has major implications for the efficiency of the service the Inspectorate is able to provide.

Table 6.2: Inspector resource usage on Section 78 work 1 August 2005 to 31 July 2006 by procedure

Procedure	Number of jobs	Days' effort
Written Representations	16,527	16,628
Hearings	2,876	9,139
Local Inquiries	995	8,301
Totals	**20,398**	**34,068**

Source: Planning Inspectorate.

6.23   Within the context of a statutory right to be heard, the Planning Inspectorate encourages the least resource intensive option when it is appropriate, and has been running, for planning appeals, an initiative over the past two years to encourage parties to change from hearings where PINS consider that the case does not need to be the subject of a hearing. This has been achieved by setting out criteria against which PINS advises parties that, unless it hears from them within a set period, their case will be dealt with by written representations. This has been successful. In the 24 months that it has been running, PINS identified over 2,800 cases where a hearing was requested that could appropriately be handled by written representations. Of these, almost 1,000 subsequently went ahead as written representations.

6.24   However, there were still a large number of cases (almost an additional 1,700) that the Inspectorate judged could be dealt with by written representations, but as it could only request a change, had no power to take further action. If the Inspectorate had the power to determine the procedure, as is being proposed in Scotland, this could result in substantial efficiency savings.[9] Estimates for how much could be saved by moving inquiries to hearings or written representations are less robust, but it could be around 10 per cent if one-day public inquiries could be conducted by hearings and a further 5 per cent by written representations. In total, therefore, this could substantially increase the efficiency of the process so that appellants would receive a better, faster service by having resources targeted where most needed. Assessments can often just as effectively be made via written representations as inquiry and hearing – they are not an inferior appeal method.

6.25   To make this change would require amending primary legislation under section 79(2) of the TCPA (1990). It is believed to be consistent with Article 6a of the European Convention on Human Rights, enshrined in UK law through the Human Rights Act; it does not appear that the

---

[9] It should be recognised, however, that if more cases currently determined by hearings were determined by written representations the ratio of resource intensiveness will change somewhat, as a result of more complex cases being determined by written representation than was previously the case.

right to a fair hearing is inconsistent with written representations (as the French experience makes clear). However, for this recommendation to be effectively delivered, it would be critical for the Inspectorate to set out clear and transparent criteria by which they would judge if it was appropriate to hear the appeal by written representation, hearing or inquiry. It would also be desirable that, when there is doubt about the most appropriate route, the Inspectorate is mindful of the wishes of the appellant and takes these into consideration. The potential for mixed routes, with a case being primarily determined by written representations with oral evidence being taken on a limited number of issues, should also be considered.

Minimising 'case-creep'

6.26   Reform is also needed to minimise 'case-creep'. Under current procedures there is the clear potential – often exploited – for either side to bring new issues in addition to those that were considered originally by the local authority. In terms of written representations, for example, some two months can be taken up by the appellants and the local planning authority making additional submissions after the appeal has been lodged, which arguably leads to the appeals system being misused. While the Inspector has the power to determine a case 'de novo', it is normally the case that the appeal should be determined on the basis of the case which was put to the LPA and not on the basis of a whole new set of evidence, unless there is a genuine and material change of circumstances.

6.27   What is required is for the Planning Inspectorate to be sent all relevant papers – the original documentation for the application, the relevant development plan provisions, the grounds for refusal from the authority, and the representations made by statutory consultees and other third-party groups. When the appeal is lodged the appellant would be expected to set out clearly the grounds for making the appeal, rather than the current system whereby parties have six weeks to make further submissions to the Inspector. These grounds have then to be copied to the main parties who have a further two weeks to make comments. Similar rules apply for hearings and inquiries. Such a process would not bind the Inspector to only considering issues put before the local authority or to limit considerations only to the stated or deemed reasons for refusal. For example, there may be a relevant change in circumstance which should be taken into account. If the information provided was considered by the Inspector to be deficient in some way, the Inspector would be able to ask for additional information to help determine the case. Parties could make suggestions in this regard in their representations. More radical reform, such as limiting the Inspector simply to assessing the soundness of the local planning authority's decision or to only considering the grounds for refusal, would not be desirable. There may, for example, be issues that the local authority should have factored in but did not take into account.

Recommendation 27

There should be a series of reforms to improve the efficiency of the appeals system. These should include:

- PINS setting out further proposals for how to increase the productivity of Inspectors, including ensuring appropriate use of support staff to free up Inspector resource;
- PINS being granted the right to determine the appeal route with a requirement to publish clear criteria for how this new power will be exercised; and
- DCLG revising regulations on appeal processes to reduce the potential for 'case-creep'. This would limit the issues and material considered to those that were before the local authority when it made its decision, subject to the Inspector retaining the power to ask for additional information as he or she sees fit in order to make a proper decision.

ENHANCING RESOURCES

6.28   In the context of sustained rising demand for a service, a public body responsible for its discharge needs to have the funds to enable it do so expeditiously. While there has been a 60 per cent rise in the number of appeals between 1999 and 2005, there has been only a 37 per cent rise in the amount of PINS funding, while additional non-appeal burdens have also been placed on the Inspectorate. Despite the proportion of PINS resource devoted to appeals remaining stable, and a growth in the number of Inspectors, there are still resource pressures, with the average resource per appeal falling from £1,590 in 1999-2000 to £1,400 in 2005-06 (although in part this may be due to welcome productivity gains).

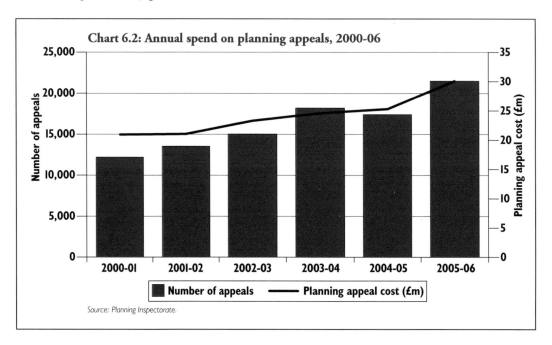

Chart 6.2: Annual spend on planning appeals, 2000-06

Source: Planning Inspectorate.

6.29   Recruiting more Inspectors is not a risk-free exercise. Salaried Inspectors are recruited from a limited labour pool shared by local planning authorities. Increasing Inspectorate resource could, over the short-term, have implications for the quality of plan-making and development control at local authority level. This is particularly the case given that the Planning Inspectorate already has to recruit to maintain current numbers, as a significant proportion of existing Inspectors are reaching an age at which they wish to work only part time or retire. Equally, it is not a 'quick fix' solution: recruiting and training highly qualified Inspectors takes time, and in the short term can in fact divert attention away from case-work activity. But, if a step-change in performance is required, this is unlikely to be achieved simply through efficiency savings, particularly in the context of rising workloads. An investment of around £3.5 million could provide an extra 57 salaried Inspectors which, on top of the efficiency gains listed above, would result in a further 9,300 Inspector days available to process appeals (disregarding the cost and time to train them). If targeted purely on appeals, it would represent an extra resource gain of over 10 per cent in additon to the overall total Section 78 English planning appeal cost of £30.1 million in 2005-06. Given the prevalence of delay, this would be expected to produce considerable economic returns from faster decision-making.

6.30   There are two possible methods of funding this extra resource. One would be through increased central government funding, drawn either from the efficiency savings derived from other recommendations in this report, the Planning Delivery Grant, or additional Exchequer funding. The second would be through additional private sector contributions. There is power to recover the Minister's costs (and hence PINS costs) for Inquiries in section 250(4) of the Local Government Act 1972 and section 42 of the Housing and Planning Act 1986. Under these powers

PINS recover the costs of Compulsory Purchase Order Inquiries and further powers exist to charge for LDF related examinations on the basis of an agreed standard daily rate (published in statutory instruments). PINS can also award costs to parties on application by one against another on the grounds of 'unreasonable behaviour leading to unnecessary expense' but cannot reclaim PINS administrative costs associated with such behaviour. There is also the potential to introduce financial penalties for parties failing to meet published timetables (the result of which can have a knock-on effect for the Inspectorate's timetabling procedures).

6.31   A further option would be the introduction of cost-recovery of foregone expenses for withdrawn applications. In 2005-06, of 22,011 cases received, 2,146 (or 9.7 per cent) were withdrawn, a proportion of which were pulled at a relatively late stage when substantial levels of public resource had already been committed to the system. Allowing the Inspectorate to charge for withdrawn appeals could generate something in the region of £1.5 million additional resource to help enhance speed of delivery. This is consistent with the principle that the appeal system should, in essence, be free at the point of need, and should be considered alongside a commitment to increase public funding of the appeals system. There are risks attached to this: in particular it could result in the perverse incentive that appellants leave an appeal to run the full course to avoid paying the cost recovery charges. This proposal should only be adopted if it seemed likely that this effect would be relatively modest. Whatever the source of the funding, a priority would be to ensure that this resulted in extra resource for the efficient running of the appeals system, rather than being diverted to other parts of the Inspectorate.

Recommendation 28

Issues relating to the resourcing of PINS should be explored by:

- considering the case for an additional £2 million of public funding for appeals conditional on the overall proportion of PINS funding on appeal work not being scaled back and on the delivery of stricter performance targets;

- introducing new powers to allow PINS to recover wasted administrative costs; and

- the introduction of cost-recovery for foregone expenses as a result of withdrawn appeals, which could result in up to £1.5 million per year, to be used for appeals.

SETTING STRETCH GOALS

6.32   The result of this package of proposals – lower demand, more resource, and greater efficiency – should enable a changed approach to performance targets. As a result of the Planning Inspectorate's inability to meet its targets for speed, those targets have been made less demanding. By the end of 2006-07 the target was for 50 per cent of all planning appeals to be decided by written representations to be determined in 16 weeks, and 50 per cent of all hearings and inquiries within 30 weeks (see Box 6.2). This implies that, if half of all hearings and inquiries take more than seven months to conduct, this is considered acceptable. However, in the context of many of these applications already having been in the local authority planning process for months or, in large cases with extensive pre-application discussions, years, this is unsatisfactory. An integrated part of any reform package must be the agreement of targets which provide a step-change in performance, not only on the part of the Inspectorate but by appellants and local authorities to resolve matters more speedily.

Box 6.2: Current key Inspectorate appeal targets

- By the end of 2006-07, to determine 50 per cent of all planning appeals decided by written representations within 16 weeks of the start date of the case;

- By the end of 2006-07, to determine 50 per cent of all planning appeals decided by hearings within 30 weeks of the start date of the case;

- By the end of 2006-07, to determine 50 per cent of all planning appeals decided by inquiries within 30 weeks of the start date of the case;

- To open all hearings and inquiries for ten or more dwellings within 20 weeks of the start date of the case, and to issue 80 per cent of decisions within ten weeks of the close of the hearing or inquiry;

- For all planning appeals and called-in planning applications decided by the Secretary of State, to open 80 per cent of inquiries and hearings within 22 weeks of the start date of the case.

6.33   As a minimum, this would involve returning to the previous targets that were so far from being met they required revision. For 2004-05 the targets had been for 80 per cent of all written representations to be determined within 16 weeks, and 80 per cent of all hearings and inquiries within 30, but this may be insufficiently ambitious. If local authorities are expected to process household developments within eight weeks, why should it take the appeals system twice as long? It should be possible for 80 per cent of written representations to be conducted in eight weeks, and for the great majority of hearings and inquiries to be conducted within four to five months. There is also a strong case for an additional goal from 2008-09 that no appeal case should take more than six months, to provide greater clarity of timescales for cases that fall outside these targets. Where exceptional circumstances arise that mean it is necessary to go beyond this six-month period, PINS should publicly state the reasons for this (which may include appellants or third parties not being able to meet the agreed timetable). Achieving these new performance targets would be highly dependent on delivery of the changes outlined above and, notably, changes in the behaviour of the parties. It is also necessary to phase the introduction of tighter targets in the light of the high demands that will be made on PINS in 2007-08 resulting from testing the soundness of development plan documents.

Recommendation 29

As a result of the efficiency and resource measures outlined, the targets for appeals processing should be tightened to bring about a step-change in performance:

- the targets for 2007-08 should include a new requirement that 80 per cent of all written representations will be dealt within 16 weeks;

- the targets for 2008-09 should state that 80 per cent of written representations should be conducted within eight weeks and 80 per cent of all hearings within 16 weeks. Inquiries should be subject to bespoke timetabling, with 80 per cent conducted within 22 weeks; and

- from 2008-09 all appeals should be processed within six months. Where it proves necessary to extend this period the Planning Inspectorate should make a public statement setting out the reasons for the delay (which may include appellants or other parties not being ready to meet timescales).

7

Improving incentives

INTRODUCTION

7.1   The previous chapters considered a number of reforms to planning policy and processes to ensure that economic benefits are fully taken into account alongside environmental and social impacts. Taken together, they should ensure greater responsiveness in recognising the benefits that development can bring, contributing to increasing income levels and raising rates of employment in all regions of the country. In addition to these reforms, however, the Review has considered the wider incentives that face decision-makers in local planning authorities to ensure that they strike the right balance between economic development and environmental and social objectives. This chapter sets out:

- why getting incentives right at the local level is so important to the planning system;

- how the range of current schemes to support and incentivise local development can be further enhanced;

- the potential for wider fiscal reforms, including tax increment financing; and

- options for further reform based on wider use of good-will and the potential use of land bids.

7.2   The issue of local government incentives is being analysed in greater depth by the Lyons Inquiry into Local Government, whose remit includes potential reforms to local government finance. This analysis is a contribution to that wider debate, focusing only on development issues.

Why incentives matter

7.3   Incentives for growth matter to the planning system, for reasons set out in the Interim Report:

- **the nature of collective benefits and costs:** the costs of new development can be immediate, visible and local – a large new high-street store may, for example, bring disruption during its construction and additional traffic congestion once completed. But the benefits may be longer term, less visible and more widely spread – in this instance the store may offer jobs to many outside the local authority boundary or contribute to lower prices for retail goods. As a result, democratic decision-making and community involvement (critical for informed decision-making) in the local authority risks prioritising those suffering immediate costs over those who would have benefited from the developments;[1]

- **political pressures and short time horizons:** there may be a bias against developments that could have long-run gain and short-term costs due to electoral cycles; and

- **direct costs to local authorities:** where a local authority has to bear the cost of additional infrastructure but receives no financial benefit, this will tend to create

---

[1] K. Barker, *Barker Review of Land Use Planning: Interim Report* (2006), p. 94.

reluctance to grant applications, particularly when there are tight financial constraints on local authorities and strong competing claims on funding.

7.4   Two related problems with the current system of local authority financing mean that it provides little incentive or flexibility to support development:

- as the Interim Report noted, the actions of a planning authority have little impact on its revenues.[2] Although new commercial and industrial developments will pay locally-collected business rates, based on local property values, these rates are redistributed nationally. Council tax revenues from new residential properties are taken into account in the allocation of government grant, but with a lag. Local people are therefore unlikely to see benefits in terms of local taxation or services from development, which will influence their views and those of their elected representatives; and

- local authorities in England have little capacity to raise tax revenues to finance the infrastructure needed to unlock development. This is in contrast to many other countries around the world, where a variety of different taxes are available to local government (see Box 7.1). The fact that, as noted above, local authorities in this country do not benefit financially from new development also eliminates future revenue streams against which they could potentially borrow. There is therefore a need to have an appropriate set of incentives so that development occurs in the right places and at the right times.

Box 7.1: International comparisons

The UK operates a very limited range of local taxes, with just property taxes being controlled locally, in the form of the council tax. Most other countries, have a variety of fiscal mechanisms that give local authorities incentives to expand their tax bases. Most EU15 countries operate some form of local income tax, and many utilise a variety of different local excise duties and charges, on everything from motor vehicles to dogs, while in the USA there are local sales taxes.[3]

Chart 7.1 shows, for comparison, how selected EU countries finance their local authorities. The UK contrasts sharply with the general experience. Moreover, there has been a general trend throughout the OECD over the past 20 years towards greater decentralisation of public-service funding, but the UK has tended to move in the opposite direction. There is therefore greater local flexibility to raise resources and better fiscal incentives available in many other OECD countries.

---

[2] K. Barker, *Review of Land Use Planning: Interim Report* (2006), p.21.

[3] NERA Consulting, *Options for Reforming Local Government Funding: A Report for the Lyons Inquiry Study Team* (December 2005), Table A.1. Dog taxes *(Hundsteuer)* are favoured in German-speaking nations; local motor vehicle taxes are prevalent in southern Europe.

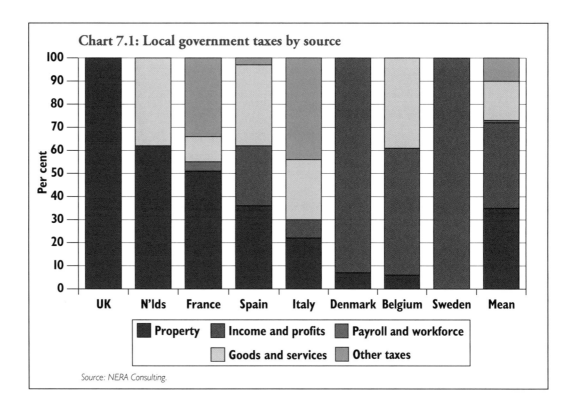

Chart 7.1: Local government taxes by source

Source: NERA Consulting.

7.5   This chapter therefore explores ways in which the incentives faced by local authorities could be better aligned with economic outcomes and how flexibilities could be provided.

ENHANCING EXISTING SCHEMES

7.6   While generally there are limited incentives and flexibilities for local authorities to support growth, some progress has been made in recent years. A number of mechanisms exist whereby some financial incentive is provided, either through one-off payments that are granted alongside planning permission or through the expansion of on-going local authority revenues from development. Ensuring that these are fully effective and fulfil their potential is therefore a useful starting point for considering improvements to the system.[4] Current schemes to offer local authority fiscal incentives include:

•   **Planning-gain Supplement (PGS):** the Barker Review of Housing Supply recommended the introduction of PGS to capture a modest portion of the land value uplift accruing to land granted planning permission. The Government has committed that a 'significant majority' of PGS revenues would be recycled back to local authorities, providing resources for the delivery of infrastructure and other public goods for new development. Consultation on its implementation took place between December 2005 and February 2006 and at present it is expected that the levy could come into effect some time after 2008;[5]

•   **Section 106 contributions:**[6] Section 106 agreements can be used in the context of a planning permission to provide mitigation against the impact of development, such as additional infrastructure, or – increasingly – to require the inclusion of

---

[4] We exclude the Local Enterprise Growth Initiative as it is a direct grant to fund certain activities locally, rather than an incentive for development.

[5] HM Treasury, HM Revenue and Customs and Office of the Deputy Prime Minister, *Planning-gain Supplement: A Consultation* (December 2005), p. 5.

[6] Planning obligations, made under s106 of the Town and Country Planning Act 1990, as substituted by the Planning and Compensation Act 1991

affordable housing requirements. Although case law and policy formally restricts their use to mitigation, compensation or prescription of development, they can in practice form an indirect incentive for local authorities to grant planning permission. Presently some 6.9 per cent of all planning permissions have planning obligations attached. Major residential developments[7] are the most likely to have section 106 agreements, with the proportion rising from 26 per cent of permissions in 1997-98 to 40 per cent of permissions in 2003-04, and a greater proportion of major applications have section 106 agreements attached in the South East (40 per cent) than in the North East (7.5 per cent). Approximately £1.15 billion worth of planning obligations were delivered across England in 2003-04.[8] Negotiated Section 106 agreements can, however, lead to delays in the granting of planning permission, and such agreements are often not applied consistently by local authorities. The Government has therefore proposed to scale back its use, coinciding with the introduction of the PGS;

- **Local Authority Business Growth Initiative (LABGI):** since 2005, local authorities have received a proportion of any increase in business rates income in their locality, subject to a minimum growth rate, in the form of a reward grant. The scheme offers local authorities discretion over how its revenues are spent, and the local authority revenue is more closely tied to business property values than was the conventional rates system. However, some aspects of the LABGI system weigh against its incentive impact. Recent reforms, including its simplification, have aimed to improve the link between LABGI revenues and local business growth. LABGI is expected to provide up to £1 billion over 3 years to 2007-08;[9] and

- **Business Improvement Districts (BIDs):** a BID scheme is a voluntary way to provide the flexibility for local businesses to pay for local infrastructure or services through the use of a small supplementary charge. The Local Government Act 2003 enables the balloting of local businesses with proposals for a BID scheme: so far, there have been 30 (out of 36) successful ballots,[10] with individual schemes raising up to £1 million per annum.[11]

7.7   These existing schemes and initiatives are to be regarded positively: they better balance the incentives faced by local authorities when considering development and provide some extra flexibility. Nonetheless, improvements can be made: Section 106 agreements, for example, have been criticised as being excessively variable,[12] increasing transactions costs for businesses, and some local authorities (such as Milton Keynes) have moved to standardise their Section 106 agreements. BID schemes, if applied with imagination and with effective business involvement, can provide additional support for regeneration within existing developed areas, but they have a long way to go before they are adopted on a similar scale as in other parts of the world.[13] Recent reforms have improved LABGI's likely impact on local authority incentives, but complexities remain within the scheme that will diminish its incentive effects. Ensuring these schemes produce the highest

---

[7] Consisting of ten or more houses.

[8] University of Sheffield and Halcrow, *Valuing Planning Obligations in England: final report* (2006).

[9] DCLG news release, 8 February 2006 at www.communities.gov.uk/index.asp?id=1002882&PressNoticeID=2071

[10] Taken from UKBIDS, 'Ballot results' at www.ukbids.org/doc.asp?doc=1568&cat=313

[11] A. Marshall, 'City Leadership: web annex 2: economic development in Britain: policy, powers and funding' (IPPR, London, December 2005), p. 15.

[12] A. W. Evans, O.M. Hartwich, *Better Homes, Greener Cities* (2006), p.42.

[13] There are estimated to be, for instance, 2,000 separate BID schemes across the US, where the system has operated since the 1960s. H. MacDonald, Why Business Improvement Districts Work in *Civic Bulletin*, no. 4 (May 1996) at www.manhattan-institute.org/html/cb_4.htm

potential impact is therefore one priority. Recently, however the focus has been on the financing possibilities associated with new development, rather than the ongoing revenue that can be secured from developing a thriving business sector.

PROVIDING INCENTIVES THROUGH THE TAX BASE

7.8   In this context there is the potential for a wider set of reforms to influence incentives. Chart 7.2, which shows the current sources of local government financing, suggests some of the areas where changes could be made.

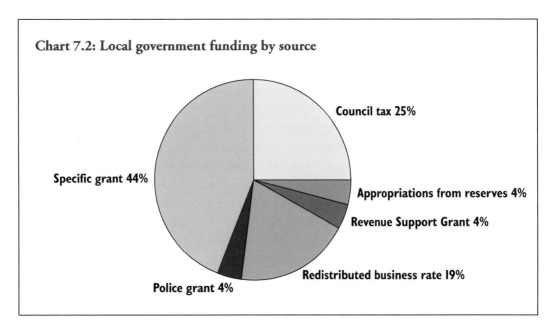

Chart 7.2: Local government funding by source

Council tax 25%

Specific grant 44%

Appropriations from reserves 4%

Revenue Support Grant 4%

Redistributed business rate 19%

Police grant 4%

7.9   Extending incentives and flexibilities through reforms to these sources would have wider implications for the local government finance system, and it raises questions about the way in which resources are distributed between different parts of the country and how tensions between equity and efficiency are addressed. Such reforms would have implications for other areas of policy and need to be considered in the context of the Lyons Inquiry into Local Government. The Inquiry is currently considering a range options for reforms to local government finance from a variety of perspectives, including economic growth, as noted in its most recent report:

> *The current system offers relatively little in the way of direct financial benefits for authorities to enhance local well-being and prosperity ... we should consider reforms to the funding system which would enable local authorities to share in the benefits of economic growth.*[14]

---

[14] M. Lyons, *National Prosperity, Local Choice and Civic Engagement: a new partnership between central and local government for the 21st century* (May 2006), para. 4.30

Box 7.2 below notes some of the areas that would seem to be most relevant from a planning perspective and perhaps worthy of further exploration by the Lyons Inquiry.

Box 7.2: Options for local fiscal incentives

The Lyons Inquiry into Local Government has published research into the considerations behind possible reforms to local authority financing. Many of these relate directly to the creation of incentives for local authorities to pursue economic development, should they so wish. This box summarises some areas of the Inquiry's previously published research.

Business rates: The current system of business rates, introduced in 1990, relies upon a system of capping and redistribution to deliver equalisation objectives, including ensuring burdens are carried fairly by local authorities and that local authorities deliver similar levels of service. At present, redistributed business rates account for 19 per cent of local authority funding. The Lyons Inquiry has highlighted some concerns that the system does not provide local authorities with the incentives or flexibility to engage in or help to fund issues relevant to economic development.[15]

Equalisation: The Inquiry has found that the English system of central government financing for local authorities offers one of the highest rates of equalisation of any developed country.[16] The Revenue Support Grant and redistributed business rates are currently disbursed by central government according to a sophisticated formula that aims to account for each local authority's population size, the assessed needs of that population and local council tax resources. This is intended to provide all areas with the resources to provide an acceptable level of provision. While noting that the equalisation process will continue to remain an integral part of the local government finance system, the Lyons Inquiry has commented on the trade-off between providing incentives for growth and redistributing resources. The Inquiry has expressed an interest in exploring these trade-offs further.[17]

Local service charges and new local taxes: One further option indicated by Lyons is the possibility of new local taxation, and greater flexibility of service charge use. For example, in Switzerland there are local and cantonal income taxes; in Spain there is a local stamp-duty tax; and in the USA there are local sales taxes. Elsewhere, this Report has recommended the use of planning fees to better enable local authorities to deliver more effective local planning; on a similar principle, allowing local authorities to use their service charges flexibly could be one means to create incentives. The Local Government Act 2003 allowed local authorities greater powers of discretionary charging, subject to certain criteria,[18] and some local authorities have already used those powers to generate revenue.[19] However, the Inquiry notes the administrative and legal difficulties around introducing new local taxes.[20]

---

[15] M.Lyons, *Lyons Inquiry into Local Government: consultation paper and interim report* (2005), paras. 2.88-2.91 at www.lyonsinquiry.org.uk/docs/051215%20interim%20report%20pt%202.pdf

[16] M. Lyons, ibid., para. 2.111

[17] M. Lyons, *Consultation Paper and Interim Report* (December 2005), p. 79.

[18] See OPDM, 'General Power for Best Value Authorities to Charge for Discretionary Services – Guidance on the Power in the Local Government Act 2003' (November 2003).

[19] Local Government Association, *Using the New Powers to Trade and Charge: local authority case studies* (October 2005).

[20] M. Lyons, op.cit., para. 2.105.

PRUDENTIAL BORROWING AND TAX INCREMENT FINANCING

7.10   Another area worth exploring is prudential borrowing. Local authorities' new prudential borrowing powers provide the potential to enhance the impact of incentives and flexibilities. One problem facing existing incentive schemes is the relatively small sums of cash likely to be available. However, borrowing money against the value of future tax revenues allows immediate access to significant sums in return for payments into the future. This is particularly useful where infrastructure projects require large fixed investments.

7.11   Large public investments are likely to produce a real increase in nearby property values: the Jubilee Line Extension, for instance, is estimated to have added some £10 billion to local property values.[21] If this anticipated increase in property value and consequent revenue flow is used to support the initial loan, it becomes possible to raise very large sums of money up-front.

7.12   Tax Increment Financing (TIF) schemes are widely used in the USA by local authorities looking to boost their spending from their tax base. A TIF area can be declared by the local authority, from which future revenues can be taken and used as security against a long-term loan, typically 20-25 years. TIFs are a popular means to fund urban regeneration as they allow large up-front payments to be made – for example, for infrastructure – in anticipation of future revenues.[22]

7.13   Borrowing requirements for local authorities in England and Wales were reformed by the Local Government Act 2003, which created the prudential borrowing regime. It removed the credit approvals that local authorities previously required to borrow money, along with centrally imposed borrowing limits. Since 2004, all local authorities can use the Public Works Loan Board, or borrow on the capital markets to as great an extent as their finances will prudently support.

7.14   Restrictions remain, including the requirement that loans only be made out for capital expenditure. The Chartered Institute of Public Finance and Accountancy (CIPFA) issue guidance for local authorities, and borrowing must be completed with regards to CIPFA's 'prudential code'. Within the terms of the code, it is possible to borrow against expected revenue streams to enable large capital borrowing.[23] Box 7.3 gives some examples where self-financing borrowing has taken place.

> **Box 7.3: Prudential borrowing**[24]
>
> Some local authorities have already taken the initiative to establish self-financing investments by utilising prudential borrowing:
>
> - **Calderdale:** additional town-centre car-parking provision has been made through use of a £200,000 prudential loan, supporting a busy town centre. Revenues from the scheme will be used to repay the loan.
>
> - **Bournemouth:** redevelopment of the Bournemouth International Centre has been undertaken through prudential borrowing, with additional income from the conference centre being used to repay the loan.
>
> - **Camden:** £3 million refurbishment of industrial buildings to create office space in the Borough has been paid with prudential borrowing. New rental income from the scheme will be used to repay the loan.

---

[21] Research summarised in A. Vigor, 'Build on land levy with egalitarian worth', *Tribune*, 2 December 2005.
[22] For details, see Minnesota House of Representatives: House Research, "How TIF Works", at www.house.leg.state.mn.us/hrd/issinfo/tifmech.htm
[23] S. Hughes, '30 Year Business Plans for Local Authorities', *Spectrum*, vol. 9 (June 2005) at www.cipfa.org.uk/pt/download/spectrum_issue09.pdf
[24] Taken from Local Government Association, *Prudential Borrowing: One Year On* (October 2005).

7.15   Since the regime's introduction in 2003, prudential borrowings by local authorities have risen to around £2.6 billion over 2006-07, and survey evidence from the Local Government Association (LGA) suggests that the great majority of councils believe the new powers to be 'very' or 'fairly' useful. However, the same LGA survey found that only 35 per cent of local authorities have made use of their prudential borrowing powers, and only 23 per cent of prudential loans taken are for self-financing schemes in the style of those given in Box 7.3. Overwhelmingly, local authorities cite the weakness of their local tax base as the biggest single barrier to their use of prudential borrowing.[25]

7.16   In the context of the planning system and where substantial infrastructure bottlenecks exist, self-financing prudential borrowing could be used to release large amounts of revenue through financing infrastructure, enabling development and economic growth.

> **Recommendation 30**
>
> That Government considers, in the context of the Lyons Inquiry into Local Government, further fiscal options to ensure that local authorities have the right fiscal incentives to promote local economic growth.

NEW POTENTIAL INCENTIVES – GOOD-WILL PAYMENTS AND LAND BIDS

7.17   As well as looking at how current initiatives can be enhanced, there is also the question of possible new means for providing better incentives. This section considers two of these: 'good-will' payments and 'land bids'. Both, potentially, can target a proportion of the financial gains from development at those affected by the planning decision but who currently receive little direct benefit.

Community good-will payments

7.18   The potential reforms described above would not directly target those affected by a development and with an interest in opposing it. These interests are likely to remain even if some indirect community benefit is derived in the form of, for example, a Section 106 payment. If a development is going to restrict a view, it may be of only limited interest to the objector to know that the developer is willing to pay for some local infrastructure – or even a new library or community centre. A more direct means of addressing this issue would therefore be to allow some form of good-will payment to the individuals concerned, alongside the planning process.

7.19   For example, a wind farm would certainly require planning permission due to the range of issues that would need to be explored in planning terms. The planning process also provides a forum for discussion of views and local democratic input. But that would not stop a developer who so chose from offering a payment to those who might be affected by the development. This payment would not be taken directly into account by the planning system.

---

[25] 86 per cent of surveyed councils cited the possibility of council tax limitations as the greatest barrier to using prudential borrowing.

7.20   Critically, the contention is not that developers must compensate directly for any loss of welfare. This would produce a number of problems, not least the incentive to mislead about the scale of harm caused in order to maximise the compensation payment, perversely increasing opposition to development. Further, it would not be right to establish the principle that development necessarily has adverse effects, or that any that do exist should always be compensated. It could also cause difficulties in terms of potential interaction with Section 106 and PGS. It is rather that those developers who choose to offer good-will payments to individuals – most likely in the form of standardised payments – in order to gain wider acceptance of their scheme should not face unnecessary restrictions on doing so. There will be some who will be unwilling to accept the development at any price; these can continue to respond to consultation processes setting out the reasons for their objection, and the planning system would continue to ensure that the applications were properly assessed on planning grounds whatever the nature and extent of the opposition.

Box 7.4: Existing good-will payment schemes in the UK

Wind farms in Scotland

Developers and operators of onshore wind farms in Scotland have established a good-will payment systems for local residents affected by the development. In most cases, these have been administered by independent local trusts, responsible for the collection and disbursement of payments.[26] South Lanarkshire Council, however, established its own fund to enable its residents to benefit directly from payments associated with a large new wind farm at Forth.[27] Where such funds have been criticised, it has been as much over the scale of compensation offered, as over the principle itself.[28]

Langeled Pipeline

The Langeled Pipeline is the longest sub-sea pipeline in the world, connecting the UK with Norwegian gas fields and supplying up to 16 per cent of the UK's peak gas demand. The developers, in consultation with the local community at Easington, Yorkshire, provided a £650,000 community hall and a local development fund worth over £360,000.[29] The local fishing industry was provided with storage facilities for its boats.[30]

---

[26] National Wind Power, for example, offered £1 million upfront and £100,000 per annum to affected communities near its windfarm sites at Strathnairn and Strathdearn in the Highlands. See Rural Gateway, 'Windfarm operator offers £1m upfront to communities', 23 August 2004 at www.ruralgateway.org.uk/cgi-bin/item.cgi?id=648&d=11&h=24&f=46&dateformat=%25o-%25b-%25y

[27] The Council's actions prompted some protests by villagers living closest to the development. BBC News, 'Village fights for windfarm cash', 16 December 2004 at news.bbc.co.uk/1/hi/scotland/4100077.stm

[28] See, for example, Regan Walters, Submission to the Renewable Energy in Scotland inquiry of the Enterprise and Culture Committee of the Scottish Parliament, 10 February 2004

[29] Pocklington Town Council, 'Langeled project helps Pocklington go green!', 7 June 2006 at www.pocklington.gov.uk/langeled-project-helps-pocklington-go-green.htm

[30] Hydro, 'In our latest pipeline, the resources flow both ways' at www.hydro.com/en/press_room/news/features/easington_aukra.html

7.21   Such schemes already operate in some form in a number of different places, sometimes called 'good-will' or 'direct community benefit' payments (see Box 7.4). In France an alternative model operates, where the central government can offer direct payments to authorities to take unpopular development. As discussed in Chapter 1, New Zealand (after significantly restructuring its planning law) allows for compensating side-payments to be made by developers to those potentially affected by development to expedite the planning application process. Good-will payments may facilitate dialogue here. Such payments could sit alongside other current initiatives, to provide a consistent model of the factors for which developers may contribute in terms of new development (see Table 7.1).

Table 7.1: Balancing developers' and community incentives

Factor	Mechanism
Windfall gain caused by granting planning permission	Planning-gain Supplement
Infrastructure costs associated with new development	Current Section 106 (local impacts); Planning-gain Supplement (wider local and regional impacts)
Environmental impact of new development needing mitigation	Current or scaled-back Section 106; wider mitigation schemes (e.g. under Habitats Directive)
Loss of amenity	Voluntary good-will payments

Land bids

7.22   In addition to the reforms outlined above, there may be some potential for innovative new incentive systems to balance better the pressures upon development – systems that, like community good-will payments, could result in direct financial benefit for those who might otherwise object. A system of housing land allocation and acquisition that enables local communities to gain when they permit more houses to be built, helping to win wider public support for much-needed new housebuilding, has been proposed by Tim Leunig of the London School of Economics (Box 7.5).

Box 7.5: A proposed land-bid scheme[31]

Tim Leunig's proposal enables local communities to gain when new development proceeds. The potential gain for local communities is massive: agricultural land in the South East is worth less than £6,000 per hectare, whereas housing land is worth £2.77 million per hectare, giving a potential gain of over £2 million per hectare for the community to capture once additional costs such as those associated with infrastructure provision have been taken into account.

Under this system, the council would invite bids from anyone in the district wanting to sell land. Farmers – and others – prepared to sell land would write to the council stating which land they were prepared to sell, and at what price. If there were no other way to get new land zoned for development many farmers may be prepared to sell their land for double its current value. The council could therefore expect a lot of land to be offered at around the £12,000 per hectare mark, and could probably buy a range of land for £36,000 per hectare. At that price a typical 90-hectare farmer would receive £3.25 million for farmland that is otherwise worth only £540,000. The council would buy land using 'best value' criteria, rather than just by considering price. It would take into account the amount of money it would make on the transaction, but would also consider other factors such as the effect on traffic or the viability of local shops and services. Protection of protected areas such as Sites of Special Scientific Interest, Areas of Outstanding Natural Beauty would remain. The council would then re-zone the land for development, and receive a large financial return. Such large council revenues could be used to support local public services, or for larger infrastructure investment, such as public transport improvements, or to reduce local taxes.

Leunig takes a hypothetical example. Assume a district covers 53,000 hectares, and has a population of around 125,000. Imagine then that the council wants to build houses for an extra 10,000 people. Assuming two people per dwelling, and 35 dwellings per hectare, the council needs 143 hectares of land. Allowing for roads, schools, parks and other facilities implies perhaps 200 hectares in all – less than 0.5 per cent of the district. It pays £36,000 per hectare for well-located land. The council then grants itself planning permission, and sells 143 hectares to developers for £2.77 million a hectare (in practice it would be a little less than this), giving a total profit of £386 million. A similar system could apply for commercial and industrial land – this scheme is not confined to housing.

7.23   In place of the current system, whereby permissions are applied for on land held, the local authority could buy land in accordance with its planned housing needs, re-zone as appropriate, and then sell it to developers. The local community would then capture a large part of the increase in value following the change in use class and disposal of the land (see Box 7.5).

7.24   There are a number of aspects of this proposal which would require modification: in particular, local authorities would not sell newly acquired land at its full value, but would need to take into account construction costs and remediation costs. As an alternate means of securing planning gain, there is a potential interaction with the PGS that would also need to be considered. It is likely, to avoid collusion, that this model could only be applied in a limited number of areas, where there are large numbers of potential sellers and numerous potential sites for development.

---

[31] T. Leunig, 'Turning NIMBYs into IMBYs', *Town and Country Planning 73/12*, December 1, 2004, pp. 357-359. Figures used are drawn from this paper.

Clearly where collusion is possible the system would not work, though the successful UK 3G auction gives reasons for believing collusion in sealed-bid systems can be difficult, even with a limited number of players.[32]

7.25   It would be useful to gain more robust estimates of the price at which farmers would be willing to sell land – although given the figures involved, even if their asking price were triple the estimates suggested there would still be a huge gain for the community. Finally, the local authority would still have to ensure that the proposed development is of appropriate quality. If these issues could be resolved, it would be worth considering a pilot study to investigate the merits of the proposal.

Recommendation 31

Business should make use of the potential to offer direct community good-will payments on a voluntary basis when this may help to facilitate development.

---

[32] P. Klemperer, 'How (Not) to Run Auctions: the European 3G telecoms auctions', *European Economic Review* (2002), at http://www.nuff.ox.ac.uk/Economics/papers/2002/w5/runauction.pdf

Summary of Recommendations

Recommendation 1

DCLG should revise the policy framework for decision-making, in the context of the plan-led system, to make clear that where plans are out-of-date or indeterminate applications should be approved unless there is good reason to believe the costs outweigh the benefits.

One way of implementing this would be to make clear that where an application for development is in accordance with the relevant up-to-date provisions of the development plan, it should be approved unless material considerations indicate otherwise. Where development plan provisions are indeterminate or where they are not up-to-date, the application should be approved unless there is a significant probability that the likely environmental, social and economic costs of the development will outweigh the respective benefits.

Recommendation 2

The Statement of General Principles should be revised to make clear that in determining planning applications due regard should be paid to the economic, social and environmental benefits of development, such as the benefits new development can bring through low average energy consumption, alongside other material considerations.

Recommendation 3

DCLG should update its national planning policy on economic development by the end of 2007. This should include:

- emphasising the critical role economic development often plays in support of wider social and environmental goals, such as regeneration;

- strengthening the consideration given to economic factors in planning policy, so that the range of direct and indirect benefits of development are fully factored into plan-making and decision-making alongside consideration of any potential costs;

- emphasising the role that market signals, including price signals, can play in ensuring an efficient use of land, both in plan-making and in development management;

- requiring a positive approach to applications for changes to use class where there is no likelihood of demonstrable harm, to provide greater flexibility of use in the context of rapid changes in market conditions;

- making clear that where a Core Strategy is in place, decisions on commercial development should not be delayed simply on the basis of prematurity;

- ensuring that development in rural communities is not unduly restrained and allows for a wide range of economic activity; and

- ensuring that in general a more positive approach is taken to applications for tall buildings where they are of very high design quality and appropriately located, and where there is the transport infrastructure to support them.

Recommendation 4

Wider planning policy should be made more responsive to economic factors. This should include:

- building on the more flexible approach to car-parking spaces for housing, by applying this less prescriptive approach to commercial development in place of the current national maximum standards per square metre of floor space;

- ensuring that any review of heritage policy builds on the recent reforms of the Heritage Review, by emphasising the critical importance of viability and proportionality, and by facilitating modernisation that does not damage the historic or architectural significance of buildings;

- supporting the 'town centre first' policy and the impact and sequential tests that help to deliver it, but removing the requirement to demonstrate need (the 'needs test') as part of the planning application process; and

- if the Competition Commission concludes that there is a problem relating to the exercise of local monopoly power as part of its current grocery inquiry, to establish how best to address these issues, either through planning or through other means.

In general, there is the need to establish a more robust evidence base for national policy, so that the costs and benefits of the policy can be better assessed. Furthermore, the Government should ensure that planning is used as a tool for delivering policy only when it is an appropriate lever and provides an efficient and effective means of delivering objectives.

Recommendation 5

The Government should engage more proactively at the policy development stage of European legislation with a potential planning impact. DCLG should resource and maintain close links with DEFRA, FCO and UKREP in particular, and other departments as necessary, in anticipating the domestic planning implications of emerging EU legislation. All departments should ensure that their negotiators take fully into account the implications of proposals for planning legislation, policy and the resulting outcomes for future development. Additions to existing domestic regulation should be avoided except where needed to address remaining areas of market failure. Where possible, transposition should use existing regulatory mechanisms.

Recommendation 6

Regional and local planning authorities should make planning for economic development a higher priority. To achieve this there should be:

- better integration of the Regional Economic Strategies (RES) and Regional Spatial Strategies (RSS), including enhanced alignment of timescales and compatibility of evidence bases, so that the RES can fulfil its role of informing the RSS. The Secretary of State should have regard to RES policies as part of her adoption procedures for the RSS;

- policies that set out how the drivers of productivity (competition, investment, skills, innovation and enterprise) will be supported. Care should be taken to ensure that plans represent the interests of small firms and potential new entrants to the market (who may not be in a position to engage with the plan);

- policies that focus, wherever possible, on desired outcomes rather than imposing the means of delivering those outcomes – for example in terms of climate change – the outcome should be to reduce the carbon footprint with the best means being flexible;

- a stronger link between plans and infrastructure provision, so that there is greater confidence that the infrastructure necessary to deliver large development will be in place;

- a marked reduction in the extent to which sites are designated for single or restricted use classes – the need to ensure provision for live-work units is relevant in this context;

- where employment land needs to be separately designated, ensuring that employment land reviews are conducted regularly, making full use of market signals, so that there is a suitable range of quality sites which provide for all sectors and sizes of firm; and

- delivery of the Government's objective of avoiding rigid local landscape designations in the context of a robust network established at national level.

Recommendation 7

Local authorities should be encouraged to work together in drawing up joint development plan documents and determining planning applications where there are significant spillovers which are likely to spread beyond the boundary of one authority. In the medium term, consideration should be given to how the London model, where strategic planning application powers are being granted to the Mayor, could be applied elsewhere.

Recommendation 8

The Government should make better use of fiscal interventions to encourage an efficient use of urban land. In particular, it should reform business rate relief for empty property and consider introducing a charge on vacant and derelict brownfield land. This reform could be considered in the context of the broader set of issues in relation to local government finance being examined by the Lyons Inquiry. In parallel with the introduction of the proposed Planning-gain Supplement, the Government should consult on reforms to Land Remediation Relief to help developers bring forward hard-to-remediate brownfield sites.

Recommendation 9

In the light of growing demand for land and the need to ensure that areas of high public value (such as sites with important or endangered wildlife) or areas at higher risk from flooding due to climate change are adequately protected:

- regional planning bodies and local planning authorities should review green belt boundaries as part of their Regional Spatial Strategy/Local Development Framework processes to ensure that they remain relevant and appropriate, given the need to ensure that any planned development takes place in the most sustainable location;

- local planning authorities should ensure that the quality of the green belts is enhanced through adopting a more positive approach towards applications that can be shown to enhance the surrounding areas through, for example, the creation of open access woodland or public parks in place of low-grade agricultural land; and

- the Government should consider how best to protect and enhance valued green space in towns and cities. In this context, the Government should review the merits of different models of protecting valued open space, including the green wedge approach.

Recommendation 10

To improve the framework for decision-making for major infrastructure to support a range of objectives, including the timely delivery of renewable energy:

- Statements of Strategic Objectives for energy, transport, waste proposals (including energy from waste) and strategic water proposals (such as new reservoirs) should be drawn up where they are not in place presently. These should, where possible, be spatially specific to give greater certainty and reduce the time taken at inquiry discussing alternative sites. Regional Spatial Strategies and local plans should reflect these national Statements and indicate, in particular, where regional facilities are needed;

- a new independent Planning Commission should be established which would take decisions on major infrastructure applications in the above areas. Decisions would be based on the national Statements of Strategic Objectives and policies set in the Regional Spatial Strategy, Local Development Documents and other relevant considerations, including local economic, environmental and social impacts;

- the Planning Commission would be comprised of leading experts in their respective fields. Proceedings would be based on a streamlined public inquiry model, using timetabling to ensure timely decision-making. Full community consultation would be carried out and decisions would be taken in a fair, transparent and even-handed manner; and

- decisions which are of local importance only, including housing and commercial applications made under Town and Country Planning legislation, should continue to be made by the local planning authority. Where appropriate, and in order to ensure successful delivery of major commercial and housing development with national or regional spillovers, Government should consider the scope for greater use of delivery bodies such as Urban Development Corporations.

Recommendation 11

In order to ensure that this new decision-making model is effective the Government should:

- rationalise consent regimes to ensure that infrastructure projects of major significance can be treated holistically and that the independent Planning Commission can take all the necessary planning decisions (if more than one is still required) on a particular scheme. Environmental consents would, however, remain separate from planning consents and be the responsibility of the Environment Agency;

- critically examine whether there are smaller infrastructure decisions currently made at the national level that should instead be determined by the local planning authority, or by the Planning Inspectorate on appeal;

- end joint and linked decision-making so that large infrastructure applications, or applications made by statutory undertakers, which would previously have been decided by two or more Secretaries of State will be transferred to the independent Planning Commission for decision. Non-strategic applications will be determined by local planning authorities or by the Planning Inspectorate on appeal; and

- as an interim measure, all Government departments with responsibilities for planning decisions, should draw up timetables based on the DCLG model, for major applications decided by Ministers before the introduction of the independent Planning Commission and to ensure that decision-making is expedited in the short term.

Recommendation 12

Measures should be taken to limit Ministerial decision-making to only those cases where there are national or wider than local spillover effects and to reduce the time taken to decide planning applications made under the Town and Country Planning legislation. The Government should:

- review the Town and Country Planning call-in directions. This should involve:

  - revising the Departures Directions so that it more clearly indicates that only those proposals that are at significant odds with the core strategy of a new Local Development Framework, or similarly significant provisions of the Regional Spatial Strategy, could be considered a departure. The departures thresholds should also be tightened so that only those schemes of national and strategic significance, which are at odds with the development plan, could lead to notification to the Secretary of State; and

  - reviewing other directions, in particular the Density, Greenfield and Shopping Directions and withdrawing them if no longer necessary. The overall aim should be to reduce significantly the number of cases referred to the Secretary of State for possible call-in;

- review the Town and Country Planning call-in policy by the end of 2007-08 and implement tighter criteria to the cases that are subsequently called-in following referral. Call-in should be used only in exceptional circumstances for those cases where significant national or wider than local issues are raised (particularly where there is no clear framework at the regional and local level to enable appropriate decision-making to be made). The aim should be to reduce the numbers called-in by 50 per cent by 2008-09;

- review the recovered appeals policy by the end of 2007-08 and so govern more strictly the appeals that are recovered, with the result that only those cases where significant national or wider than local issues are raised, are recovered for Ministerial decision;

- reduce the amount of time it takes to decide whether or not to call-in an application. In particular, the Government Office's secondary target of seven weeks should be reduced to no more than five weeks; and

- amend secondary legislation to remove the remaining categories of transfer excepted appeals: Listed Buildings in receipt of Grant Aid, Enforcement appeals accompanied by Environmental Statements, Tree Preservation Order appeals and Hazardous Substances appeals.

This Review does not recommend that there should be a change to Ministerial decision-making under the Town and Country Planning legislation. In the future, it may be appropriate for the Government to look again at the need for Ministerial involvement in decision-making on planning applications made under the Town and Country Planning legislation.

Recommendation 13

The Government should consolidate the secondary legislation related to planning. A priority is to consolidate the General Development Procedure Order and its subsequent amendments – this should be undertaken in 2007.

Recommendation 14

There should be a substantial streamlining of national policy, delivering previous commitments. The Government should publish proposals by summer 2007. This should include consideration of the potential to remove some of the current range of Planning Policy Guidance and where necessary replace through an expanded PPS1. Any new policy should be consistent with the green paper principles of being strategic, concise and not mixing policy with guidance. Any new guidance should be published ideally alongside or otherwise within four months of publishing national policy. A desirable goal would be to reduce over 800 pages of policy to fewer than 200 pages.

Recommendation 15

Local planning authorities and regional planning bodies should continue to develop their development plans as expeditiously as possible to provide a clear planning framework for decisions.

DCLG should urgently review the regulations and guidance behind the new plan-making system to enable the next generation of Development Plan Documents to be delivered in 18-24 months in place of the current 36-42 months, while ensuring appropriate levels of community involvement. Draft guidelines should be published by summer 2007, drawing on the views of other stakeholders including the Better Regulation Executive. This will involve:

- streamlining of Sustainability Assessment (SA) processes including removing or reducing requirements where a related higher tier policy has already been subject to SA and exploring how SA requirements can be streamlined for Supplementary Planning Documents;

- streamlining of Local Development Scheme processes to a short programme of intended development documentation by local planning authorities;

- refashioning the Statement of Community Involvement into a corporate 'comprehensive engagement strategy' along with removal of the need for independent examination, as proposed in the Local Government White Paper 2006;

- increasing the speed with which Supplementary Planning Documents can be delivered;

- regional and local planning authorities and Inspectors should ensure that regional and local plans deliver against the original objective of being short documents that do not duplicate national policy;

- the removal of a formal requirement for an issues and options phase of plan-making, leaving the Preferred Options and Submitted stage. Preferred Options should be generated via effective and focused engagement with stakeholders, especially those vital to the delivery of the plan;

- a reform of the challenge provision so that if a plan or part of a plan is quashed in the Courts the plan can be amended without the plan-making process having to begin from the start; and

- ensuring that the new Examination in Public process enables an effective scrutiny and a testing of the evidence base of policy.

Local authorities should explore the potential for efficiency gains (which could be in excess of £100 million over a three-year period) to be reinvested in enhancing the quality of their planning service provision.

Recommendation 16

The Government should formally commit to the gradual unification of the various consent regimes related to planning following the proposed unification of scheduled monuments and listed building consents, and should set out proposals in 2007. One option would be to bring together the heritage and planning consents.

Recommendation 17

The Government should, as a matter of priority, work with local planning authorities and other bodies such as the Better Regulation Executive to reduce substantially the information requirements required to support planning applications. The principle should be to move towards a risk-based and proportionate approach to information requests. Action should include:

- a review of the guidance on validating planning applications including the introduction of proportionality thresholds and the phasing of information required at different stages of the application process;

- the introduction of strict criteria to be fulfilled by Government, regional planning bodies and local planning authorities before any additional information requirements on applicants are introduced;

- an examination of the potential to raise the thresholds for EIA applications and limit the paperwork associated with Environmental Statements;

- a tighter enforcement of processes aimed at ensuring that resource transfers and training provision occur before other government departments implement policy via planning; and

- formal monitoring of progress based on representative samples of volumes of information, and associated costs, for like-with-like cases for both major and minor developments across a range of sectors. The first assessment should be published in 2009, benchmarking against 2006 volumes and costs.

Recommendation 18

There should be a rebalancing of the focus of planning on the cases that matter most, in line with the principles of risk-based regulation by:

- a widening of permitted development rights for minor consents by extending the 'impact' principle of the Householder Development Consent Review, so that in future only those cases where there will be non-marginal third-party impact will require planning permission, with the objective of an appreciable reduction in volumes of applications. This should be completed within the next two years; and

- the development of a voluntary new system of negotiated side-agreements between affected parties, so that where agreement can be reached a full planning application will not be required. This is likely to be most practical with smaller scale applications.

The permitted development rights should also be widened to help combat climate change. In particular, proposals to extend rights to domestic microgeneration should be extended to commercial settings.

Recommendation 19

The planning application system should be made more efficient so that high quality outcomes are delivered through a value-for-money process. This should include:

- more widespread use of pre-application discussions, which are often of great value to both planning departments and applicants. Where appropriate these should be used as an opportunity for early community involvement. Local authorities should charge for these only when this is unlikely significantly to reduce demand for the service;

- the roll-out of Planning Delivery Agreements (PDA) to ensure all applications are dealt with in a reasonable time frame. There should be a requirement for local authorities to offer these for large applications – revising the current thresholds for 'majors' by separating them from medium-sized applications would help here. Where a PDA has been agreed the application would be removed from the current national targets;

- a review of the statutory consultee arrangements to improve efficiency, to include consideration of the thresholds at which these bodies become involved with applications and better incentives to ensure a quicker response to enquiries;

- early engagement from statutory consultees such as Natural England, the Environment Agency and English Heritage. In particular, the Highways Agency should ensure that it adopts this approach rather than relying on late use of Article 14 holding powers; and

- speeding up the final stages of the application process, in particular by earlier negotiation of Section 106 agreements or use of tariffs, and discharging planning conditions.

Businesses should engage with pre-application discussions to enable issues to be identified at an early stage and ensure that they submit complete applications.

Recommendation 20

The Government should review current resource arrangements for local planning authorities, related authority services (such as conservation) and key agencies. This should take account of the efficiency gains to be derived from other recommendations. In particular it should explore:

- raising the £50,000 threshold for fee payments on a tapered basis;

- making it easier for applicants to pay for a premium service or to pay for additional resource/consultants to help process their application expeditiously, if this can be done in a manner that avoids anti-competitive effects; and

- maintaining a form of Planning Delivery Grant beyond 2007-08, ensuring some form of benefit for commercial speed and delivery outcomes alongside other goals.

Any fee increase should only be allowed on the basis of a clear mechanism for indicating the higher quality of service that will be delivered as a result.

Recommendation 21

The skills of decision-makers and others involved with the planning system should be enhanced and more effectively utilised. To achieve this:

- the Government should ensure continued funding for the Planning Advisory Service to promote continuous improvement, raise underperformance and facilitate joint working;

- the Government should work with the RTPI, TCPA and other bodies to ensure a continued focus on getting new entrants into the profession. Postgraduate bursaries funded by DCLG should be tied to a number of years of public sector service, so that a return is provided for the public purse;

- the Goverment should raise the status of the Chief Planner within local authorities, potentially on a statutory basis, to reinforce the status of the profession for all parties, including members;

- wider use of business process reviews and best practice guidance to ensure that the time of more qualified planners is freed up to focus on the most complex cases;

- compulsory training for planning committee members, focusing resources in the first instance on new members, with increased training for officers; and

- the LGA and POS should establish a change management strategy/programme to help deliver culture change in local authorities.

Recommendation 22

Local planning authorities should enhance the quality of service provided by their planning department through more effective interaction with external organisations, via:

- the introduction of more 'shared services' by local authority planning departments (or contracting to more efficient LPAs) to enable economies of scale and scope;

- increased use of outsourcing and tendering for development control services, so that private sector expertise is more effectively leveraged; and

- exploring the potential for greater use of accredited consultants to carry out technical assessments for selected tasks.

The Government should also expand the role of ATLAS both in scope, to remove bottlenecks in the delivery of large commercial development as well as housing developments, and in geographic range, so that the benefits of this model can be felt beyond southern regions.

Recommendation 23

A robust system of performance management should be put in place to address continued poor performance, in line with proposals in the Local Government White Paper. DCLG should:

- conduct a review of measures to judge effectiveness of planning departments in the context of local government reform. A review should consider how best to measure the quality of service by the planning system, including consideration of development outcome measures and labour productivity figures, alongside a greater emphasis on customer satisfaction survey evidence. In addition, the end-to-end time taken to process the larger applications that fall outside current targets should be included in the DCLG annual publication of development management statistics;

- encourage the development of stronger sector-led support and intervention models;

- use the new performance framework to set improvement targets in the worst performing authorities; and

- encourage and, where necessary, direct local authorities that continue to underperform to tender their planning function, along the lines of the successful Urban Vision model or to contract with other more successful authorities to provide or share services.

For 2007-08, DCLG should require the chief executives of persistent poor performers to discuss improvement programmes with senior officials and, where appropriate, Ministers.

Recommendation 24

Decision-makers should give higher priority to ensuring that new development has high design standards – both for function and appearance:

- design coding may be used strategically and carefully in the context of master-planning to assist good design. Care is needed to ensure that design codes do not become formulaic or exclude contemporary architecture so that innovation and originality are restricted;

- pre-application discussions should be acknowledged as one tool in ensuring good design;

- design champions with high-level skills and expertise should be encouraged at all levels;

- design review panels should be facilitated at the local level and integrated within the pre-application discussion process; and

- local planning authorities and Inspectors should be encouraged to turn down poorly-designed proposals, particularly where the costs of bad design will be high.

Recommendation 25

DCLG should establish a planning mediation service to act as an alternative dispute resolution mechanism within the planning system. PINS should also explore further means of reducing the demand for the appeals system. This should include greater use of powers to charge for unreasonable behaviour leading to unnecessary expenses.

Recommendation 26

The Department of Communities and Local Government should reduce the non-appeal demands made on the Planning Inspectorate. This should include working with local planning authorities to reduce both the number and the length and complexity of their Development Plan Documents, so that there is a reduction in the proportion of resources devoted to testing their soundness.

Recommendation 27

There should be a series of reforms to improve the efficiency of the appeals system. These should include:

- PINS setting out further proposals for how to increase the productivity of Inspectors, including ensuring appropriate use of support staff to free up Inspector resource;

- PINS being granted the right to determine the appeal route with a requirement to publish clear criteria for how this new power will be exercised; and

- DCLG revising regulations on appeal processes to reduce the potential for 'case-creep'. This would limit the issues and material considered to those that were before the local authority when it made its decision, subject to the Inspector retaining the power to ask for additional information as he or she sees fit in order to make a proper decision.

Recommendation 28

Issues relating to the resourcing of PINS should be explored by:

- considering the case for an additional £2 million of public funding for appeals, conditional on the overall proportion of PINS funding on appeal work not being scaled back and on the delivery of stricter performance targets;

- introducing new powers to allow PINS to recover wasted administrative costs; and

- the introduction of cost-recovery for foregone expenses as a result of withdrawn appeals, which could result in savings of up to £1.5 million per year, to be used for appeals.

Recommendation 29

As a result of the efficiency and resource measures outlined, the targets for appeals processing should be tightened to bring about a step-change in performance:

- the targets for 2007-08 should include a new requirement that 80 per cent of all written representations will be dealt within 16 weeks;

- the targets for 2008-09 should state that 80 per cent of written representations should be conducted within eight weeks and 80 per cent of all hearings within 16 weeks. Inquiries should be subject to bespoke timetabling, with 80 per cent conducted within 22 weeks; and

- from 2008-09 all appeals should be processed within six months. Where it proves necessary to extend this period, the Planning Inspectorate should make a public statement setting out the reasons for the delay (which may include appellants or other parties not being ready to meet timescales).

Recommendation 30

That Government considers, in the context of the Lyons Inquiry into Local Government, further fiscal options to ensure that local authorities have the right fiscal incentives to promote local economic growth.

Recommendation 31

Business should make use of the potential to offer direct community goodwill payments on a voluntary basis, when this may help to facilitate development.

Recommendation 32

That DCLG publish a progress report on delivery against these recommendations by the end of 2009, drawing on the views of key stakeholders and users of the planning system.

B Local authority performance improvement case studies

Introduction

1.1 A number of local authorities have made significant improvements over recent years to the timeliness and quality of service they provide. This annex details four best-practice case studies: Windsor and Maidenhead, West Berkshire, Mid Devon and Harrow. All of these authorities had previously been identified by the Government as Planning Standards Authorities because their performance was below standard for one or more of the national targets. As the cases illustrate, there are a number of means to enhance performance to improve the full range of quality outcomes and not just speed of decision-making, though of course there is no panacea (see Box B1 below).

Box B1: Examples of action taken to improve performance

- **Leadership** was an important driver of change and vital to raising the status of planning within authorities. All cases had a new head of planning, and in some cases a corporate planning role was created. The authorities also developed and implemented improvement plans to help deliver change.

- **Resource** issues were addressed through new and more flexible ways of working (such as working from home and hot-desking), restructuring teams, recruitment (often using Planning Delivery Grant funds) and skills initiatives (such as improving the performance of planning staff through on-the-job training and cross-team working, day release for formal qualifications and creating more room for personal development).

- **Efficiency** became paramount. Backlogs were dealt with so officers were free to concentrate on new applications. Administrative teams were restructured around validation and dispatch. Process reviews were undertaken: delegation schemes were simplified, 'hit' teams were created to chase up applications due for completion, and flexible support was involved.

- **Customer management**, such as a dedicated customer service manager and call centres, took away administrative burdens from planners. There was increased use of pre-application discussions, sometimes with fees attached. Planning advice and customer service teams were also effective. E-planning developments also assisted, allowing applicants to track progress of their proposal online.

- **Improved communications** also featured heavily, with the people within the department sharing information about workloads and achievements, which encouraged more team-working. Use of newsletters, team meetings, team updates on performance and education about changes in national policy were pivotal. Relationships with local authority members were also enhanced.

- **An improved working environment** was also beneficial. Some authorities made improvements to the planning departments through repositioning teams and others moved into new premises. One authority used Planning Delivery Grant money to modernise the office environment and create an open-plan office space.

The Royal Borough of Windsor and Maidenhead

Background 1.2   The planning authority for Windsor and Maidenhead receives about 3,000 applications a year. Meeting Government performance targets was proving very difficult. Officer time was taken up with administration and handling complaints. The team was split across two offices – one in Windsor and one in Maidenhead.

Actions taken 1.3   A new head of planning was brought in. An improvement plan was developed and the planning service became a pilot within the council for a corporate-wide 'Delivering Excellence' scheme. The planning teams were brought together into one location and, internally, the teams were structured to replicate the workflow of a planning application. A hot-desking system was introduced and officers were allowed to work from home when appropriate to allow for flexible ways of working and cut down on office space requirements. To focus minds on performance each individual officer was given an externally facilitated development plan from which all training was checked for relevance. The council realised it was important to develop their own planners and introduced two trainee officer posts. To reduce the time spent managing customers a customer service group was formed within the support services team (this has since been incorporated into a new corporate-wide Customer Service Centre). Alongside this a new tailor made IT system, drawing from the council's database, enabled officers to track their applications over time and allowed performance management information to be made available. A database of Section 106 payments that can be interrogated was developed, and a structured pre-application service with a degree of charging was introduced.

Outcomes 1.4   The authority came off 'standards' for all types of planning applications and is now showing good performance. Further improvements could be made with a higher rate of delegation: currently about 10 per cent of applications still go to two panels (down from four panels before the improvements were introduced and alterations made to the scheme of delegation).

Mid Devon District Council

Background 1.5   Mid Devon is a small rural authority, with the local economy largely comprising agriculture and tourism. The authority deals with about 35-45 major applications per year out of about 1,400 applications. At the end of 2002 it was made a Planning Standards Authority because of its poor performance. The department was under resourced and overworked and a large backlog of planning applications had built up with the result that officers were unable to concentrate on new applications – 170 of these applications were over 13 weeks old. A complicated delegation scheme did not help officers to determine applications quickly. Staff retention became a pressing issue for the authority – at the end of 2004 four planners left the department, and at one point, 50 per cent of the professional planning roles were vacant.

Actions taken 1.6   In April 2003 an improvement plan was drawn up and agreed with the local authority's members. A new head of planning started, who instilled a strong team work ethic into the department. A move to new premises also helped with team cohesion. The department was reorganised into three area teams, which made room for promotion by creating more higher-grade posts. The administrative team was split into dispatch and validation. New planners were hired and the authority implemented a system for 'growing your own' talent to help address resource and performance issues. A focus on performance was created through monthly, quarterly and annual monitoring and individual performance reviews.

1.7   The backlog was tackled so officers could focus on processing new applications and meeting targets. For example, 'blitz meetings' were held to tackle large volumes of straightforward applications in one go. Other process improvements were introduced, such as a simplified delegation system, an improved IT tracking system and the use of e-planning. A range of communications tools were used to improve customer relations and a customer services officer post was created to ensure planning officer time was used most productively. Members were kept fully informed of the changes by quarterly reporting on the agreed improvement plan.

Outcomes 1.8 By mid-2004 the department had a full staff complement and quality had improved. Retention is good and there have been a number of promotions within the planning department. The DCLG target for improved performance was June 2005 and the department had met this target by May 2005. The time taken to make decisions has improved dramatically. For example, in 2001–02 only 27 per cent of major applications met DCLG targets. By 2004–05 this had improved to 62 per cent, and by October 2006, there was a further improvement to 76 per cent. The depatment also has a good system of delegation. Before 2003 about 87 per cent of applications went to members for decision but now about 94 per cent are delegated to officers.

West Berkshire Council

Background 1.9 West Berkshire Council is a unitary authority responsible for the full range of local authority services. It was created in April 1998 when the former Newbury District Council took on responsibilities from Berkshire County Council, which was abolished. However, there was a 25 per cent increase in planning applications over three years. Combined with concerns about resources, poor relationships between members and officers and complaints about poor performance and high turnover resulted in West Berkshire becoming a Planning Standards Authority. At one point only 2 per cent of applications were processed within the national targets. IT systems were poor. Weak performance led to a large number of complaints, which then created a further drain on resources. In a two-year period there were four different heads of planning. Finding planners with good management expertise proved difficult. Authority Members were reluctant to put money into planning. In the development control team 50 per cent of the positions were vacant and five out of sixteen staff were off work with stress. Morale was low. Planners were dealing with a very large case load, in some instances as much as 350 cases per year.

Actions taken 1.10 A new head of planning joined the team and a corporate role for planning was created. Officers were promoted on their management ability and the department focused on developing planners internally. Staff were encouraged to embark on professional training and the authority paid for employees to attend day-release courses and gave time and space for studying. In addition, existing staff were given priority when vacant posts arose within the service to gain promotion. All non-planning tasks were taken away from qualified officers; a call centre and registration team contributed to this. Rigorous process reviews were undertaken, including the production of a process map which enabled the planning team to identify weaknesses in the administration of applications. Where areas of duplication and time wasting were identified, these were quickly addressed to streamline the process. A 'formula' approach for managing Section 106 agreements was created, and a 'Major Applications Developer's Pack' was produced, which provided advice for applicants, set out the level of service the planning authority would provide and made clear what was required from the developer.

1.11 Member relations were seen as an important part of the improvements, taking ownership of a part of the improvement plan. In addition, a Member Reference Group, chaired by the Chief Executive, was created. Reduction in the number of Area Committees from five down to two dramatically saved time and costs for officers and Members, and reduced the confusion of managing so many Committees for all involved in the development control process. Finally, significant changes were made to the Scheme of Delegation, which resulted in approximately only 6–10 per cent of the applications received being reported to the Area Committee. These changes provided more certainty for all involved and helped avoid applications missing a particular

Committee because applications could be called to Committee late in the process. Planning Delivery Grant funding was essential in providing additional resources.

Outcomes   1.12   The overall performance of the development control team remains consistently high. In the first two quarters of 2006-07 the team met its targets in 94 per cent of major applications, 83 per cent of minor applications and 94 per cent of others. These all exceed the national targets.

London Borough of Harrow

Background   1.13   Harrow is located in the north-east of the West London Sub-Region, identified in the London Plan as the 'Western Wedge', and is a vibrant part of the London economy. The sub-region will see continued growth, both in population and employment terms, in the foreseeable future. Harrow will have to accommodate an appropriate share of this growth. There is considerable partnership working between a wide range of agencies, bodies and groups in the sub-region, and importantly between the six local authorities which comprise the West London Alliance. Various strategies, plans and programmes on a variety of subject matters are developed jointly between the Boroughs. Planning was seen as a regulatory function, and not a tool for policy delivery. The planning team had a lack of experienced staff and inefficient processes. Between 1998 and 2004 there was extremely poor performance. The Best Value Review in 2001 by the Audit Commission gave the department a one star rating with uncertain prospects for improvement. Systems and procedures were not as efficient as they should have been, but there was little time to address them due to officers carrying caseloads of over 220 applications to determine compared with a recommended 150 cases.

Actions taken   1.14   A new corporate role for planning was created and the improvement plan provided a good way of focusing Members on the issues. This, combined with a new head of planning, helped raise the status of planning within the council. Planning Delivery Grant funding was used to good effect. IT improvements enabled an excellent e-planning service. The council was able to develop a better recruitment and retention package so that it could compete effectively within a very competitive market. Staff were educated about the importance of performance and customer focus. Teams were restructured around targets (major, minor and other) to help create a performance culture. All systems and procedures were reviewed and a planning advice team was created to improve efficiency. Career development was made an important part of working in the department and officers were encouraged to work across teams to learn new skills.

Outcomes   1.15   The team restructuring and cultural change had a big impact on improvements. Targets are now being met, although major applications are still a concern due to low numbers received and increasing complexity. The authority now considers that, relative to other services, planning provides good value for money.

C Consultation process

Following the publication of the Interim Report, Kate Barker and the Review team carried out further consultation with interested parties, through a series of one-to-one meetings, seminars, regional and international visits, workshops and consultation panels. In addition, many organisations and individuals wrote with further comments for consideration. Kate Barker and the Review team are very grateful to all those who have contributed to this Review.

PANEL OF EXPERTS

Sir Howard Bernstein:	Manchester City Council
Andrew Beshaw:	Siemens Real Estate
Professor Paul Cheshire:	London School of Economics
Dr Rachel Griffith:	Institute for Fiscal Studies
Sir Peter Hall:	University College London
Mike Hayes:	West Northamptonshire Development Corporation
Nathalie Lieven QC:	Landmark Chambers
Professor Colin Lizieri:	University of Reading Business School
David Lock:	David Lock Associates
Sir Michael Lyons:	Lyons Inquiry into Local Government
Adrian Penfold:	British Land
Mark Southgate:	The Environment Agency

ACADEMICS SEMINAR

Phil Allmendinger:	University of Reading
Heather Campbell:	Sheffield University
Paul Cheshire:	London School of Economics
Tony Crook:	Sheffield University
Tim Leunig:	London School of Economics
Mark Pennington:	Queen Mary College, University of London
Christine Whitehead:	Cambridge Centre for Housing and Planning Research

INTERNATIONAL VISITS

Paris

Kate Barker and team conducted a study visit to Paris. Individuals met included:

Christian Curè:	Ministère de l'Equipement, des Transports, de l'Amenagement du territoire du Tourisme et de la Mer
Christophe Jacomin:	Avocat associé at Lefèvre Pelletier et associés
Francois Remoué:	Chargé de Mission, Direction des Affaires Economiques, Financiéres et Fiscales, Mouvement des Entreprises de France
Geneviève Bogeat-Tardieu:	Mission des Affaires internationals, Ministère de l'Equipement, des Transports, de l'Amenagement du territoire du Tourisme et de la Mer
Marc Drouet:	Sous-directeur de l'Urbanisme et de la Construction, Préfecture de Paris
Phillippe Grand:	Chef du service de l'Aménagement et de l'Urbanisme, Ministère de l'Equipement des Transports, de l'Amenagement du territoire du Tourisme et de la Mer
Phillipe Pelletier:	President du Conseil d'Administration, Agence Nationale pour l'Amelioration de l'Habitat

REGIONAL VISITS

Southampton

Kate Barker and team visited Southampton and attended a seminar organised by the Hampshire Economic Partnership. While there, they visited the Southampton Science Park with Don Fox, Chief Executive of Southampton Science Park.

West Midlands

Kate Barker and team visited the West Midlands with Advantage West Midlands. While there, they met with interested parties in the region and visited Ansty, the Ricoh Arena and developments in Birmingham.

CASE STUDY VISITS

The Barker Review conducted four case study visits to investigate performance improvements at the local level, facilitated by:

Andy Parson and Graham Jones:	London Borough of Harrow
Jonathan Guscott and Shane Broad:	Mid Devon District Council
David Trigwell and Paul Butt:	Royal Borough of Windsor and Maidenhead
John Ashworth and Gary Lugg:	West Berkshire Council

WORKSHOPS

The Barker Review undertook a number of workshops focusing on local plan-making and development control, facilitated by Lynda Addison of Addison Associates.

Birmingham

John Acres:	Redrow Homes
Bruce Braithwaite:	Staffordshire County Council
Nick Bubalo:	Sandwell Metropolitan Borough Council
Dave Carter:	Birmingham City Council
Patrick Clifton:	Knight Frank LLP
Gillian Griggs	GVA Grimley
Jon Harris:	Owen Williams (Amey)
Simon Hodge:	Birmingham City Council
Samantha Holder:	Arup
Lawrence Jackson:	Sandwell Metropolitan Borough Council
Doug Lee:	Birmingham City Council
Sue Manns:	Arup
Andy Plant:	Chase Midlands
Stuart Sage:	Advantage West Midlands
Savinder Sahota:	West Midlands Regional Assembly
Alison Smart:	Birmingham City Council
Peter Wright:	Birmingham City Council

Plymouth

Tim Bacon:	Sutton Harbour Company
Tim Baker:	Strategic Land Partnerships
Paul Barnard:	Plymouth City Council
Jonathan Bell:	Plymouth City Council
Simon Bettis:	Gervas Property
Peter Ford:	Plymouth City Council
Graham Lobb:	Form Design Group
David Lobban:	Penrilla Consultants
Jan Molyneux:	Terence O'Rourke
John Oakes:	South Hampshire District Council
Clive Perrin:	Plymouth City Council
Jessica Potter:	South West Regional Development Agency
Chris Shipley:	Chris Shipley Planning
John Steven:	Wykeham Group
Jon Turner:	Sutton Harbour Company

London

John Allen:	London Thames Gateway Development Corporation
Philip Booth:	Dept. of Town and Regional Planning, University of Sheffield
Peter Bovill:	GVA Grimley
Simon Brown:	Government Offices London
Roger Chapman:	Government Offices London
Pat Cox:	London Borough of Hammersmith and Fulham
Michael Crook:	Cushman & Wakefield
Bob Dolata:	London Borough of Hackney
B. Hartley-Raven:	Cushman & Wakefield
Nigel Hawkey:	Quintain Estates
Mike Kiely:	London Borough of Tower Hamlets
Jackie Leask:	Planning Advisory Service
Andrew McIntyre:	GVA Grimley
Kelvin MacDonald:	Royal Town Planning Institute
R. MacQueen:	Westminster City Council
Bruno Moore:	Planning Advisory Service
Brian O'Donnell:	London Borough of Camden
Jamie Ounan:	London Borough of Tower Hamlets
Adrian Penfold:	British Land
Tim Pugh:	Berwin Leighton Paisner
Ted Rayment:	City of London
Joanne Russell:	Home Builders Federation
Howard Sheppard:	Canary Wharf Group
Barry Smith:	Westminster City Council
David Soloman:	Greater London Authority Transport Group
M. Tewdwr-Jones:	University College London/Royal Town Planning Institute

MEETINGS WITH STAKEHOLDERS

In addition to the workshops and formal seminars Kate Barker or members of the Review team undertook a number of meetings with stakeholders following the publication of the Interim Report.

Organisations and individuals met included:

Addison Associates

Air Track Ltd

Architects Journal

ASDA

Association of Convenience Stores

British Property Federation

British Shopping Centre Council

British Urban Regeneration Association

Commission for Integrated Transport

Competition Commission

Confederation of British Industry

Demos

Sir Rod Eddington

English Partnerships

English Partnerships (ATLAS)

Europe Economics

Friends of the Earth

Professor Sir Peter Hall

IDeA

Institute for Public Policy Research

John Lewis Partnership

Home Builders Federation

London Borough of Harrow

London Borough of Tower Hamlets

London First

Nick de Lotbinière

Sir Michael Lyons

Mid Devon District Council

National Planning Forum

Natural England

NERA Economic Consulting

Office of Fair Trading

Planning and Development Association

Planning and Environmental Bar Association

Planning Inspectorate

Royal Borough of Windsor and Maidenhead

Royal Institute of British Architects

Royal Society for the Protection of Birds

Royal Town Planning Institute

J Sainsbury plc

St George plc

Tesco plc

OTHER MEETINGS

Kate Barker spoke at a number of events, organised by: CBI East of England, RIBA East, Faculty of Building Anglia Branch, A. S. Biss, CBI London, British Urban Regeneration Association and the Architects Journal.

COMMENTS ON THE INTERIM REPORT

Kate Barker and the Review team received numerous comments on the interim Report, which was published on 4 July 2006, in addition to receiving some response to the call for evidence after the 28 March 2006 deadline:

Advantage West Midlands

Chris Allington

Association of Consultant Architects

Association of Convenience Stores

Association of Gardens Trust

Sir Howard Bernstein

Geoff Beacon

Birmingham City Council

Campaign to Protect Rural England

Capital Shopping Centres plc

Chris Goodall

City of Westminster

Commission for Integrated Transport

Core Cities Group

John Corkindale

Country Land and Business Association

W. H. Deakin, OBE

E.ON UK

Ecotricity

East Midlands Development Agency

English Heritage

English Partnerships

English Partnerships (ATLAS)

Food Poverty Project

Andrew Fraser

Freight on Rail

Freight Transport Association

Friends of the Earth

Green Issues Communications

Hampshire County Council

Heritage Link

Independent Retailers Confederation

Industry Forum

Institute of Historic Building Conservation

Kingsley Smith Solicitors LLP

Live/Work Network

London Borough of Tower Hamlets

London First

Marks & Spencer Group plc

National Grid

Office of Fair Trading

One NorthEast

Planning and Environment Bar Association

Planning Officers' Society

Planning Summer School

Quarry Products Association

Royal Institute of British Architects

Royal Society for the Protection of Birds

Royal Town Planning Institute

J Sainsbury plc

Brian Skitrall

Alastair Smith

Stanhope plc

Tesco plc

Town and Country Planning Association

Transport 2000

Urban Forum

West Midlands Chief Engineers and Planning Officers Group

West Midlands Planning Transportation

Wildlife and Countryside Link

D Interim report executive summary

Context and terms of reference

1.1   The Chancellor and the Deputy Prime Minister commissioned an independent review of the land use planning system in England in December 2005. The terms of reference were:

> *To consider how, in the context of globalisation, and building on the reforms already put in place in England, planning policy and procedures can better deliver economic growth and prosperity alongside other sustainable development goals. In particular to assess:*
>
> - *ways of further improving the efficiency and speed of the system;*
>
> - *ways of increasing the flexibility, transparency and predictability that enterprise requires;*
>
> - *the relationship between planning and productivity, and how the outcomes of the planning system can better deliver its sustainable economic objectives; and*
>
> - *the relationship between economic and other sustainable development goals in the delivery of sustainable communities.*

1.2   This report sets out the initial analysis of the review. Its focus is on understanding how the planning system impacts on economic growth and employment, by analysing the direct and indirect impacts of policy and processes on the key drivers of productivity – enterprise, competition, innovation, investment and skills. It also sets out areas that will be explored further in the final report. This will be submitted to the Chancellor and Secretary of State for Communities and Local Government in late 2006.

1.3   The Planning and Compulsory Purchase Act 2004 addressed large parts of the plan-making process in particular, but this is not the whole of the picture. There are still other questions to ask in the context of the wider challenges to the planning system which are set out in this report. Globalisation, for example, is intensifying – according to the OECD there was a 27 per cent increase in global foreign direct investment in 2005 alone, to $622 billion.[1] And there is the need to look at how the planning system as a whole will fit with the potential recommendations of related government reviews and studies to enable policy-making to move forward in a properly joined-up way.

The planning system plays a key role in the delivery of sustainable development

Aims and Objectives   1.4   The planning system has a profound impact on our quality of life. Its outcomes influence almost every aspect of our life, from the quality of our urban environment to the size of homes we can afford, the employment opportunities available to us, and the amount of open countryside we can enjoy. By addressing deficiencies in the free market for land use and development, the planning system can work towards the delivery of sustainable development objectives that maximise net welfare to society. It does this by integrating and, where necessary, balancing complex sets of competing economic, environmental or social goals within the framework of democratic accountability. Overall sustainable development goals can be hard to define and to measure. However, the planning system broadly aims to deliver a range of outcomes to help deliver sustainable development:

---

[1] OECD, *International Investment Perspectives*, September 2006 (forthcoming).

- economic objectives – plan-making can support the economy by providing greater certainty for investors about the likely shape of future development in a locality or region; it can help deliver public goods such as transport infrastructure; it can promote regional inward investment by supporting regeneration and enabling comprehensive redevelopment where the landowner has monopoly power, for example via compulsory purchase orders;

- social objectives – positive planning can also help deliver important social objectives, including protecting the vitality of town centres, providing new housing, aiding regeneration, and protecting our historic built environment in part via the listing of 370,000 buildings. Planning authorities can play a positive role in shaping our towns and cities through, for example, urban design coding; and

- environmental objectives – there are benefits to the environment more widely, though protecting and enhancing the countryside and natural environment, minimising the effects of, or influencing the location of, developments that create noise, pollution or congestion and using mitigation measures to limit the flood risk potentially associated with new developments in certain areas.

1.5   But while planning policies and processes aim to address market failures, there can also be costs associated with government intervention. Where information is imperfect, plans may under or over-provide for certain non-market goods, while the transaction costs of intervention may be high. There may also be unintended consequences of policy. The planning system therefore needs to ensure it tackles market failures in an efficient and effective manner.

How the system 1.6   The principal framework through which planning is delivered is the Town and Country
operates Planning Act (TCPA) 1990, as recently modified by the Planning and Compulsory Purchase Act (PCPA) 2004. Both are based on the first comprehensive planning legislation that was introduced in 1947. The TCPA 1990 is plan-led system of land use regulation, with important roles for participation and democratic accountability. Other planning consent regimes with separate legislation exist for certain sectors such as transport and energy infrastructure. Key elements of the town and country planning system are:

- a hierarchical structure of guidance and plans at national, regional and local level against which planning applications are assessed – following the PCPA 2004, the plan-framework comprises a Regional Spatial Strategy and a Local Development Framework (LDF);

- the requirement for planning permission for any development of land. Planning applications are normally determined by local planning authorities. Under the plan-led system, decisions on planning applications are made in accordance with the development plan unless there are material considerations sufficient to overrule the plan;

- extensive powers for the Secretary of State (DCLG) enabling the direction and shaping of planning policy at both the national and regional level, and of determining a very small but high-profile number of planning applications through use of 'call-in' powers; and

- strong policies protecting the countryside and containing urban areas. Only 8.3 per cent of land in England is urban, as a result of a number of policies including density targets and the designation of large areas of land for the protection of biodiversity, important landscapes or to prevent urban areas coalescing (see Table 1).[2] The UK has around double the OECD average of the proportion of protected land.[3]

Table 1: Designations and other land uses in England

	Number of sites	Hectares	% of total land
Sites of Special Scientific Interest (SSSIs)	4110	1,072,540	8.2
Special Protection Areas (SPAs)	77	609,240	4.7
Special Areas of Conservation (SACs)	229	809,199	6.2
Areas of Outstanding Natural Beauty	35	2,040,000	15.6
Green Belt		1,678,200	12.9
National Parks		994,000	7.6
Urban Areas		1,100,000	8.3

Source: Environment Agency; DEFRA; DCLG; JNCC; National Association of AONBs.

But the changing context of planning means more is likely to be demanded of it in coming decades

1.7 In every country, planning involves making difficult and complex decisions. This is particularly the case in England, where a relatively high population density of 383 per square kilometre combined with high levels of average per capita income leads to strong demand for travel, retail, recreation, and housing. With so many people in a relatively confined space, decisions on land use and development will often affect many others.

Long term challenges 1.8 Making these trade-offs is likely to become more challenging over the coming decades, as the planning system will need to adapt to a number of key trends. These include:

- *globalisation and technological change:* The global economy is in the midst of a radical transformation, involving far-reaching changes in technology, production and trading patterns. Emerging and developing countries are forecast to have increased their share of global output from 15 per cent in 1980 to 31 per cent in 2015.[4] This is resulting in significant structural change in the English economy. Demand for commercial land is increasing, while businesses need to respond with increasing speed to changes in the market. A flexible, responsive, and efficient system of plan-making and development control can help business respond to these changes. Some 79 per cent of respondents to a recent CBI survey stated that planning, as a public service, is important to supporting their competitiveness;[5]

- *climate change and environmental limits:* The clear evidence of changes in the global climate requires that the planning system at all levels plays its role in helping the UK meet its targets for greenhouse gas emissions through, for example, helping deliver renewable energy. Spatial plans can also help address the consequences of

---

[2] Some of these designations overlap. In particular SACs and SPAs often fall within SSSIs.

[3] OECD, *Environmental Data Compendium.*

[4] Consensus Economics, Inc., Consensus Forecasts: Long-term Forecasts (2004); International Monetary Fund, *World Economic Outlook 2004* (Washington DC, 2004).

[5] CBI *Public Services Survey* 2006.

climate change – for example by taking full account of the flood risk associated with new development. The need to protect the wider environment is also a growing challenge given the changing understanding of environmental issues;

- *demographic change:* Rising population levels also pose important challenges for planning. More people require more homes, infrastructure, workplaces and retail premises. The population of England expanded from around 43 million in 1951 to 51 million today. Current projections suggest the population will grow to 56.8 million by 2031, when there may be 435 people per square kilometre. Demographic changes, such as an increase in the proportion of single-person households, will also affect demand for space; and

- *increased prosperity:* The planning system also has to respond to the challenge of a more prosperous population. The more affluent people become, the more they seek larger homes, the more they are likely to travel both at home and abroad, and the more they are likely to consume leisure and other goods and services. A trend growth rate of even just 2.5 per cent per annum implies a doubling of national income in less than 30 years.

Implications for planning 1.9   All four of these factors are subject to considerable uncertainty. Economic change, population growth, climate change and other resource pressures can only be projected with a wide margin over long time frames. The 2006 household projections, for example, show average household growth of 209,000 per year, compared with 189,000 and 153,000 in the 2002 and 1996-based projections respectively.[6] The Government Actuary's Department variant projections show how sensitive these projections are to different variables. A low estimate for life expectancy results in a projected average annual household growth of 196,000 and a high estimate for life expectancy in 221,000.[7] This poses particular challenges for a planning system that operates on the basis of long-term plans, which on a regional level involve making estimates for housing or employment land needs over a 15 to 20 year time-period, though these estimates are reviewed typically every five years. A key question is whether the planning system provides the right balance between certainty for those making long-term decisions and responsiveness for those seeking to respond to changing circumstances.

1.10   In addition, while increased wealth and population growth implies pressure for development, environmental constraints make the location of this development increasingly sensitive. Many of these trends involve increased demand for space – ensuring the planning system releases space horizontally (through supplying sufficient land) or vertically (through permitting upward build) to respond to these pressures, while delivering its environmental responsibilities, is a major challenge. At the same time, there is pressure for efficient public service delivery to minimise costs to businesses associated with uncertainty and delay, and to maximise taxpayer value for money.

Despite some progress, more could be achieved in terms of efficient delivery of timely and transparent decisions

1.11   Planning decisions involve gauging individual and community preferences to factor non-market values into the decision-making process. Ensuring decisions are informed by the relevant economic, social, environmental and resource considerations through proper consultation is likely to be both costly and time-consuming, particularly for major projects. This is a necessary part of

---

[6] Office for National Statistics, *Population Trends 123* (London, 2006).
[7] DCLG statistical release available at http://www.opdm.gov.uk/index.asp?id=1002882&PressNoticeID=2097.

the planning process. Equally, the window of commercial opportunity for business tends to be rapidly shrinking. Firms therefore require a value-for-money service that is timely and transparent. A recent select committee inquiry found that the majority of concerns expressed by business around the planning system related to 'day-to-day operational issues such as delays, direct costs to firms, and uncertainty.'[8] The challenge is therefore to improve efficiency without compromising the effectiveness of outcomes.

Reform to date 1.12 The planning system has experienced substantial reform in recent years, as the Government has aimed to help planners respond to the changing circumstances in which land use regulation is operating and to address longstanding concerns surrounding the efficiency of the planning system – including tackling delays to plan-making and decision-making, and increasing transparency. These include:

- the introduction of PCPA 2004, which aimed to create a simple, transparent, efficient and effective system of plan-making, aiming to halve the 5-7 years which local authorities previously took to update their plans. Reforms included the removal of one of the three tiers of plans and the introduction of a new spatial approach that aims better to integrate planning into wider policy delivery;

- the introduction of the Planning Delivery Grant (PDG) to help local planning authorities respond to the needs of applicants in the context of rising case loads – almost 700,000 planning applications were determined in 2004-05. £600m of additional funding has been provided in this form. PDG has also enabled local planning authorities to manage the process of change regarding the introduction of new Local Development Frameworks. It operates alongside targets to incentivise authorities to determine planning applications within 8 and 13 week targets; and

- reforms to the national policy framework, including the introduction of Planning Policy Statements aimed at reducing the volume of national policy to reduce levels of complexity within the system in the context of a Green Paper that found that 'the sheer amount of guidance imposes considerable burden on the planning system and reduces its effectiveness as a means of communicating national policy priorities'.[9]

Delays 1.13 There has been some significant progress in terms of local authority development control processes as a result of recent reforms. Almost 80 per cent of all planning applications are now decided in eight weeks (Chart 1) and of the 18,800 applications for major developments in 2004-05, 57 per cent were made in 13 weeks – up from 49 per cent in 1999-2000. As volumes have also risen, there has been a more than 60 per cent increase in the number of applications determined within the 13-week target for major applications and a 50 per cent increase in the number of applications determined within the eight-week target.[10] Reforms have also been successful at reducing the length of the time to decision for 'call-ins' and major appeals decided by the Secretary of State (DCLG) with over 80 per cent of cases now decided within the 16 week target from the close of the public inquiry.

---

[8] Housing, Planning, Local Government and Regions Committee, Fourth Report, *Planning, Competiveness and Productivity* (London, 2003).
[9] Office of the Deputy Prime Minister, *Planning: Delivering a Fundamental Change* (London, 2002).
[10] DCLG, Development Control Statistics 2004-05.

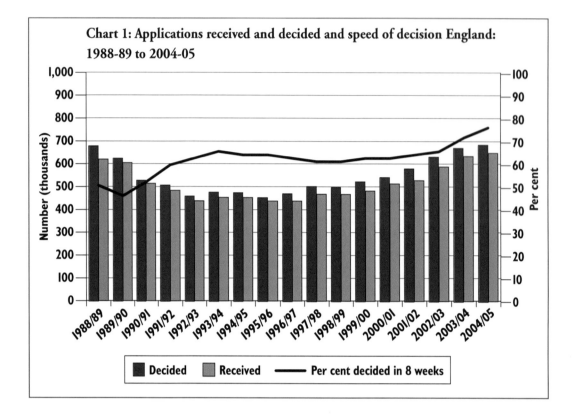

Chart 1: Applications received and decided and speed of decision England: 1988-89 to 2004-05

Legend: ■ Decided ■ Received — Per cent decided in 8 weeks

1.14 There will always be a limit to how quickly complex planning decisions can be made, particularly given the importance of consulting with a number of parties and the need for democratic accountability. But in the context of a survey suggesting that 69 per cent of businesses are dissatisfied or very dissatisfied with the record of local government in improving the planning system,[11] more could be achieved:

- the appeal system has become slower in recent years, in part due to rising case loads: six per cent of planning inquiries took over a year to determine in 2001-02; by 2005-06 this had risen to 34 per cent, with increases in processing times for other types of appeal. Given that some of the most economically significant cases go to appeal this is a cause for concern;

- in terms of applications to local planning authorities, around a third of local planning authorities (130 in total) are not meeting their target of 60 per cent of major applications being determined in 13 weeks (though this number is falling) while over 20,000 minor applications take more than 13 weeks to process. Some recent reports have suggested perverse outcomes from the local authority targets, such as late registration of planning applications, though the nature and scale of this issue is disputed;[12] and

- start-end times for larger or more controversial applications, which often include lengthy pre-application discussions or section 106 negotiations. Reliable data here is limited but according to a major housing developer large applications now take around 14 months to process, compared to 12 weeks 25 years ago.[13] Major infrastructure delays – often determined under separate legislation such as the Electricity Act – are also still common. These cases are often very complex, and so

---

[11] CBI Public Services Survey 2006.

[12] See, for example, Audit Commission, *The Planning System: Matching Expectations with Capacity* (London, 2006).

[13] Barratts Response to the *Barker Review of Land Use Planning* – Call for Evidence.

it is perhaps not surprising that they take considerable time to be determined. But the question of whether timings are excessive needs to be addressed. Transport and energy decisions can take several years (see Table 2) – the North Yorkshire power line took an exceptional six and a half years to determine. In this context it has been argued that a clearer articulation of national policy could reduce delays.

Table 2: Case studies of major transport decision timings (months taken)

Scheme	Years	Application to Inquiry	Length of Inquiry	Close of Inquiry to receipt of report	Receipt of report to decision	Total time
M6 Toll Road	1992-1997	28	16	17	4(+20*)	65(85)
Heathrow Terminal 5	1993-2001	27	46	21	11	86
London International Freight Exchange	1999-2002	13	7	6	15	41
Upgrade of West Coast main line	2000-2003	11	11	7	8	37
Dibden Bay Port	2000-2004	14	13	9	7	43
Camden Town tube rebuilding	2003-2005	11	5	5	6	27

The additional time was the result of a legal challenge
Source: DfT, PINS

Complexity   **1.15**   Planning often involves making complex judgements and there will inevitably be some complexity of process in decisions involving many interests. But in this context it is particularly important that unnecessary complexity is avoided. This is the rationale behind recent reforms aimed at simplifying the national policy framework and plan-making process, and re-engineering the planning application process through, for example, the introduction of e-planning. It is too early to conclude what the impact of many of these reforms will be. A layer of plans has recently been removed, but there still appears to be substantial complexity in the system, which is adding to costs for both taxpayers and businesses, and increasing resource strain on local authorities:

- while some of the new planning policy statements are shorter than their predecessors, they are sometimes accompanied by lengthy guidance notes. Partly due to the range of interests to be considered, it has taken over two years to update just nine of the 25 national policy guidance notes – completing the task could take another five. There are still thousands of pages of national policy and guidance, including circulars;

- the new framework of plan-making needs time to bed down, and while it may deliver increased flexibility at the local level and should deliver quicker plan-making (the aim is a three year process) there are some concerns that Local Development Frameworks are jargon-laden and over-engineered; and

- in terms of the planning application process, the extent of supporting evidence, the range of players involved, the extent of conditions and the number of consent regimes (12 within the Town and Country Planning Act legislation alone) all add to complexity. Documentation can provide vital information but planning officers need the time and expertise to assess them.

1.16   For the reasons set out earlier, where it promotes the quality of the planning system in a proportionate manner, complexity should not be reduced nor speed arbitrarily increased. Indeed complexity can add to certainty for investors when it provides useful additional information. However, unnecessary delays and complexity result in additional costs for business and local authorities. Though planning costs typically are a small proportion of overall development costs, planning fees, for example, now cost over £200 million per annum, with hundreds of millions also being spent on consultants' and lawyers' fees. Very large applications (involving consultancy and legal fees) can cost millions of pounds – the recent Dibden Bay application, for example, cost £45 million. If further progress can be made to increase efficiency without compromising effectiveness this would therefore be desirable, although there are a number of constraints here.

The planning system can be made more responsive to the needs of sustainable economic development

1.17   In the context of globalisation, planning should help deliver productivity growth, where this is consistent with delivery of wider sustainable development goals. The review has therefore explored the potential impact of planning on investment, competition, enterprise, innovation and skills.

Planning and   1.18   There are a number of ways in which planning policies and processes can support
investment   investment. They can:

- *provide compatible land uses.* One of the economic benefits of planning is certainty of land use. A hotel, for example, can be built in the confidence that an unsightly or noisy industrial plant will not be given permission to build next door;

- *help provide regeneration and place-shaping.* Proactive planning, used effectively in conjunction with other tools and working alongside other private and public sector bodies, can help provide regeneration and to create places where people want to live and work. This can aid inward regional investment as in the city centres of Manchester, Birmingham and Liverpool. It can also help deliver the Sustainable Communities agenda, principally in the major growth areas of Thames Gateway, Milton Keynes/South Midlands, London/Stansted/Cambridge/Peterborough and Ashford; and

- *generate valued public goods.* Planning improves the physical environment through infrastructure provision and through helping deliver a sense of place and space. It thereby helps to make England an attractive place to come to work and to do business. It plays an important role, for example, in stimulating the £74 billion tourism industry.

1.19   The system can, however, work to the detriment of investment. Refusal rates have been growing in recent years. The proportion of refusals for major applications has grown substantially from around 13 per cent in 1998-99 to 25 per cent in 2004-05, with minor application rejections (which do not include householder consents) rising from 15 per cent to 24 per cent. Major non-residential application refusals have been rising for the past five years from under nine per cent to 13 per cent though over a ten-year horizon they have been stable.[14] Total applications withdrawn or turned away have grown from 22,000 in 1995-96 to 48,000 in 2004-05.

1.20   A proportion may be resubmitted, and in certain circumstances the investment loss will only represent the difference between preferred investment and the alternative, rather than the value of the whole investment. Conversely, there are likely to be some lost investment opportunities from applications which are not brought forward, but it is hard to measure the extent of this, or how it is changing. But there was a 36 per cent drop in the number of commercial properties built 1991-2001 compared to 1981-1991 and a 20 per cent drop in new floorspace in the same period, and the question of whether the planning system has played a role in this needs to be considered.[15] In terms of foreign direct investment, according to UK Trade and Investment, planning is consistently one of the top six concerns of companies looking to invest in the UK.

---

[14] DCLG Development Control Statistics, 2004-05.

Factors at issue 1.21 While it may impose economic costs, it is right that the planning system turns down inappropriate proposals or imposes necessary conditions. This is a vital function of development control. Investment objectives need to be balanced against other objectives. But while some factors work to the advantage of applicants – large firms, for example, may have financial resources available to them that work in their favour – there are also a number of factors that may work in the other direction:

- there is currently *little financial incentive* for plans and decisions to promote economic development, particularly in the economically stronger regions of England. With the exception of section 106 payments, whereby developers pay local authorities for costs related to the development which would otherwise be refused, and initiatives such as the Local Authority Business Growth Initiative, the local government finance system may provide little incentive to adopt a growth agenda. This is in contrast to countries such as Germany, where a combination of local taxation and per capita grants provides a strong incentive for local authorities to promote growth;

- related to this, there are often *local interests against development*. These can be for good reason, and community involvement and democratic legitimacy are vital to planning. But plan-making and development control can favour smaller and more concentrated special interest groups at the expense of more diffuse interests. If a development will, for example, lower prices by improving the efficiency of a firm, it will do so for a wide group who each gain marginally, but may more directly affect a small group who may feel increased costs of higher congestion in the area. Evidence suggests that 60 per cent of planning changes brought about by the process of public participation result in a reduction in the amount of development proposed as against 13 per cent where development targets are increased.[16] A recent survey suggests there is broad opposition to development (see Table 3);

Table 3: Public attitudes towards hypothetical developments being proposed in their area

	Strongly oppose or oppose	Somewhat oppose	Somewhat support	Strongly support or support	Net opposition
Waste collection/land fill site	80	6	3	9	–73
Power plant or utility	77	6	5	8	–70
Quarry	75	7	5	7	–70
Office	53	14	11	17	–39
Retail park	54	7	9	27	–24
Department store	50	8	9	29	–19
Supermarket	50	7	10	31	–16
Social residential – flats	39	13	15	27	–10
New road project	36	8	15	36	7
Govt office, church, non-profit	33	7	20	34	13
Private residential – housing	24	9	23	38	28
School	10	8	15	61	54

Source: Saint Index, March 2006 [17]

---

[15] Derived from DCLG data used for publication of the Commercial and Industrial Floorspace Statistics series.

[16] D. Adams, *The Urban Development Process* (1995)

[17] Percentages may not sum to 100 due to rounding.

- similarly, *the nature of political pressures and time-horizons* means that there can be a bias against developments that could have long-run gain and short-term costs: development may, for example, result in short-term local disruption to traffic (particularly with major infrastructure projects such as airports) even though the benefits it supports directly or indirectly may be felt over many years to come – though this can also work against certain long term environmental interests;

- *perceptions about development* are not always accurate. The public cannot be fully informed about the nature of a number of specialised policy processes, of which planning is one. For example, even twenty years ago two-thirds of the population believed that 65 per cent or more of the UK surface area is urban, when only eight per cent of England is urban today;[18] and

- finally, the *administrative boundaries* currently in place for planning authorities can exacerbate some of these tendencies. Local planning authorities for towns and city centres will frequently be smaller than the travel to work area, or wider city-region catchments, where benefits of economic development will be felt and this may therefore result in sub-optimal outcomes. New plan-making arrangements that provide opportunities for regional/sub-regional plan making and local development documents covering more than one area may help to address this issue.

Planning, competition and enterprise   1.22   There are a number of ways in which planning can help promote competition and enterprise. Compulsory purchase orders can be used to overcome barriers to new development. And it can also be used to provide wider public goods such as busy and attractive high streets. Where planning is delivering effective infrastructure and regeneration this can also support competition in specific locations, while providing employment land can support the development of new enterprises. But planning can also have some adverse effects, though their overall significance is hard to evaluate:

- the complexity of the planning system provides insider-power, as incumbent firms are able to exploit their knowledge of the system when making applications and objecting to proposals from competitors. Similarly the plan-led system may enable incumbent firms with the strongest lobbying powers to influence the location and availability of development sites. Large firms are more able to pay for quality consultants and legal fees; while delays provide rival firms with time to react to the threat of entry. Only 51 per cent of Small and Medium Sized Enterprises (SMEs) were satisfied with how their contact with Government in terms of planning permission process had been handled – the lowest levels of satisfaction of any of the ten areas surveyed;[19]

- planning requirements may lead to development being constructed below an economically optimal size, shape, condition or in a sub-optimal location, leading to higher cost structures and/or lower revenue flows. Similarly other restrictions to the use and development of property can preclude the efficient use of capital and lower competitive intensity, though they may be justified by wider goals such as cultural heritage; and

---

[18] B. Cullingworth and V. Nadin, *Town and Country Planning in the UK* (London, 1988), p. 184.
[19] Small Business Survey, *Annual Survey of Small Business 2004-05* (London, 2005), Table 8.2a. Base: 674.

- to the extent that restrictions to land supply raise land values and property prices, this raises the cost of entry to the market. Equally, the targets for development of previously developed land may mean that only larger developers are able to handle complex issues, such as site decontamination, tend to be able to enter some markets. Land supply restrictions also increase the potential for strategic barriers to entry to foreclose markets by closing off access to land – for example by purchasing land options. A recent report also found that local authorities also sometimes appear to favour the interests of firms indigenous to the area, for example by giving preference to local firms at particular sites.[20]

1.23   The impact on competition and choice may affect some sectors more than others. There is evidence that the hotel sector experiences difficulties with planning and that this might in part account for the age of England's hotel stock.[21] A number of studies have also concluded that land supply constraints are lowering retail productivity by raising barriers to entry and inhibiting the ability of more efficient firms to benefit from economies of scale.[22] A Competition Commission report in 2000 found that there were substantial economies of scale in stores up to 3000 square metres, but that the average store size in the UK is less than 500 square metres, with the planning system being partly responsible for this.[23] Recent reforms to planning policy on town centres may go some way to addressing these issues and any costs associated with the impact need to be assessed against potential wider benefits. The relationship between town centre vitality, transport, and 'town centre first' policy is more complex than often assumed. Growing consumer expenditure, for example, suggests there is not always a zero-sum game between town centre vitality and development beyond the centre, and *Planning Policy Statement 6* considers this.

Planning, skills and labour flexibilty   1.24   There is less evidence of the impact of the planning system on the demand and supply of skills than for other productivity drivers. But it can be used to facilitate the expansion of the education sector at a time of growing demand for higher-level skills. It can aid labour market flexibility through its impact on housing supply and transport infrastructure. And it can be used to influence the types of employment and hence skill-base likely to be employed in a given locality:

- in terms of facilitating the expansion of schools, colleges and universities the picture is varied. The biggest difficulties often relate to land supply issues, with planned expansions at Bath, Surrey and York all taking several years to negotiate their way through the planning system;

- in terms of influencing labour mobility there is evidence that regional house price-to-earnings ratios influence net migration between the South East and the rest of England, in part as homeowners from lower-priced regions cannot afford to move to higher-priced areas. Similarly, delays to transport infrastructure provision can influence labour market flexibility; and

---

[20] ECOTEC Research and Consulting Ltd and Roger Tym and Partners, *Planning for Economic Development: A Report for the Office of the Deputy Prime Minister* (2004), pp. 9,81.

[21] Better Regulation Task Force, *Tackling the Impact of Increasing Regulation – A Case Study of Hotels and Restaurants* (London, 2000).

[22] See among others, M. Maher and M. Wise, 'Product Market Competition and Economic Performance in the UK', OECD Economics Department, Working Paper no. 433 (Paris, 2005) and R.H. McGuckin, M. Spigelman and B. van Ark, *The Retail Revolution: Can Europe Match US Productivity Performance?* The Conference Board (Groningen, 2005).

[23] Competition Commission, *Supermarkets: A Report on the Supply of Groceries from Multiple Stores on the United Kingdom* (London, 2000).

> - planning policies can also influence the demand for skills through the plan-framework that can influence the type of employment in a certain area. Policies to encourage jobs that suit the needs of low-skilled residents, for example, may limit the growth of new enterprises.

Planning and innovation 1.25   The planning system has the potential to influence the size and development of agglomerations of economic activity. Larger towns and cities may reap benefits in the form of labour market pooling and supplier specialisation. Where planning constrains city growth it may constrain these benefits – recent research has suggested doubling the size of a city can result in productivity gains of three to eight per cent.[24]

1.26   In terms of innovation, the UK has persistently spent less on research and development (R&D) than key competitors – in the last five years the UK has spent 1.8 per cent of GDP on R&D while Germany and France have spent over 2.5 per cent. There are a wide range of potential explanations for this, most of which are unrelated to planning. The Government has responded in a number of ways, including introducing a ten-year science and innovation investment framework. But in recent years there has been growing interest in spatial explanations and the cluster benefits from proximity to similar firms – 54 per cent of high-tech firms finding local access to innovative people, ideas and technologies of value to their business.[25]

1.27   Planning is only one factor among many in determining the success (or otherwise) of innovative clustering. Local authorities that choose to adopt pro-growth policies aimed at promoting clusters can be instrumental in ensuring their development and continued success, as the City of London illustrates. But the system does not always play this positive role in the development of successful clusters:

> - the Cambridge cluster, for example, now employs over 30,000 people, but, until the early 1990s, regional and county planning guidance aimed to disperse economic activity;
>
> - Oxford also developed a strategy of displacement, in the context of a tight city boundary which limits available employment land and raises house prices; and
>
> - for 'Newcastle Science City' the planning framework and administrative boundary issues may also be slowing development aimed at attracting 100 new technology start-ups to Newcastle and the surrounding area by 2010.

1.28   There is therefore evidence of land use regulation impeding the development of clusters that could have developed quicker or more extensively – a report for the DTI concluded that planning restrictions can be a 'significant barrier' to cluster growth.[26] This is true both in terms of land designated for the purpose of cluster formation, and wider policies relating to planning such as the need to ensure an adequate supply of housing to support local labour markets. Where the wider conditions exist for cluster formation, the planning system needs to ensure that it does not act as an impediment within the context of its wider sustainable development objectives.

---

[24] S. S. Rosenthal and W. C. Strange, 'Evidence on the Nature and Sources of Agglomeration Economies', in J. V. Henderson and J-F. Thisse (eds.), *Handbook of Regional and Urban Economics*, vol. 4 (2004).

[25] D. Keeble, C. Lawson, B. Moore and F. Wilkinson, 'Collective learning processess, networking and 'institutional thickness' in the Cambridge Region', *Regional Studies*, 33/4 (1999), p. 325.

[26] Lord Sainsbury, Biotechnology Clusters: report of a team led by Lord Sainsbury, Minister for Science (1999), p.41.

There are issues around the responsiveness of the planning system to price signals

1.29   There are large differences in land values for different uses in England. For England and Wales (excluding London) the average value of mixed agricultural land is around £10,000 per hectare.[27] But land values for other uses with more limited supply (see Chart 2) are much higher. Average costs are £2.6 million per hectare for housing land, £660,000 for industrial and warehousing, and £780,000 for general office class B1.[28] In certain parts of the country this differential is even higher. In the South East, for example, while agricultural land is worth £12,000 on average, general business class B1 land is worth £1.7 million and housing land £3.2 million per hectare.[29] On average it is not surprising for there to be a large discrepancy in land values between certain use classes. But research suggests this discrepancy is also found at the border between use classes.

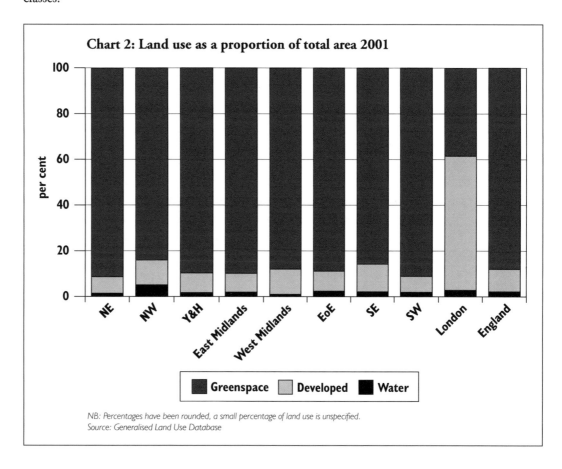

Chart 2: Land use as a proportion of total area 2001

Greenspace   Developed   Water

NB: Percentages have been rounded, a small percentage of land use is unspecified.
Source: Generalised Land Use Database

1.30   While there are non-market values of land to be taken into account, which can be substantial (rising to over £10 million per hectare for urban core public space) it is not clear that wider social or environmental benefits can always account for the level of discrepancy in land value for different use-classes.[30] In terms of traffic emissions, for example, although it is often suggested that there is a link between density and emissions – and that one justification for high price differentials between urban and agricultural land may therefore be the need to reduce emissions – the nature and extent of this link is disputed. Over the long term, other policies, including road-pricing, may help to achieve the desired goals more efficiently. Equally, there may be wider costs associated with limiting the growth

---

[27] Valuation Office Agency, *Property Market Report 2006*.

[28] Valuation Office Agency, *Property Market Report 2006*.

[29] Valuation Office Agency, *Property Market Report 2006*.

[30] Eftec and Entec, *OPDM Appraisal Guidance, Valuing the External Benefits of Undeveloped Land: A Review of the Economic Literature*, A Report for the Deputy Prime Minister (London, 2002).

of towns and cities, as in some instances when sites of higher biodiversity within urban areas may be developed in favour of less valuable open space beyond the city boundary.

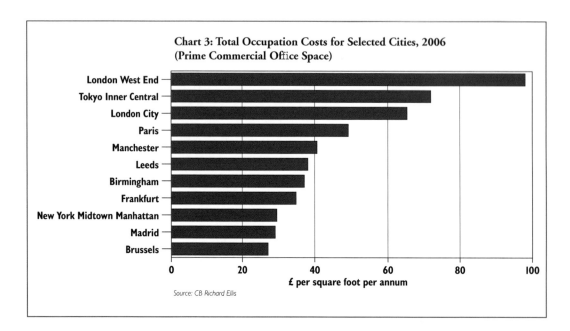

Chart 3: Total Occupation Costs for Selected Cities, 2006 (Prime Commercial Office Space)

Source: CB Richard Ellis

1.31 Land supply restrictions (only 0.6 per cent of land is developed to non-domestic buildings) combined with height restrictions such as tall buildings policies or protected views, are likely to have a hidden cost of increasing business rents – usually the second highest component of business costs after wages. It is clear that there is some relationship between price and supply of space – developers are, for example, revising down their rent estimates in certain Central London locations in the light of the anticipated 5.2 million square feet of space coming on stream at the nearby King's Cross development. Though precise rankings vary in part due to exchange rate fluctuations, England has some of the highest occupation costs in the world (see Chart 3):

- of the world's 15 most expensive prime commercial property locations, five are in England;

- London West End occupation costs of £98 per square foot are the most expensive in the world. They are around 40 per cent more than any other city in the world, and double that of Paris, the next most expensive European city; and

- prime site occupation costs in Manchester and Leeds are around 40 per cent more than mid-town Manhattan.[31]

1.32 While land is limited in England and demand is high, the magnitude of the differentials means it is difficult to account for the figures above in terms of these factors alone. Nor do construction costs appear to be higher in England than elsewhere. Research commissioned for the review on 14 local office markets going back to 1973 suggests that regulation – including planning – plays a significant role in determining price.[32] And the need to deliver land for housing may be having a knock-on effect of distorting the market for employment land.

---

[31] CB Richard Ellis, *Global Market Rents*, January 2006.

[32] P. Cheshire and C. Hilber, 'The Cost of Regulatory Constraints on the British Office Market', Report for the Barker Review of Land Use Planning, May 2006.

1.33   But there is other data to consider. There is evidence that suggests that planning is not a major constraint on the supply of space. In London, for example, the stock of available permissions greatly exceeds the average rate of new construction starts, while in areas such as Yorkshire and the Humber there appears to be an oversupply of employment land. So in addition to supply constraints there may also be issues relating to the operation of the land market. In short, this is a complex area and research in the field is fairly limited. But though the degree is uncertain, planning restrictions are likely to be contributing, along with other factors, to high occupation costs in England.

NEXT STEPS

1.34   Planning often involves making difficult decisions, and reaching judgements can be controversial. There are a number of ways in which the planning system appears to be integrating and where necessary balancing competing interests in an effective manner. The extent of open countryside, the degree of heritage protection, the vitality of many town and city centres, the successful separation between land uses such as heavy industry and housing, the ability to reach consensus about the nature and extent of development via community involvement, and the regeneration of many deprived areas are just some of the ways in which proactive planning actively contributes to wider quality of life goals. Many recent reforms should also help in the delivery of key outcomes – the new system of spatial planning, for example, should also help ensure that planning is better integrated with other policy goals at a regional and local level.

1.35   But more can be done to ensure the planning system responds more effectively to the challenges of globalisation. While there are important economic benefits associated with effective planning, there seem to be some negative direct and indirect effects, to varying degrees, on all five of the main drivers of productivity, though the literature in this area is often not extensive and it can sometimes be hard to isolate the impact of planning from other factors. This does, however, suggest that improvement in the performance of the planning regime could – where justified – help to close the productivity gap between the UK and other developed countries.

1.36   Responding to this challenge does not and should not imply prioritising the needs of business over other interests. Indeed, it may be that there are reforms that could also enhance environmental and social outcomes so that an overall better set of outcomes can be achieved. But it means improving a system whereby, according to a recent study commissioned by the Government, 'in general, planning for economic development is a lower priority and has a lower profile compared to other major areas of the planning system, notably housing and retail development. A culture of positive proactive planning for economic development is not firmly embedded, although there are positive examples where it does occur.'[33]

1.37   Among the issues that the review will explore in making its final recommendations are:

1.   *Efficiency of process* – how can the planning system be made more efficient, so that it delivers high quality and sustainable outcomes while providing value for money? The review will consider how unnecessary delays and complexity in the planning system at all levels – national policy, regional and local plan-making and development control – can be further reduced, and how the skills of decision-makers can be enhanced and how to ensure they are able to focus those skills on the most significant issues. Where planning policies seek to deliver important Government priorities, it will explore whether any might more appropriately be

---

[33] ODPM (now DCLG) Planning Research, *Planning for Economic Development: Report for the Office of the Deputy Prime Minister* (2004), p. 7.

tackled, at least in part, by other policy routes or whether there are ways to deliver more joined-up policy.

2.   *Efficient use of land* – many of the ways that planning impacts on the economy – including the expansion of universities, the impact on occupation costs, the development of innovation clusters, the setting up of small enterprises – relate to the supply of land. This raises questions about whether sufficient land supply is designated for development. In addition there are environmental concerns about whether the right land is being used for new development.

3.   *Flexibility and responsiveness* – can the planning system be made more responsive to price-signals and changing economic circumstances at a local and regional level, while also providing the certainty that businesses value? In this context the issue of the incentives facing decision-makers will be explored – for many local planning authorities there is often little financial incentive to adopt pro-growth strategies or enhance competition. The issue of the level at which decisions are best made will also be explored, considering how the principle of subsidiarity might best be applied.

1.38   In drawing its conclusions, the review will take note of emerging findings from related reviews, including the Lyons Inquiry, the Energy Review and the Eddington Transport Study. In considering potential reforms to address these problems, the review will also take into account four critical background issues:

- it is important that participation and democratic accountability is maintained within the system;

- in an age of increased legal challenge, risk-aversion among public bodies and private sector applicants is to be expected and this will necessarily have an impact on the speed and complexity of the planning system;

- beyond an assessment of evidence relating to gold-plating, the potential for reform of European legislation is constrained; and

- there have been a number of changes made to the planning system in recent years, and constant change bears its own costs.

1.39   There are complex sets of trade-offs to be made in planning and there are unlikely to be simple magic bullet solutions to many of these issues. Nor will reform be suggested for reform's sake. And given that the new plan-making process is bedding down, the focus of the final report will not be on this aspect of the system. But in the context of the issues identified, and the economic costs that may be being imposed on businesses and consumers as a result, the final report will consider how and whether planning can improve the efficiency and effectiveness of sustainable economic development while protecting or enhancing its wider sustainable development goals.

E Glossary of terms

APM (Adopted Proposals Map): a component of a Local Development Framework and an important part of the development plan, or a Development Plan Document (DPD) itself, showing the location of proposals in all current DPDs, on an Ordnance Survey base map.

AAP (Area Action Plan): a type of development plan document (DPD) focused upon a specific location or an area subject to conservation or significant change (for example major regeneration).

AMR (Annual Monitoring Report): a report submitted to the Government by a local planning authority or Regional Planning Bodies assessing progress with and the effectiveness of a Local Development Framework.

ATLAS (Advisory Team for Large Applications): a team set up in 2004 as a pilot scheme by the Office of the Deputy Prime Minister (ODPM) to provide an independent advisory service to local authorities in London and the wider South East, who were experiencing the pressures of increased development activity flowing from the Sustainable Communities Plan. ATLAS is part of the Planning Advisory Service (PAS). The team is being provided by English Partnerships. Its success has led to an expansion of its duties.

BVR (Best Value Reviews): local authority performance is continuously monitored, partly through adherence to locally and statutorily determined Best Value Performance Indicators (BVPIs), and results are disseminated annually through Best Value Performance Plans (BVPPs).

CPA (Comprehensive Performance Assessment): conducted by the Audit Commission, measures how well councils are delivering services for local people and communities. A CPA looks at performance from a range of perspectives and combines a set of judgements to provide both an easily understood rating and a more complete picture of where to focus activity to secure improvement.

CPO (Compulsory Purchase Order): an order issued by the Government or a local authority to acquire land or buildings for public interest purposes, for example for the construction of a major road or the redevelopment of certain brownfield sites.

CPRE (Campaign to Protect Rural England)

CS (Core Strategy): A development plan document setting out the spatial vision and strategic objectives of the planning framework for an area, having regard to the Community Strategy (see also DPDs).

CWO (Compulsory Works Order): an order made by the Secretary of State in the form of a statutory instrument. A water company may apply for a CWO under Section 167 of the Water Industry Act 1991 where it is proposing, for the purposes of its function as a water undertaker, to carry out any engineering or building operations or to discharge water into an inland waterway or underground strata. A CWO allows for a variety of authorisations to be given in a single instrument, and has the benefit of bringing together the application and decision-making for these consents and authorisations into one streamlined procedure. A CWO can confer such powers and such authorisations as the Minister considers necessary or expedient for the works in question.

DPDs (development plan documents): prepared by local planning authorities to outline the key development goals of the Local Development Framework (LDF). The local development framework should include the following development plan documents: the Core Strategy; Site-specific Allocations of Land; and Area Action Plans (where neeeded). There will also be an Adopted Proposals Map (APM) which illustrates the spatial extent of policies that must be prepared and maintained to accompany all DPDs. All DPDs must be subject to rigorous procedures of community involvement, consultation and independent examination, and then adopted after receipt of the Planning Inspector's binding report. Once adopted, development control decisions must be made in accordance with them unless material considerations indicate otherwise. DPDs form an essential part of the LDF. There are three required DPDs: the Core Strategy which sets out the spatial 'vision' for the local area; the Adopted Proposals Map which show the location of proposals in all current DPDs, on an Ordnance Survey base map; and Site-Specific Allocations.

DTI (Department of Trade and Industry)

EIA (Environmental Impact Assessment) and ES (Environmental Statement): applicants for certain types of development, usually more significant schemes, are required to submit an 'environmental statement' with the planning application. This evaluates the likely environmental impacts of the development, together with an assessment of how the severity of the impacts could be reduced.

GDPO (General Development Procedure Order): the Town and County Planning (General Development Procedure) Order 1995 describes the procedure that local authorities have to follow when dealing with planning applications and certificates of lawful use, as well as the procedure they must follow with applications that are a departure from the development plan.

GPDO (General Permitted Development Order): a set of regulations made by the Government which grants planning permission for specified limited or minor forms of development.

LDF (Local Development Framework): this sets out in the form of a 'portfolio', the local development documents which collectively deliver the spatial planning for the local planning authority's area. It includes development plan documents (DPDs); a project planning document called the Local Development Scheme (LDS); an Annual Monitoring Report (AMR); a document outlining the consultation process called the Statement of Community Involvement (SCI); and supplementary planning policy documents (SPDs).

LDO (Local Development Order): an order made by a local planning authority extending permitted development rights for certain forms of development, with regard to a relevant Local Development Document (LDD).

LDS (Local Development Scheme): a local planning authority's time-scaled programme for the preparation of its Local Development Documents which must be agreed with Government and reviewed every year.

LGA (Local Government Association)

LPA (Local Planning Authority): the local authority or council that is empowered by law to exercise planning functions; usually the local borough or district council. National Parks and the Broads Authority are also considered to be local planning authorities. County councils are the planning authorities for waste and minerals matters.

LSP (Local Strategic Partnerships): an overall partnership that brings together organisations from the public, private, community and voluntary sector within a local authority area, with the objective of improving people's quality of life.

PARSOL (Planning and Regulatory Services Online): the PARSOL National Project has developed a range of standards, toolkits, specifications, schemas, systems and software to assist local authorities in building effective and transparent online planning and regulatory systems.

PAS (Planning Advisory Service): a service set up by the Government to help and advise local planning authorities struggling to meet best value performance targets for development control.

PCPA 2004 (Planning and Compulsory Purchase Act 2004): the Act updates elements of the 1990 Town and Country Planning Act. The PCPA 2004 introduced:

- a statutory system for regional planning;

- a new system for local planning;

- reforms to the development control and compulsory purchase and compensation systems; and

- removal of crown immunity from planning controls.

PDA (Planning Delivery Agreement): the local planning authority and planning permission applicant agree a time frame within which an application will be decided.

PDG (Planning Delivery Grant): a central government grant is providing about £605 million over six years (2003-2008), to resource and incentivise Regional Planning Bodies and local authorities to improve the planning system and deliver sustainable communities. Allocations are based on assessment of performance across a range of planning functions.

PINS (Planning Inspectorate): PINS is an executive agency of the Department for Communities and Local Government (DCLG). It is the government body responsible for:

- the processing of planning and enforcement appeals;

- holding inquiries into local development plans;

- listed building consent appeals;

- advertisement appeals;

- reporting on planning applications called in for decision by DCLG or in Wales by the National Assembly for Wales;

- examinations of development plan documents (DPDs) and Statements of Community Involvement;

- various Compulsory Purchase Orders and rights of way cases; and

- cases arising from the Environmental Protection and Water Acts and the Transport and Works Act and other highways legislation.

The work is set in agreement with the Department for Transport, the DCLG and the National Assembly for Wales.

POS (Planning Officers Society)

Planning Policy Statements (PPS) and Planning Policy Guidance (PPG): Planning Policy Guidance notes (PPGs) and their replacement Planning Policy Statements (PPSs) are prepared by the Government after public consultation to explain statutory provisions and provide guidance to local authorities and others on planning policy and the operation of the planning system.

RDA (Regional Development Agency): nine RDAs were set up in the English regions as non-departmental public bodies. Their primary role is as a strategic driver of regional economic development in their region. The RDAs aim is to:

- coordinate regional economic development and regeneration;

- enable the regions to improve their relative competitiveness; and

- reduce the imbalances that exist within and between regions.

RES (Regional Economic Strategy): statutory strategies that take an integrated and sustainable approach to economic development and regeneration by tackling business competitiveness, productivity and the underlying problems of unemployment, skills shortages, social exclusion and physical decay. They provide:

- a regional framework for economic development, skills and regeneration to ensure better strategic focus for, and coordination of, activity in the region, whether by the agency or by other regional, sub-regional or local organisations;

- a framework for the delivery of national and European programmes and influence the development of government policy; and

- the basis for the RDAs' detailed action plans.

RSS (Regional Spatial Strategy): a strategy for how a region should look in 15 to 20 years' time and possibly longer. An RSS identifies the scale and distribution of new housing in the region, indicates areas for regeneration, expansion or sub-regional planning and specifies priorities for the environment, transport, infrastructure, economic development, agriculture, minerals and waste treatment and disposal. Most former Regional Planning Guidance is now considered to be part of an RSS and forms part of the development plan. RSS are prepared by the Regional Planning Bodies.

RTPI (Royal Town Planning Institute)

SA (Sustainability Appraisal): an appraisal of the economic, environmental and social effects of a plan, from the outset of the preparation process, to allow decisions to be made that accord with sustainable development principles.

SCI (Statement of Community Involvement): sets out the processes to be used by the local authority in involving the community in the preparation, alteration and continuing review of all local development documents and development control decisions. The SCI is an essential part of the new Local Development Frameworks (LDFs).

SEA (Strategic Environmental Assessment): an environmental assessment of certain plans and programmes, including those in the field of planning and land use, which complies with EU Directive 2001/42/EC. The environmental assessment involves the:

- preparation of an environmental report;

- carrying out of consultations;

- taking into account of the environmental report and the results of the consultations in decision-making; and

- provision of information when the plan or programme is adopted;

and shows that the results of the environment assessment have been taken into account.

SSA (Site Specific Allocation): a development plan document (DPD) which show where land is allocated for specific uses, including mixed uses. Policies in relation to the delivery of site-specific allocations, such as critical access requirements or broad design principles, must be set out in a DPD.

SME (Small to Medium Sized Enterprise): an independent business managed by its owner or part owners and having a small market share, either by number of employees or turnover.

SPDs (Supplementary Planning Document): a local development document that may cover a range of issues, thematic or site specific, and which provides further detail of policies and proposals in a 'parent' development plan document (DPD).

SPZ (Simplified Planning Zone): an area in which a local planning authority wishes to stimulate development and encourage investment. SPZs operate by granting a specified planning permission in a zone without the need for an application for planning permission or the payment of planning fees.

Standards Authority: a local planning authority that is required to produce an improvement plan, having failed to meet one or more government Best Value performance targets for development control relating to efficient processing of planning applications.

TCPA (Town and Country Planning Association)

UDC (Urban Development Corporation): non-departmental public bodies which were established under the Local Government, Planning and Land Act 1980. They are limited-life bodies tasked with a broad remit to secure the regeneration of their designated areas.

UDP (Unitary Development Plan): An old-style development plan prepared by a metropolitan district and by some unitary local authorities which contains policies equivalent to those in both a structure plan and local plan. These plans will continue to operate for a time after the commencement of the new development plan system, by virtue of specific transitional provisions.

Bibliography

Databases   Department for Communities and Local Government, Table 401, Household Estimates and Projections: Great Britain, 1961-2021. Live table, http://www.communities.gov.uk/index.asp?id=1156099, accessed 07 November 2006.

DCLG, New Projections of households for England and the Regions to 2026, DCLG Statistical Release 2006/0042, 14 March 2006.

DCLG, live tables on housing stock, table 117, http://www.communities.gov.uk/pub/23/Table117_id1156023.xls, accessed 07 November 2006

DCLG, Development Control Statistics 2005-06, table 3.5, http://www.communities.gov.uk/index.asp?id=1503632.

EC, Corine Land Cover 2000, http://dataservice.eea.europa.eu/dataservice/

Generalised Land Use Database, available at http://www.communities.gov.uk/pub/87/GLUDfor LocalAuthoritiesExcel104Kb_id1146087.xls

Office of National Statistics, Table 1.2, *Population Trends 2006*.

Primary and secondary works   *Charles Church Developments Limited v. South Northamptonshire District Council,* JPL Planning Law Case Reports, vol. 46 (2000).

First Corporate Shipping v North Somerset District Council, England and Wales Court of Appeal Civ 693.

Advisory Team for Large Applications, 'Planning Delivery Agreements Report' http://www.englishpartnerships.co.uk/publications.htm#programmesandprojects (January 2006).

J. Andersson, N. Gallent, R. Oades and M. Shoard, Bartlett School of Planning Report for the Countryside Agency, 'Urban Fringe – Policy, Regulatory and Literature Research. Report 2.3: Green Belts' (2003).

S. Angel, D. Civco and S. Sheppard, World Bank, 'The Dynamics of Global Urban Expansion' (2005).

Arup Economics+Planning, The Bailey Consultancy, Addison & Associates and Professor Malcolm Grant, 'The Planning Service: Costs and Fees. A Report for the Office of the Deputy Prime Minister' (November 2003).

Association of British Insurers, 'Flooding and Insurance', http://www.abi.org.uk/flooding.

A. B. Atkinson and J. E. Stiglitz, *Lectures in Public Economics* (New York, 1980).

Audit Commission, 'The Planning System: Matching Expectations and Capacity' (2006).

Audit Commission, 'Recruitment and Retention – A Public Service Workforce for the 21st Century' (2002).

M. Balen, *Land Economy,* a report for the Adam Smith Institute (2006).

E. Balls and J. Healey (eds.), *Towards A New Regional Policy: Delivering Growth and Full Employment* (2000).

K. Barker, *Review of Housing Supply. Delivering Stability: Securing our Future Housing Needs. Final Report – Recommendations* (2004).

K. Barker, *Review of Housing Supply. Delivering Stability: Securing our Future Housing Needs. Interim Report – Analysis* (2003).

K. Barker, *Review of Land Use Planning. Interim Report – Analysis* (2006).

J. Barlow, *Public Participation in Urban Development: The European Experience* (Policy Studies Institute, 1995).

BBC News, 'Village Fights for Windfall Cash' http://news.bbc.co.uk/1/hi/scotland/4100077.stm, 16 December 2004.

BMG, 'Report of Wave 1 Survey: Lyons Inquiry into Local Government' (2005).

S. Bond, K. Denny, J. Hall and W. McCluskey, 'Who Pays Business Rates?' *Fiscal Studies,* 17/1 (1996), pp. 19-36.

M. Breheny, 'The Compact City and Transport Energy Consumption', *New Transactions of the Institute of British Geographers,* vol. 20 (1995), pp. 81-101.

J. Brueckner, 'Urban Growth Boundaries: An Effective Second-Best Remedy for Unpriced Traffic Congestion', mimeo, University of California at Irvine (2006).

R. Burdett, T. Travers, D. Czischke, P. Rode and B. Moser, *Density and Urban Neighbourhoods in London: Summary Report* (Enterprise LSE Cities, 2004).

E. Burton, 'Measuring Urban Compactness in UK Towns and Cities', *Environment and Planning B,* vol. 29 (2002), pp. 219-250.

D. Carswell, *Paying for Localism,* a report for the Adam Smith Institute (2004).

J. Caulfield, *Local Government Finance in OECD Countries* (University of New South Wales, 2000).

Centre for Urban Policy Studies, University of Manchester and Centre for Urban and Regional Development Studies, University of Newcastle, 'A Framework for City-Regions. Working Paper 1: Mapping City-Regions. A Report for the ODPM' (2006).

P. Cheshire and S. Sheppard, 'The Introduction of Price Signals into Land Use Planning Decision-Making: A Proposal', Research Papers in Environmental and Spatial Analysis, no. 89, London School of Economics (2004).

P. Cheshire and S. Sheppard, 'Land Markets and Land Market Regulation: Progress towards Understanding', *Regional Science and Urban Economics,* 34/6 (2004), pp. 619-637.

P. Cheshire and S. Sheppard, 'Taxes Versus Regulation: The Welfare Impacts of Policies for Containing Sprawl', mimeo, Williams College (2004).

P. P. Combes, G. Duranton and H. G. Overman, 'Agglomeration and the Adjustment of the Spatial Economy', mimeo, London School of Economics (2005).

Commission for Architecture and the Built Environment, 'The Cost of Bad Design' (2006).

Commission for Architecture and the Built Environment, 'Design and Access Statements: How to Write, Read and Use Them' (2006).

Commission for Architecture and the Built Environment, 'The Impact of Office Design on Business Performance' (May 2005).

Commission for Architecture and the Built Environment, 'Public Attitudes to Architecture and Public Space: Transforming Neighbourhoods: Final Report. Research Study Conducted for the Commission for Architecture and the Built Environment' (2004).

Commission for Architecture and the Built Environment, Office of the Deputy Prime Minister and English Partnerships, 'Design Coding: Testing its Use in England' (2005).

Commission for Architecture and the Built Environment, 'Housing Audit: Assessing the design quality of new homes in the North East, North West and Yorkshire & Humber' (2005).

Competition Commission, 'Annual Report and Accounts 2005/2006' (2006).

Competition Commission, *Safeway PLC and Asda Group Limited (owned by Wal-Mart Stores Inc.); Wm Morrison Supermarkets PLC; J Sainsbury PLC; and Tesco PLC: A Report on the Mergers in Contemplation* (2003).

Competition Commission, *Supermarkets: A Report on the Supply of Groceries from Multiple Stores in the United Kingdom* (2000).

Confederation of British Industry, *Planning Reform: Delivering for Business?* (2005).

Confederation of Business Industry, *Public Services Survey* (2005).

P. Davies, 'Spatial Competition in Retail Markets: Movie Theaters', working paper, MIT Sloan (2001).

Department for Communities and Local Government, 'Circular 01/06: Guidance on Changes to the Development Control System' (2006).

Department for Communities and Local Government, 'Design Coding in Practice: An Evaluation' (2006).

Department for Communities and Local Government, 'Development Control Statistics, England, 2005/06' (2006).

Department for Communities and Local Government, 'Land Use Change in England: Residential Development to 2005' (2006).

Department for Communities and Local Government, 'News Release' http://www. communities.gov.uk/index.asp?id=1002882&PressNoticeID=2071 (8 February 2006).

Department for Communities and Local Government, Planning Policy Guidance 2: Green Belts.

Department for Communities and Local Government, Planning Policy Statement 10: Planning for Sustainable Waste Management (July 2005).

Department for Communities and Local Government, 'Results from the National Land Use Database of Previously-Developed Land ' (2006).

Department for Communities and Local Government, 'Strong and Prosperous Communities: The Local Government White Paper' (2006).

Department for Communities and Local Government, 'Commercial and Industrial Property Estimated Vacancy Statistics: England, 2004-05' (2006).

Department for Communities and Local Government, 'Previously-developed land that may be available for development, England 2005: Results from the National Land Use Database of Previously-Developed Land' (2006).

Department for Environment, Food and Rural Affairs, 'Economic Note on UK Grocery Retailing' (2006).

Department for Environment, Transport and the Regions, Commission for Architecture and the Built Environment and UCL Bartlett School of Planning, 'The Value of Urban Design' (2001).

Department of Environment, Transport and the Regions, 'Strategic Gap and Green Wedge Policies in Structure Plans' (2001).

Department of Environment, Transport and the Regions, 'The Use of Density in Urban Planning' (1998).

Department of the Environment, 'Planning Policy Guidance Note 1: General Policy and Principles' (1988).

Department for Transport, 'The Future of Air Transport' (2003).

Department for Transport, Local Government and the Regions, 'Planning: Delivering a Fundamental Change' (2002).

Department of Trade and Industry, *The Energy Challenge* (2006).

Department of Trade and Industry, '2005 Guidance to RDAs on Regional Strategies' (2005).

Department of Trade and Industry, 'Updating the Electricity Generating Stations and Overhead Lines Inquiry Procedure Rules in England and Wales' (November 2006).

T. Edmundson, 'Planning Research: An Investigation of Potential Measures to address London Local Planning Authorities' Recruitment and Retention Problems. Report for the Association of London Government, the RTPI London Branch, and the Association of London Borough Planning Officers' (April 2004).

M. Elson, *Green Belts: Conflict Mediation In The Urban Fringe* (1986).

M. J. Elson, 'Green Belts: The Need for Re-Appraisal', *Town & Country Planning*, 68/5 (1999), pp. 156-158.

ENTEC, 'A Sustainability Impact Study of Additional Housing Scenarios in England, Report for the Office of the Deputy Prime Minister' (2005).

ENTEC, EFTEC and Richard Hodkinson Consultancy, 'Study into the Environmental Impacts of Increasing the Supply of Housing in the UK. A Report to DEFRA' (2004).

Environment Agency, 'Development and Flood Risk Report 2004/05' (2006).

A. W. Evans, '"Rabbit Hutches on Postage Stamps": Planning, Development and Political Economy', *Urban Studies*, 28/6 (1991), pp. 853-870.

A. W. Evans, 'No Room! No Room!' IEA, Occasional Paper 79 (1988).

A. W. Evans and O. M. Hartwich, *Better Homes, Greener Cities* (2006).

A. W. Evans and O. M. Hartwich, *Unaffordable Housing: Fables and Myths* (London, 2005).

S. Evans and A. Oswald, 'The Price of Freedom: A Non-Technical Explanation of the Case for Road Pricing', *Transport Review* (1999-2000), pp. 28-29.

Friends of the Earth, 'Listen Up: Community Involvement in the Planning System - 7 Case Studies' (2006).

A. Gilg, *Planning in Britain: Understanding and Evaluating the Post-War System* (London, 2005).

E. Glaeser and M. E. Kahn, 'Sprawl and Urban Growth', NBER Working Paper No. 9733 (2003).

Greater London Authority, 'Interim Strategic Planning Guidance on Tall Buildings, Strategic Views and the Skyline in London' (2001).

GLA Economics, 'More Residents, More Jobs? The Relationship between Population, Employment and Accessibility in London' (2005).

R. H. Haines-Young et al. 'Accounting for nature: assessing habitats in the UK countryside. A Report for the Department for Environment, Transport and the Regions' (2000).

Halcrow Group, 'Valuing Planning Obligations in England: Final Report. A Report for the Department for Communities and Local Government' (2006).

Halcrow Group and Office of the Deputy Prime Minister, 'Unification of Consent Regimes' (2004).

J. Hall and S. Smith, 'The Feasibility of a Local Sales Tax', Local and Central Government Relations Research, vol. 32 (1995).

P. Hall, *The Land Fetish* (2005).

P. Hall and K. Pain, *The Polycentric Metropolis: Learning from Mega-city Regions in Europe* (2006).

P. Hall, R. Thomas, H. Gracey and R. Drewett, *The Containment of Urban England. Volume One: Urban and Metropolitan Growth Processes or Megalopolis Denied* (1973).

W. Heinz, 'City and Region – Co-operation or Co-ordination? An International Comparison' (2000).

C. Hepburn, 'Regulation by Prices, Quantities or Both: A Review of Instrument Choice', *Oxford Review of Economic Policy*, 22/2 (2006), pp. 226-247.

J. Hermansson, TRANSLAND, 'Greater Copenhagen: 'The Finger Plan'. A Report for TRANSLAND' (2000).

HM Treasury, HM Revenue & Customs and Office of the Deputy Prime Minister, 'Planning-gain Supplement: A Consultation' (2005).

HM Treasury, Department of Trade and Industry and Office of the Deputy Prime Minister, 'Devolving Decision Making: 3 – Meeting the Regional Economic Challenge: The Importance of Cities to Regional Growth' (2006).

House of Commons, Select Committee on Transport, Ninth Report, Session 2005-06 (2006).

House of Commons, Select Committee on Planning, Housing, Local Government and the Regions, 'The Role and Effectiveness of CABE. Fifth Report of Session 2004-05' (2005).

S. Hughes, '30 Year Business Plans for Local Authorities', *Spectrum*, vol. 9 (2005) http://www. cipfa.org.uk/pt/download/spectrum_issue09.pdf

IFF Research Ltd, 'The Impact of Rates on Businesses: Report for the Department of the Environment ' (1995).

Institute for Fiscal Studies, 'The Relationship Between Rates and Rents: An Analysis of the Relationship between Non-Domestic Rates and Commercial Rents. A Report for the Department of the Environment' (1995).

M. L. Katz, 'Multifirm Monopoly in a Spatial Market', *Bell Journal of Economics*, 11/2 (1980), pp. 519-535.

J. A. Kay and M. A. King, *The British Tax System* (Oxford, 5th edition, 1990).

P. Klemperer, 'How (Not) to Run Auctions: The European 3G Telecoms Auctions', *European Economic Review*, vol. 42 (2002), pp. 757-759.

Land Use Consultants, Oxford Brookes University, CAG Consultants and Gardiner & Theobald, 'Adapting to Climate Change Impacts – A Good Practice Guide for Sustainable Communities. A Report for DEFRA' (2006).

T. Leunig, 'Turning NIMBYs into IMBYs', *Town and Country Planning*, 73/12 (2004), pp. 357-359.

Local Government Association, 'Prudential Borrowing: One Year On' (2005).

Local Government Association, 'Using the New Powers to Trade and Charge: Local Authority Case Studies' (2005).

Local Government Association and Office of the Deputy Prime Minister, 'Skills Base in the Planning System' (2004).

London School of Economics for Development Securities, 'Tall Buildings: Vision of the Future or Victims of the Past?' (2002).

London School of Economics, Proceedings of the LSE London Density Debate, http://www.lse.edu/collections/londonDevelopmentWorkshops/density%20debate/report.doc

M. Lyons, *Lyons Inquiry into Local Government: Interim Report and Consultation Paper* (December 2005).

M. Lyons, *National Prosperity, Local Choice and Civic Engagement: a new partnership between central and local government for the 21st Century* (2006).

H. MacDonald, 'Why Business Improvement Districts Work', *Civic Bulletin*, vol. 4 (1996), pp. http://www.manhattan-institute.org/html/cb_4.htm.

A. Marshall, 'City Leadership: Web Annexe 2. Economic Development in Britain: Policy, Powers and Funding,' a report for IPPR (2005).

Mayor of London, 'Housing in London: The London Housing Strategy Evidence Base 2005' (2005).

N. Mehdi, 'The Capitalisation of Business Rates: An Empirical Study of Tax Incidence in Six London Boroughs', PhD Thesis, London School of Economics (2003).

Ministry of Housing, Spatial Planning and the Environment, Netherlands, 'National Spatial Strategy: Creating Space for Development' (2006).

Minnesota House of Representatives: House Research, 'How TIF Works', http://www.house.leg.state.mn.us/hrd/issinfo/tifmech.htm.

MORI Survey for the Campaign to Protect Rural England, http://www.cpre.org.uk/news-releases/news-rel-2005/49a-05.htm, (2005).

C. Mynors, 'Planning Law and the Need for Reform', paper presented to the Planning Summer School, Canterbury (2006).

National Board of Housing, Building and Planning, Sweden, and Ministry for Regional Development of the Czech Republic, *Housing Statistics in the European Union 2004* (2005).

B. Needham, 'The New Dutch Spatial Planning Act: Continuity and Change in the way in which the Dutch Regulate the Practice of Spatial Planning', *Planning Practice and Research*, 20/3 (2005), pp. 327-340.

NERA Consulting, 'Options for Reforming Local Government Funding: A Report for the Lyons Inquiry Study Team' (2005).

Office of the Deputy Prime Minister Neighbourhood Renewal Unit, *Under-served Markets: Preliminary Research Findings* (2003).

Office of the Deputy Prime Minister, 'Creating Local Development Frameworks: A Companion Guide to PPS 12' (2004).

Office of the Deputy Prime Minister, 'General Power for Best Value Authorities to Charge for Discretionary Services – Guidance on the Power in the Local Government Act 2003' (2003).

Office of the Deputy Prime Minister, 'Generalised Land Use Database Statistics for England' (2005).

Office of the Deputy Prime Minister, 'Planning for Economic Development: Study and Scoping Study' (May 2004).

Office of the Deputy Prime Minister, 'Starting out with Local Development Schemes. Spatial Plans in Practice: Supporting the Reform of Local Planning' (2006).

Office of the Deputy Prime Minister, 'Strong Local Leadership – Quality Public Services. White Paper on Local Government Finance' (2001).

Office of the Deputy Prime Minister, 'Sustainable Communities: Building for the Future' (2002).

Office of the Deputy Prime Minister, 'Urban and Rural Definitions: A User Guide' (2002).

Office of Fair Trading, *Grocery Market: Proposed Decision to Make a Market Investigation Reference* (2006).

Office of Science and Technology, 'Future Foresight: Flood and Coastal Defence', http://www.foresight.gov.uk/previous_projects/flood_and_coastal_defence/index.html (2004).

Organisation for Economic Co-operation and Development, *Economic Policy Reforms: Going for Growth* (2005).

M. Parkinson et al, *State of the English Cities: A Report for the Department for Communities and Local Government* (2006).

Peter Pendleton and Associates, 'PPA Planning Website Survey: A Report for the Office of the Deputy Prime Minister', http://www.pendleton-assoc.com/images/Dec2005resultspdfs/EnglishandWelsh_Website_Review_Report_2006.doc (December 2005).

M. Pennington, 'Liberating the Land', a report for the Institute of Economic Affairs (2000).

M. Pennington, *Planning and the Political Market: Public Choice and the Politics of Government Failure* (2000).

Pocklington Town Council, 'Langeled Project Helps Pocklington Go Green!' http://www.pocklington.gov.uk/langeled-project-helps-pocklington-go-green.htm (7 June 2006).

A. Power, L. Richardson, K. Seshimo and K. Firth, *A Framework for Housing in the London Thames Gateway* (London, 2004).

Renaisi and ANCER SPA, 'Workspace Supply and Demand in the City Fringe: A Study for City Fringe Partnership Final Report' (April 2003).

Lord Rodgers and Urban Task Force, *Towards an Urban Renaissance* (London, 1999).

D. A. Rodriguez, F. Targa and S. Aytur, 'Transport Implications of Urban Containment Policies: A Study of the Largest Twenty-five US Metropolitan Areas', *Urban Studies*, vol. 43 (2006), pp. 1879-1897.

Royal Town Planning Institute, 'Green Belt Policy: A Discussion Paper' (2000).

Royal Town Planning Institute, 'A Survey of Discipline Knowledge and Generic Skills of RTPI Corporate Members' (2005).

Royal Town Planning Institute, *Uniting Britain: The Evidence Base – Spatial Structure and Key Drivers* (2006).

D. Rudlin and N. Falk, *Building the 21st Century Home: The Sustainable Urban Neighbourhood* (1999).

Secretary of State for Trade and Industry, Energy statement on need for additional gas supply infrastructure to the House of Commons, (http://www.dti.gov.uk/files/file28954.pdf (May 2006).

H. Smith, 'Store Characteristics in Retail Oligopoly', working paper, Department of Economics, University of Oxford (2005).

H. Smith, 'Supermarket Choice and Supermarket Competition in Market Equilibrium', *Review of Economic Studies,* 71/1 (2004), pp. 235-263.

Social Exclusion Unit, 'A New Commitment to Neighbourhood Renewal: National Strategy Action Plan' (http://www.socialexclusionunit.gov.uk/downloaddoc.asp?id=33, January 2001).

M. Spence, 'Product Selection, Fixed Costs, and Monopolistic Competition', *Review of Economic Studies*, vol. 43 (1976), pp. 217-235.

D. Stead, 'Relationships between Land Use, Socio-Economic Factors, and Travel Patterns in Britain', *Environment and Planning B*, vol. 28 (2001), pp. 499-528.

Steer Davies Gleave, *Northern Way and the Transport Strategic Direction* (forthcoming, 2006).

N. Stern, *Stern Review on the Economics of Climate Change* (London, 2006).

M. Stubbs, 'A New Panacea? An Evaluation of Mediation as an Effective Method of Dispute Resolution in Planning Appeals', *International Planning Studies*, 2/3 (1997), pp. 347-365.

J. Tirole, *The Theory of Industrial Organisation* (Cambridge, MA, 1988).

S. Titman, 'Urban Land Prices under Uncertainty', *American Economic Review*, 75/1 (1985), pp. 505-514.

Town and Country Planning Association, 'Policy Statement: Green Belts' (2002).

Urban Task Force, *Towards a Strong Urban Renaissance* (2005).

A. Vigor, 'Build on Land Levy with Egalitarian Worth', *Tribune* (2 December 2005).

R. Walters, Submission to the Renewable Energy in Scotland Inquiry of the Enterprise and Culture Committee of the Scottish Parliament (2004).

M. Welbank, N. Davies and I. Haywood, 'Mediation in the Planning System. A Report for the Department of Environment, Transport and the Regions' (2000).